Museums and the Public Sphere

To Caitlin Miranda

Museums and the Public Sphere

Jennifer Barrett

A John Wiley & Sons, Ltd., Publication

This paperback edition first published 2012
© 2012 Jennifer Barrett

Edition history: hardback 2011

Blackwell Publishing was acquired by John Wiley & Sons in February 2007. Blackwell's publishing program has been merged with Wiley's global Scientific, Technical, and Medical business to form Wiley-Blackwell.

Registered Office
John Wiley & Sons Ltd, The Atrium, Southern Gate, Chichester, West Sussex, PO19 8SQ, United Kingdom

Editorial Offices
350 Main Street, Malden, MA 02148-5020, USA
9600 Garsington Road, Oxford, OX4 2DQ, UK
The Atrium, Southern Gate, Chichester, West Sussex, PO19 8SQ, UK

For details of our global editorial offices, for customer services, and for information about how to apply for permission to reuse the copyright material in this book please see our website at www.wiley.com/wiley-blackwell.

The right of Jennifer Barrett to be identified as the author of this work has been asserted in accordance with the UK Copyright, Designs and Patents Act 1988.

Library of Congress Cataloging-in-Publication Data

Barrett, Jennifer.
    Museums and the public sphere / Jennifer Barrett.
       p. cm.
    Includes bibliographical references and index.
    ISBN 978-1-4051-7383-4 (hardcover : alk. paper); ISBN 978-1-118-27483-5 (paperback)
 1. Museums–Social aspects. 2. Museums–Philosophy. 3. Public
spaces–Social aspects. 4. Public spaces–Philosophy. 5. Community life.
 I. Title.
  AM7.B35 2011
  069'.68–dc22
                                                              2010011916

A catalogue record for this book is available from the British Library.

Set in 10/12.5pt Galliard by Thomson Digital, Noida, India
Printed in Malaysia by Ho Printing (M) Sdn Bhd

01   2011

Contents

List of Images   vii

Introduction   1

1   The Public Sphere   15

2   Historical Discourses of the Museum   45

3   The Museum as Public Space   81

4   Audience, Community, and Public   118

5   The Museum as Public Intellectual   143

Conclusion   164

References   175

Acknowledgments   191

Index   193

List of Images

1   Thomas Struth, *Hermitage 1, St Petersburg, 2005*   2

1.1   Louis-Léopold Boilly, *The Public in the Salon of the Louvre, Viewing the Painting of the "Sacre"* begun 1808, Woodner Collection   17

1.2   Étienne-Louis Boullée, *Cénotaphe de Newton*, 1784   19

1.3   Hubert Robert, *Projet d'aménagement de la Grande Galerie du Louvre en 1796*, 1796   31

1.4   Honore Daumier, *Free Admission Day – Twenty-Five Degrees of Heat*, 1852   35

2.1   John Tenniel, *The Sunday Question. The Public-House; or, The House For The Public?*, 1869   59

2.2   Louis-Léopold Boilly, *Interior of a Parisian Café, c.1815*   66

2.3   Edgar Degas, *Mary Cassatt at the Louvre: The Etruscan Gallery*, 1879–80   69

2.4   Jacques-Louis David, *Le Serment des Horaces*, 1784   73

2.5   Jacques-Louis David, *The Tennis Court Oath, 20th June 1789*, 1791   75

3.1   *Forecourt, British Museum*, 2005   92

3.2   *Turbine Hall, Tate Modern*, 2004   93

4.1   Installation view, *The Arts of Islam: Treasures from the Nasser D Khalili Collection*   125

5.1   *Belongings* homepage 2009. Migration Heritage Centre New South Wales   144

5.2   *Talkback Classroom 'Political Satire' forum with John Safran and cartoonist David Pope*   154

5.3   *Garden of Australian Dreams, opening day at the National Museum of Australia*   157

5.4   Jean-Marie Tjibaou Cultural Centre, New Caledonia   158

5.5   Exhibition *People, Power, Politics: The first generation of anthropologists at the University of Sydney*, 2008   161

5.6   *Makarr-garma: Aboriginal collections from a Yolngu Perspective, Macleay Museum* 2009   161

5.7   Book cover *The Changing Presentation of the American Indian: Museums and Native Cultures* by the National Museum of the American Indian   162

6.1   Thomas Struth, *Tokyo National Museum, 1999, Tokyo*   168

Introduction

Museums are highly visible institutions in contemporary societies and their ongoing existence and claims for resources are often justified on the grounds of "relevance." To what, and to whom, are they relevant? The common answer is "the public." Within the museum context the term *public* is often used to invoke a generalized body of people: an audience, a represented community or certain non-visitor interest groups. It is employed to lay claim to and convey the museum's status as an open, democratic institution for and of "the people." However, for all its centrality to the museum sector's talk about itself, the term "public" is often used loosely. At other times it is used strategically, with a particular political purpose that may suggest clarity, even precision, but is actually tendentious, even opportunistic. In the literature, one finds a surprising lack of sustained critical reflection upon the term: little awareness of its etymology, its political meaning, or the reasons why it has had such an expansive influence upon the museum world.

This book seeks to offer such a reflection. What are the many ways in which the museum is, or is not, public? How can the museum be understood as a critical sphere of public debate? How do museums facilitate, respond to, support, and intersect with wider public discourse? These questions are the key to understanding and redefining the very parameters of the museum.

Reworking the idea of the museum is critical in a world in which museums compete for the representation and interpretation of cultural heritage with other related "public" forums and sites, including community cultural centers, public halls and the Internet. In this world of increasingly diversified media, what can museums offer to our experience of being *in public*? This book examines the implications of a more complex understanding of how the public is realized, invoked, and understood in the museum context. An examination of the way museums themselves use the term "public,"

Museums and the Public Sphere   by Jennifer Barrett
© 2010 Jennifer Barrett

Image 1 Thomas Struth, *Hermitage 1, St Petersburg, 2005.* C-print, 114.0 × 144.5 cm. © 2010 Thomas Struth. (Image from Struth's project, *Museum Photographs*, where he foregrounds the public in iconic museums.)

as well as other critiques of the public, will enhance the capacity for museums to engage with "publics" in more complex, productive ways.

This book emerges from my long-term engagement with what constitutes public culture, who produces it, where is it represented and by whom. My interest in this area has included community cultural practices, where communities of interest engage, practice, and produce culture, both for themselves and sometimes others. The museum was not always present in these practices, or surrounding discourses. In recent years, however, sites of community culture have also attracted museum professionals. Communities are identified as a new audience, or alternatively as producers of culture with the potential to renew the role of the museum. What this shift implies about the pre-existing location and nature of community cultural practices is often left unspoken in museum studies.

One of the first questions about the relationship between the museum and the idea of the "public" is how the museum's public remit has altered over time. The utopian or idealist goals of the late eighteenth- and nineteenth-century democracies included using museum spaces to civilize and educate people. Museums also symbolized a nation's achievements (military, cultural, or economic). The role of the "modern museum" at this time was caught up with the new experience of being *public*. More recently, as museums re-examine what it meant to be a public institution, the term has been called upon to reflect inclusivity and diversity, in contrast to the historical singularity of "the public." The contemporary museum often struggles to negotiate between the remnants of an earlier rhetoric of "public" and new practices and types of spaces designed to attract new audiences, engage new communities and respond to the locality or nation within which they are situated.

Central to this adjustment, and to the reconfiguration of the museum, was Peter Vergo's (1989) invention of "the new museology." The idea emerged at a time when museums (in common with other public institutions such as libraries) were suffering funding pressures and cut-backs, often because they were perceived to be elitist and inaccessible. The new museology, as a response to this situation, argued for an increased emphasis on the visitors and their experience and for new thinking about museum education and the importance of accessibility. Authors included in the new museology, such as Nick Merriman (1989) and Peter Wright (1989), were directly influenced by Pierre Bourdieu's original works (1969 and 1979). These were translated from French in 1990 and 1984 respectively and were based on research on museums in Europe in the late 1960s and 1970s and his sociological approach to understanding who visits museums and why. His research found that museums reproduced for visitors the existing class-based culture, education, and social systems. Bourdieu maintained that the museum, rather than welcoming the broad spectrum found in social life, instead reinforced existing social and cultural distinctions and maintained social inequality, particularly in Europe in the second half of the twentieth century where class determined the capacity to be comfortable or not in the museum. This theory, based on empirical research and new theories about learning in the museum is discussed in Chapter Four. It informed new practices within the museum context, practices which purported to engage with the public differently from the universalizing exhibiting practices of previous centuries. It attempted to "democratize" the museum by advocating multiple ways of interpreting the world and its history, and by emphasizing the importance of consultation with communities, in particular in devising exhibits.

Thematic approaches, rather than chronological interpretative modes of displaying techniques, are preferred (Barker, 1999a; Clifford, 1999). The desired effect is to demystify the authoritative function of the museum, represent diversity and attract new publics to the museum. Museum practice is dispersed rather than centralized, and has multiple voices rather than being singularly authoritative.

The rhetoric of the new museology attempts to position the museum as not only having a new relationship with the public but also, significantly, a new relationship with its own history. One of the significant outcomes has been the development of specific education and public programs in museums. In this context, the public is identified as "audience" or "visitor," considered as active subjects in the making of the museum's purpose. The new museology becomes a key way of thinking about the way in which audiences are differentiated and organized into categories of disadvantage, synonymous with identity groups of the period (gender, disability, ethnicity, class, geography) that gave rise to social policies. Understanding forms of difference (rather than an undifferentiated "public") becomes a key way for museums to interpret their charter, to study visitors and to develop their capacity to be responsive.

The new museology promoted the need to develop strategies to redress the exclusivity and centralized authority of the museum. Since the late twentieth century, changes in museums have been shaped as much by the other global currents in the cultural sector and political life as by this discourse. Parallel movements in other cultural sectors promoted increased access to, and increased recognition of, the culture of working-class communities, migrant communities, women, and people with disabilities, among others. The differences between cultural democracy and democratic culture were much debated in the 1980s against a backdrop of cultural movements, with community arts movements advocating social change and the need for greater recognition of the diversity of cultures in social life (as well as condemning capitalism and the increasing consumerism during the Reagan and Thatcher eras). Over the past three decades concerns about greater access and participation in the museum sector have preoccupied many museum practitioners around the world (Karp et al., 1992; Sandell, 1998). These concerns ran parallel to discourses about access to libraries, universities, theatres, urban regeneration programs, and culture more broadly. Museums in the late twentieth century were affected by changes in economic, social, and education policies of the period: they were not immune to the broader political contexts of the times.

The physical structures, types of exhibits, collection policies and management of many museums have changed over the past three decades to accommodate the developments of both the consumerist and the cultural-pluralist aspects of museums (Benhamou and Moureau, 2006; Karp et al., 2006; McIntyre, 2006; Message, 2006). They have also expanded to include museum shops, cafés, cinemas, and restaurants, meeting Thomas Krens's formula for the twenty-first century museum: "great collection, great architecture, a great special exhibition, a great second exhibition, two shopping opportunities, two eating opportunities, a high-tech interface and economies of scale via a global network" (Krens, 1999). Krens's view is, in fact, close to what many people now experience in the contemporary museum, and reflects – if paradoxically – the values for which the new museology stands.

Museums have also sought to attract sectors of the public that do not – historically – attend museums. In this way, they acknowledged that they have neither acted as, nor been perceived as, being "for the public," despite a history of being *public institutions.* Competing notions of the public within the museum have emerged. In one, it is assumed that the visitor comes to the museum with knowledge, and contributes to knowledge-creation in the museum. In the other, the public is treated to populist presentations and approaches from museum staff with the aim of making the museum accessible to as many people as possible. In response, museums have applied the science of "visitor studies" to an understanding of why some (people, communities, and other types of public) simply do not visit museums. At the same time, communities with a developing interest in museums have also generated greater capacity to relate to and challenge the practices of museums. Underlying these developments, and still unre-solved, is the nature of the "public" which the museum still purportedly serves.

Any visit to a museum (physical space or an online site) reveals that the term "public" is used in multiple ways to describe not only the institution itself but also the culture represented and managed by it. It also includes the people who visit it (and even those who do not visit). In this context, the term "public" may be convenient, but not always accurate or useful. The easy recourse to it encapsulates both the potential and the problem of being a contemporary museum. Today the museum is about as many things as there are people who could visit it. It is about the word public and the sentiments attached to it in relation to museums having a defining history in the late eighteenth century. This history remains central to understanding what it is that renders museums *public.*

This book investigates the role of museums engaging in public dis-course, and gauges their ability to operate as sites of democratic public space. International debates on these themes are central concerns of this book. Insights from other disciplines, including geography, social theory and political science, also help to better understand what constitutes a public and what forms and processes in social life facilitate public interaction and discourse. I draw upon current debates in museum studies and research undertaken about museums across the disciplines of art history, geography, cultural studies, sociology, anthropology, social history, natural history, and science and technology to investigate the potential and limitations of museums and their capacity to engage with notions of "the public."

As we have seen, many recent developments in museums are driven by the need to engage with the public in new and innovative ways, as opposed to the universalist exhibition practices of previous centuries (Karp et al., 2006; Koster, 2006). Yet, often traces of the historical development of the museum internationally can be found in these new approaches. Recent aspects of museum development reveal a desire to be more reflexive, attempting to understand the museum as advocating multiple ways of interpreting the world and its history, by emphasizing the importance of consultation with communities in devising exhibits, and to understand the visitor as a contributor to knowledge about museum collections, whether that is through direct visitation or electronically. As one of the essential aims of recent museology has been to demystify the authoritative function of the museum, as necessary to represent diversity, to attract new publics to the museum, and to encourage new forms of visitation and engagement via electronic means, the museum demonstrates an awareness of the history of its practices.

This ongoing quest to attract and be relevant to the public is not new. It has been a concern for museums since their invention as a public institution in the late eighteenth century (see Anderson, 2004). At this time, as outlined in Chapter Two, the state developed a new relationship with culture and cultural institutions. This historical shift is now well known and documented (Bennett, 1995, 2004; Hooper-Greenhill, 1992; McClellan, 1994). In late eighteenth-century Europe, in particular, a tendency to conflate the state with "the public" becomes common. To this day, this conflation is still often assumed. This tends to be one of key tenets in the history of museums where their role is perceived as both an institution of the state (representative) and of the public (of the people). With this also comes an assumption that the museum is a public space: for the public, of the public. In this sense, the discourse about the museum and the public sphere intersects with discourses central to modern democracies, their cultures and institutions. The influence of this understanding of museums as public spaces lingers in the twenty-first century, even while it is assumed that the museum, as public space, functions as a site of public discourse in new ways.

Central to my consideration is the influential work of Jürgen Habermas, particularly his *Structural Transformation of the Public Sphere* (Habermas, 1989). Habermas's work is one of the most influential contributions to thinking about the public sphere. By association, the public sphere and Habermas's work have been used to understand public space (Smith, 1993; Warner, 2002; Staeheli and Mitchell, 2007; Iveson, 2008). The concept of the public sphere is a tool to help us understand the social world in which we live. Understanding what the public sphere is relies on thinking about the notion of *being public*.

Being Public

Before considering some of the more complex aspects of public sphere and public space, it will be useful to clarify some of the distinctions surrounding the term "public" as used in this book (the different formations of the public sphere are discussed in Chapter One). The term "public" is slippery and evasive, paradoxically, despite the assumption that its meaning is accessible. Perhaps this slipperiness and this mutability – the process of forever attempting to be democratic – is in fact what characterizes "the public," and the way in which it articulates itself, its expectations, and its institutions. The notion and associated practices change over time and space.

The term "private," meaning that which is not "public," is a crude yet basic binary, often used to fix the meaning of the term "public." To be *private* is to be with oneself, to be an individual, to be particular. The private sphere is also more often feminized, because it also connotes the domestic familial sphere (Landes, 1988, 1995; Fraser, 1992; Ryan, 1992; Meehan, 1995; Warner, 2002). The concept of private can relate to the private interests of the individual, or to a privatized market economy. The exclusion of private interests in Habermas's public sphere, according to Nancy Fraser, demonstrates "this clear separation of society and state that was supposed to underpin a form of public discussion that excluded 'private interests'" (Fraser, 1992: 113). To be public with other individuals in public spaces is to be outside of, or apart from, one's private realm, and to be engaged in social relations with others. For Richard Sennett (1992: 4), that which is outside of the private realm is the "grand psychic system" that lies beyond the individual. As discussed later in this book, the term "community" could also be interpreted as lying outside the personal or individual. This, however, is a contentious and yet crucial point in critical thinking about the terms "public," "private," and "democracy." Private persons and their particular concerns are often presumed to be separate from the public realm; the concept of community unsettles this dichotomy. It has been strongly argued that "[n]otions of 'the public' and public democracy were 'played off' and developed dialectically with notions of private property and private spheres" (Mitchell, 1995: 115). In this scenario the public is considered the realm of the political, the private that of the personal or non-political. In more recent times, as I discuss later, it is also conflated with "the state." Where, however, does the private person end and the public begin? Where does the private person attain an understanding of how and what it means to be public, as opposed to private? What are the impacts of these concepts of the private and public spheres upon that other realm – civil society?

Civil society is, according to John Keane, distinct from the state and the public sphere:

> In the most abstract sense, civil society can be conceived as an aggregate of institutions whose members are engaged primarily in a complex of non-state activities – economic and cultural production, household life and voluntary associations – and who in this way preserve and transform their identity by exercising all sorts of pressures or controls upon state institutions. . . . [C]ivil society has no natural innocence; it has no single eternally fixed form. It has a vital additional meaning. It has the potential to become a non-state sphere comprising a plurality of public spheres – productive units, households, voluntary organizations and community-based services – which are legally guaranteed and self organizing. (1988: 14)

It is from civil society that the public sphere emerges, and it lies within and between the state (Keane, 1988). Habermas's account of civil society in relation to the public sphere tends to fit with Keane's interpretation of the public sphere as "specifically a part of 'civil society'" (Habermas, 1989: 3, 20, 23). Nevertheless, as indicated above, Keane understands civil society as "comprising a plurality of public spheres" (Keane, 1988: xiii), an idea that I will examine in the following chapters. Civil society plays a formative role in the development of the public sphere, as well as the private sphere and the community. The implications of these considerations will also be explored in relation to public space in the following chapters of this book.

Public Space

Public spaces, it is often argued, are vital to a truly democratic society (Sennett, 1990, 1994; Wilson, 1991; Sorkin, 1992; Zukin, 1995). Public space is thought to be accessible, in both a material and an abstract sense, to all members of society. The material form of public space must be available, it is thought, in order for people to have the opportunity to participate in democratic processes. The right to protest and demonstrate, to have a "speakers' corner," is considered by these authors as a material and symbolically significant sign of a democratic society. Within some academic disciplines, such as cultural studies and geography, this is known as *traditional* public space (discussed in Chapter Three). The existence of public space is thus said to support democracy because it facilitates public discourse. Absent from most of these accounts, however, are museums as sites of public discourse.

Some urban planners, geographers, sociologists, and architects also warn of the dangers of a city without public space; a sign of decline in civic cohesion (Sorkin, 1992; Harvey, 1993; Mitchell, 1995, 2003). Threats to the existence of public space are often interpreted as a sign that democracy itself is under threat. This interpretation implies a particular concept of public space where people are free to meet, congregate, demonstrate, sit, walk through or perform whatever functions they, as members of the public, determine. This book explores how these conditions have an impact on the concept of the public sphere, the use of public spaces and the notion of the museum as being "public." It does so by considering the relationship between concepts of the public sphere and public space and how public spaces are used, produced, reproduced, and understood.

The public sphere may also be a "metaphorical term" for a space where people can interact (McKee, 2005). Alan McKee identifies the Internet as a public sphere because this is where "minds meet" to discuss matters public. In other words, the topic and form of discussion render the sphere public. Spaces of the public sphere are not necessarily virtual, although this is occurring increasingly with electronic technology, but may also be physical spaces. Ways of identifying and comprehending the public sphere rely on understanding representations of the public and its reproduction. An important site for the public sphere is public space: main streets, town squares and halls, public parks, and gardens, generally understood as spaces where people may congregate, without discrimination, for recreation or to engage in public address.

Museums, I argue, are also a site for and of the public sphere. In doing so, I explore the different ways in which the museum functions as a space of public address. That is, I ask how the "public" is invoked within the museum context and how the museum itself sees its role in defining or prescribing how that public should be constituted.

Much debate about public space has been about those kinds of spaces that are now being reclaimed or rediscovered as significant for communities. These are more overtly political spaces or community spaces related to distinct political struggles. The community is often identified with or characterized by a struggle with government or private economic interests, reinforcing its separateness from both "private" and "public." Yet, irrespective of their overt connection to the sphere of government at local, regional and national levels, references to museums as public spaces are persistent. To a great extent, this then renders the claim to *publicness* less convincing. It suggests that the museum is less worthy than the communities that are identifiable as, or characterized by, the site of political struggle.

How, then, can a museum be defined as *truly* public and yet capable in a political sense? Small community heritage projects are, in fact, no less susceptible to political and state influences than are the large, open public space projects. The tension between public and political remains, however, a crucial issue to be addressed when considering museums as facilitators and forms of public address.

There is a general reluctance to interrogate the term "public" within both museums and museum studies: it is simultaneously too amorphous and too obvious. This broad, ubiquitous term may perhaps be thought more useful if left elusive, and undefined. However, with the more recent validation of the term "community," the imperative to understand why *public* is no longer sufficient is increased. As we see later in this book, a shift to the term "community" has significant implications for our understanding of "the public" in the museum context. Although the desire to be more relevant "to people" may be at the heart of such a shift, it is important at the same time to understand what is inadequate about the term "public" so as not to end up inflicting the same type of misuse on "community," thereby rendering it less meaningful than intended.

What does it matter that these distinctions are not made or that the terms to which they refer are slippery and evasive? It does matter. A genuine engagement with the public by a cultural institution like a museum requires an understanding of the key terms that define it, the history of their use and how they work now. Without this, museums may of course still engage "a public." The problem is that where issues of *publicness* are considered they are generally framed around, and are indeed interchangeable with, a more general concept of the audience. Alternatively, "state" cultural institutions are assumed to be "public," undermining their claim to be a viable and important public sphere. In the current international climate, a more rigorous understanding of the term renders it productive if used strategically in the museum context. Rather than simply undermining the claim of many museum proponents that the museum is "public," I suggest that the distinctive meanings of the term render it increasingly powerful.

The museum, it is claimed, is not only a public space, but a place where public discourse takes place. Claims about the public nature of museums can be found in museology and professional accounts analyzing and describing the significance of the museum (Bennett, 1995; McClellan, 1994, 2008; Weil, 2002; Heumann Gurian, 2005). In turn, the public, as audience, assumes that the space of the museum *is* public space. The exhibitions are conceived for the public, and the subject matter is therefore considered to be of public importance.

In each of these contexts, the term "public" is used in different ways, with a general intention of being symbolic of, and relevant to, democratic societies. This book provides a critical reflection on this important idea of being public, examines the impacts of slippage in the use of this term and identifies how it can be used in the development of museums in the future.

Methodology and Structure

As I outline below, the methodology draws on the discourse of the term "public" as it is debated in political science, as well as its use within historical discourses about museums. Subsequently, the spatial practices of the museum as a material space and as space of representation are examined. This is followed by an account of the way in which museology and museum studies have adapted the term "public" since the late 1980s in the form of an institutional critique of curatorial practices and the subsequent institutional response: namely, "visitor studies."

Chapter One uncovers the implicit but unexplored discourses of democracy in Habermas's concept of the public sphere as it relates to museums. It is through the identification and development of these discourses that his concept can be reconsidered and reformed to engage more fully with the exclusive characteristics of his reasoned and "rational public sphere" (Habermas, 1989). In a reconsidered framework, the public sphere can more adequately accommodate a more diverse, site-specific concept of the public sphere; that is, a sphere that is made up of groups in continual motion. The potential of Habermas's public sphere, particularly its modification by Habermas and his critics, from the original concept, is a valuable consideration in the context of museums. It is also the most often cited reference to the notion of "public" as it is used and understood in relation to museums.

Significantly, as noted above, the concept of the public sphere in the museum context emerges historically during the same period in which the museum develops a new relationship to the state. Chapter Two explores the historical discourses of the museum as part of the public sphere. Indeed, the use of the term "public" in the museum context is not new to the twenty-first century. Debates about the public nature of the museum – in relation to audience and public discourse – have occurred since the late eighteenth century. This chapter charts how the museum has been historically constituted, representing the transition from the princely collection to the public – in short, democratizing culture. It examines how the museum emerges from the nineteenth century as a cultural institution with an important role, working with competing notions of the term "public" as it engages with the state. These ideas are presented in the broader context of the merging public sphere, as imagined and represented through visual discourses. In particular, I look at the work of Louis-Léopold Boilly (1761–1845) and Jacques-Louis David (1748–1825) and highlight how their art was important in the emergence of an understanding of what is "public." The importance of *vision* in the development of representations of the public sphere and in museums is also considered in this chapter, despite visual discourses being dismissed by Habermas.

The historical development of the modern museum reveals spaces, formerly ecclesiastical or aristocratic, opening up to the people. The form of presentation and representation still mimics the traditional forms of collection and display in place before the revolution in Paris. Chapter Three examines the museum as public space and considers the way in which assumptions about the public nature of museum space are based on an idea of democracy (historically, politically, and ideologically) upon which museums were formed. Yet, the relationship between the materiality of democratic public space and the discourses about democracy is little understood in museology. This chapter discusses the limitations of the public sphere and outlines the relationship between space and democracy in the museum context. Some of the key questions are: how does the museum profession engage with the notion of audience in relation to the concept of the public? How do museums function as a site of public space within which public discourse can occur?

In considering the different ways in which museums are public, Chapter Three explores the spatial aspect by examining the role of space as it relates to the public sphere. First, if we analyze the spaces in which the public sphere operates, and the way in which it is practiced, we may recognize how citizens and publics are shaped conceptually in the museum itself. We can see how, by practicing *being* a public in this way, people may *constitute* themselves as a public. Second, while in this state, people involved in the practices of *being a public* are not autonomous but, rather, in their very practices, are reshaping what it means to be a public and in turn are being shaped by the public.

In the late twentieth and early twenty-first centuries, investigating the views, experience and interests of visitors to museums has become a significant strategy used by museum professionals around the world. This has resulted in the introduction of visitor studies, audience research, and myriad methodologies. One key influence has been the pioneering work of Pierre Bourdieu in the 1960s and 1970s. As we see in Chapter Four, in effect museums have developed ways of articulating the audiences' concerns with the public function of the museum to address concerns about accessibility, programming, and accountability.

The consequences of museums identifying their "public," and the reason this is equated with audience, are central concerns of this book. How museums use the term "public" to think about audiences – as community, and as individuals – is as central to the museum as the collection. Many museums use visitor studies to understand their audiences as "the public" even when visitors are not always performing in this way. By investigating the role of subjectivity in visitor studies programs and related material produced by museums, this chapter reveals the limitations of the methodologies used to identify and understand the public as audience. Recent developments in social media also signal new ways in which the public can comment in independent forums about museums, opening up new avenues for communication and negotiation about the role of museums.

In many ways, the desire "to know" the public has been a response to assumptions about perceptions of the role of curators. We see the role of curator coming under scrutiny in new ways. The so-called lack of engagement by audiences is attributed to a sense of alienation from the museum, particularly in terms of how audiences are addressed and assumptions made by curators about the knowledge and experience audiences bring to the museum. Questions in museum studies and within the profession are asked about the tendency to mask the curator's role. The primary producer of knowledge within the sector was, up until the 1980s, assumed to be the curator. In an effort to reveal the rationale for particular exhibitions and collections displays, the curator's role since then has been reconfigured (sometimes renamed) in an attempt to render the role more "accountable" and insist on models of exhibition development and curatorial practices that involve all roles in the museum profession.

In Chapter Five, The Museum as Public Intellectual, I discuss the intellectual function of the museum as a site of public culture. I examine the role of the museum professional and the role of the public intellectual or producer and facilitator of public culture. This chapter investigates the changing role of curators as public intellectuals.

The book concludes that, notwithstanding the dilemmas associated with the term, museums are, and have been for many years, a form of public space and an important part of the public sphere. There are limitations to what museums can do. These are derived from the relationship of museums to the state and society. A failure to understand these limitations means that museums suffer from unrealistic expectations. Invariably, museums fall short. By showing the relationship between public and *community*, I advocate greater recognition and understanding of the terms "community," "public," "public space," and the "public sphere" as a means to reconcile ideas about the function of the museum with contemporary practices, as well as to understand the possibilities and limitations of future practices.

An exploration of the public sphere and museums is particularly challenging given the multitude of ways that museums engage with the idea of the public. Methodologically, it is equally challenging to do justice to the multiple ways in which museums exist, in scale, divergent political contexts, disciplinary focus, media, and location. For this reason this book takes the form of a discussion about an idea central to museums and their constituents. That idea, while problematic, also enables a connection to be drawn between the work of museums across cultural institutions and cultural forms: from princely collections, to public museums and community cultural centers, and across time, from the private collections of royalty to the virtual museum in the digital age.

1

The Public Sphere

The term "public" is pivotal in the museum context. As suggested in the introduction, the multiple applications and pervasive use of the term may appear – misleadingly – to render it useless. I examine in this chapter the complexity of the term in order to reveal both its shortcomings and its potential in the context of museums. I also explore possible ways to extend its use in that context.

Apart from the general everyday references to the museum's public nature or function, the most frequently cited reference to the term "public" in museum studies is to the work of Jürgen Habermas (1989). There is a certain irony here, as I detail later, in that Habermas does not himself make the link between culture, spatial practices or aesthetics often assumed in such citations. But inaccuracies in the ways in which Habermas's work is employed in discussions about museums are less important than an understanding of how his work may lend itself to a deeper exploration of museums, in particular of the way in which they attempt to be democratic and genuine institutions of, and for, the public. In this sense, I rework Habermas's "public sphere" as a *cultural* public sphere to reveal the significance of "the cultural" in understanding the public realm. I will begin with a detailed consideration of the key tenets of the idea of the "public sphere," and then work towards an understanding of how museums are relevant to the concept.

The notion of a "bourgeois public sphere" was proposed by Jürgen Habermas in 1962. *The Structural Transformation of the Public Sphere* (*STPS*) was translated from German in 1989 and has received considerable attention from critics since. There has been a resurgence of interest in critical theories of the public sphere, particularly theories that have emerged from the Frankfurt School – from Habermas, Oskar Negt and Alexander Kluge (Koivisto and Valiverronen, 1996; Johnson, 2006). These critical theorists, as we see later in this chapter, have refocused the attention of academics in the Western world on the political implications of the public sphere, because of the way the concept of the public sphere engages with concepts of democracy and societal organization (Johnson, 2006).

Habermas identified literary discourses of the bourgeois public as most prevalent and influential in his historical model and theory. (This may be because of his background in journalism.) I suggest this is a relatively narrow conception, in which the literary discourse and literary "publics" are prioritized at the expense of other "publics." Those that challenge Habermas's model or are not included in his concept may, however, be understood by investigating cultural discourses other than literary ones. The significance of cultural disciplines is not sufficiently apparent to Habermas. Though he claims that interdisciplinarity is necessary for considering the public sphere and discourses on democracy, Habermas himself fails, importantly, to draw on those disciplines that are concerned with cultural institutions and practices in civil society and democracy.

The idea of the "public," as defended in this book, intersects with notions of "public" in several academic disciplines and related professions. We find, however, a number of poorly conceived understandings of the public sphere in these other disciplines, particularly in understanding the intersection between museums and museum studies, and history, colonialism, urbanism, and visuality. A new, cultural understanding of the public sphere acknowledges many different ways of "being in public." The public is not an amorphous or homogenous grouping of subgroups or individuals. Nor is public space merely a simple nostalgic representation of the public sphere (see Chapter Three). The production of the public sphere involves complex exchanges and negotiations between different forms of communications and practices of *being in public*. This is not a notion that rests upon difference, bracketed off from an otherwise all-inclusive idea of the public. I will suggest that, from a perspective that is cultural, spatial, and intersectional, it is also possible to identify the emergence of new publics.

Many critical accounts of the term "public" investigate specific or actual sites in their search for evidence of the existence of a public sphere (Iveson, 2008; Mitchell, 2003; Smith and Low, 2007). However, these actual sites are often given marginal status in critical accounts of the public sphere, as such. This is despite the potential centrality of visual and spatial discourses to various formations and understandings of the public sphere. It is essential to consider these discourses (and their limitations) as iterations, as practices, of public address and potentially representative discourses of the public sphere. The *performative* aspect of democratic sites is often overlooked, while the existence of physical space is prioritized over the practice of democracy. The practice of being part of the public in the space

Image 1.1 Louis-Léopold Boilly, *The Public in the Salon of the Louvre, Viewing the Painting of the "Sacre"* begun 1808, Woodner Collection. Image courtesy of the Board of Trustees, National Gallery of Art, Washington, USA

of the museum – recognizing how being a citizen in the museum constitutes the public – is valuable for understanding the democratic nature of the museum. To understand democracy we also need to recognize that many different versions of democracy exist. There are, however, some key or core characteristics, including a particular form of rhetoric (see Held, 1996). By investigating actual spaces and places of the public in which this rhetoric is performed, it is possible to see how public spaces constitute a critical visual discourse of the public sphere. These spaces include the museum.

Habermas and the Public Sphere

The idea of the public sphere has received renewed critical attention since the translation of Habermas's foundational text, *The Structural*

Transformation of the Public Sphere, coincided with major world events including the fall of the Berlin Wall, the reunification of Germany, and the Tiananmen Square Massacre in China (Koivisto and Valiverronen, 1996). The work of Jürgen Habermas, a critical theorist, member of the Frankfurt School and foremost commentator on the public sphere, is also considered valuable because of its strengths relative to other theoretical approaches. Benhabib (1992a), for example, proposed three distinct models of the public sphere, and favored Habermas's over the Arendtian and liberal (Kantian) conceptions, because "questions of democratic legitimacy in advanced capitalist societies are central to it." "Nevertheless," she added, "whether this model is resourceful enough to help us think through the transformation of politics in our kinds of societies is an open question" (Benhabib, 1992a: 74). A discussion of the relevance of Habermas's theory to the museum will provide one point of entry to answering this question.

Habermas's work has received significant critical responses from many disciplines (including sociology, philosophy, media studies and cultural studies). Of particular interest in this present discussion is how his work and that of his critics intersect with space and vision, or with the spatial and visual discourses of the public sphere.

In Habermas's *STPS*, the argument about the central role of discourse on public matters in the formation of the public sphere became in particular the basis of his later work on "communicative action."[1]

Habermas repeatedly uses the term "public sphere" but does not elaborate on its spatiality in either a material or theoretical sense. Despite this, the notion of a public sphere invokes certain spatial metaphors, the most obvious being a *spherical* form, such as a globe or a ball. Specific forms of architectural space have historically represented political and cultural concerns in social or public life. For example, in Western cultures, the sphere, seen in Étienne-Louis Boullée's 1784 project for a memorial to Isaac Newton (see Image 1.2, *Cénotaphe de Newton*) and in his museum and library designs, has been purposely used historically to represent democratic space in its "natural" form (Boullée, n.d.). The significance of such cultural forms and expressions of public space is, as we will see, overlooked in Habermas's writing, and yet his concept of the public sphere both suggests and ultimately depends on spatiality.

The public sphere is not represented as an actual space in Habermas's theory; instead, it refers to the conduct of public discourse, understood primarily as literary and discursive. It may therefore be found on the pages of an eighteenth-century pamphlet or in discourse about public matters in coffee houses, market places or literary salons. While Habermas's historical

Image 1.2   Étienne-Louis Boullée, *Cénotaphe de Newton*, 1784. Bibliothèque nationale de France

model cites *places* where such discussion occurs (European coffee houses or market places, among others), the centrality of actual space for the public sphere is not, in itself, considered significant. This is examined later in Chapter Three.

Habermas's research into the emergence of the liberal bourgeois public sphere in eighteenth-century France led to the theory of the bourgeois public sphere as a "site" where the interests of the state, the commercial class and the bourgeoisie intersect. This model then became generalizable for Habermas as the "liberal public sphere" or "public sphere." The public sphere exists between the state and the private body of persons; it functions to rationally contemplate matters of public importance. Habermas's public sphere is not an "actual" body of people; yet it has the potential to have "real" power. The mechanism by which it becomes real is discourse or debate about matters of public importance. In this model these debates affect public opinion and have influence on government policy and its implementation. The spatial context itself is, Habermas implies, not relevant to, or constitutive of, such discussion.

To speak simply of influence is insufficient for understanding what is at stake. Nancy Fraser (1992: 134) distinguishes between "strong" and "weak" publics and argues that the public sphere – as a sphere between government and civil society – is weak because those "whose deliberative practice consists exclusively in opinion formation and does not encompass decision making" cannot claim to have real influence. For Fraser, deliberative practices do not necessarily translate into actual social change. The capacity to influence and the power to implement actual change is essential, she concludes. This requires a reworking of Habermas's model to take into account the real-life processes of democracy. Fraser's critique offers a model for subjecting Habermas's theory to an analysis built around the centrality of cultural space. Indeed, if we consider Fraser's argument in the museum context, we see that the capacity of the museum to exist between government and civil society is in many countries compromised by the state's interest (via funding and policy) in the role and function of the museum. The museum's capacity to be democratic, in Fraser's sense, may be limited to opinion formation but not actual decision making and may not actually effect social change: in this manner the museum is rendered a "weak public." As we will see, however, the capacity of the museum as a public sphere is more complex than this. It may be weak in its relationship with the state, but powerful in serving as a site for community and democratic "publics."

Habermas's concept of the public sphere remains valuable, however, despite inconsistencies in his use of the concept. Where he is clear, though, is in identifying literary discourses as media where the primary articulation of – and the formation of – the public sphere occurred: "The medium of this political confrontation was peculiar and without historical precedent: people's public use of their reason (*öffentliches Räsonnement*)" (1989: 27). He continues:

> The "town" was the life center of civil society not only economically; in cultural-political contrast to the court, it designated especially an early public sphere in the world of letters whose institutions were the coffee houses, the salons, and the Tischgesellschaften (table societies). (Habermas, 1989: 30)

define

He defines "public spaces" as sites where public discourse occurs. "The commons was public, publica: for common use there was public access to the fountain and market – loci communes, loci publica" (Habermas, 1989: 6). (Today this would also include print and electronic media with the actual physical space being secondary to the function of discourse on public matters.) Thus, while he emphasizes the "virtual" nature of the public sphere, concealed in the processes and exchanges of discourse, debate and communication, he also notes the physical spaces in which these processes took place. He fails, nonetheless, to recognize the significance of these

cafes, salons, markets

spaces. The importance of this recognition, however, should not be overlooked. It will be of significance in understanding the nature of the *cultural* and *spatial* public sphere.

For Habermas, the public sphere becomes known through the process of promotion and publicity generated by an emerging bourgeois public involved in reading societies and lending libraries, talking in coffee houses and clubs, seeking new ways to participate in the governance of their society. Habermas elaborates on the structured way in which the bourgeois public sphere developed into another platform from which the public could represent itself: "through the vehicle of public opinion it put the state in touch with the needs of society" (1989: 31). Publications and the development of the mass media became (and remain) critical conduits for such publicity. Publicity in Habermas's work refers to the way in which the public sphere is disseminated: through the "world of letters," where "rational critical debate which originated in the ... conjugal family, by communicating with itself, attained clarity about itself" (1989: 51). The public articulation of arguments, presented in written form in letters, books and papers, became for Habermas a technical and cultural context in which the bourgeois public sphere was constituted (Warner, 1992).

Access to the public sphere of representation came to be considered a basic right of citizens, but for Habermas, representation in the public realm was conditional upon the public use of reason.[2] Sentiment, for Habermas, is too personal, irrational and particular in this model, and becomes a significant point of contention in critiques of the *STPS*. Relying on the "natural" goodwill of citizens will not guarantee, Habermas concludes, that the private interests of individuals will not determine their deliberation on public matters. To participate in public discussion citizens had to be willing to compromise, to transform their views. According to Habermas, then, new problems arose historically, as different sectors of society demanded access to the public sphere as a "basic right," without necessarily understanding the rational form of discussion that was required for democracy to work.

The will to participate in democratic processes was not itself sufficient for democracy to work. In the practices of Habermas's public sphere in the late eighteenth century, citizens were required to participate, and comply with, recognizable forms of interaction in the public sphere, where the notion of freedom (of speech, of the press) was indeed limited, and contingent upon public norms that were subject to change. The mode of discourse allowed negotiation, hence change, to occur if there was consensus. To understand these basic rights and forms of representation, citizens needed to be literate in the structure of public discourse and democracy. Habermas's concept of the bourgeois public sphere relied on the ability of citizens to recognize particular norms and forms of representations in the public sphere, namely the literary and the print media.

Habermas's claims about the necessity and universality of "rationality" have been subject to criticism (Young, 1990, 1992; Robbins, 1993; Ingram, 1994; White, 1995). Inclusion in the public sphere, in Habermas's model, requires reasoned and rational discourse on matters of public concern. Inclusion, however, does not ensure equality. Despite the rhetoric of inclusivity, a public sphere based on these principles, I argue, will be precarious. "Oppositional" public spheres, according to Habermas, should modify their forms of discourse to comply with apparent normative conditions of the "mainstream" public sphere. I argue, however, that this modification does not acknowledge the contested nature of the public sphere itself. The representation as well as recognition of the public sphere in spatial and visual discourses illustrates contestation of the public sphere. It serves to underline the relationship of the public to democratic forms, which are themselves based on contestation.

Despite such shortcomings in Habermas's idea of the public sphere, Nancy Fraser concedes that "[t]he idea of 'the public sphere' in Habermas's sense is a conceptual resource that can help overcome ... problems arising from 'less precise' understandings and uses of the term" (1992: 110). For Fraser, "Habermas's idea of the public sphere is indispensable to critical theory and democratic social practice" because it illustrates the "distinctions among state apparatuses, economic markets, and democratic associations," which are central to democratic theory (1992: 111). This is useful for an understanding of the public role of the museum.

Richard Sennett (1992) has also written extensively on the history of the term "public" and its uses. According to Sennett, the practice of public life has shifted from an extrinsic to a more intrinsic individualistic practice. This, he argues, is to the detriment of both the individual and society. Sennett claims that confusion and difficulty can arise with the term "public" when individuals work out "in terms of personal feelings public matters that can be dealt with only through codes of impersonal meaning" (1992: 5). The individual, for Sennett, can act or engage on the public stage with the "greater" social good in mind, demonstrating a public conscience. This is distinct from self-gain. Sennett further argues that a problem emerges when notions of democracy are negotiated on an individualistic basis, because it is likely that such notions are being negotiated to satisfy individual needs rather than for the "common public good." Yet what does it mean for something to be a "common" good? The use of the term "public" often "betrays a multiplicity of concurrent meanings" (Habermas, 1989: 1). Such multiplicity is apparent in the museum context too.

Reasoned and rational discussion, according to both Habermas and Sennett, performs a normalizing function. It allows individuals to enter the public sphere as equals to negotiate public matters for the public good. However, while reason and rationality appear to be enabling in Habermas's and Sennett's models, they are also used to exclude individuals from the public sphere. Habermas's model also excludes the dynamic way in which contestation between competing publics about what constitutes the public sphere may be an effective way for the public sphere to remain relevant in social life. It is Habermas's requirement for reason and rationality that obscures these dynamics, and attracts most criticism from critics (and critical supporters alike). Both Habermas and Sennett recognize, however, that though rationality and reason are key principles of modern liberal democracy and the public sphere, they are not necessarily always employed. Nor are they used in the same way all the time. We consider this further, below.

The different types of public spheres that arise from this discussion of the *bourgeois* public sphere and the way in which the term "public" functions in relation to democracy are discussed below. The tensions between the empirical (historical) and abstract (theoretical) modes in the *STPS* must also be considered. To explore these tensions, I draw on Habermas's critics, for whom the public sphere is exclusionary, and expand on their work to consider the importance of visual and spatial discourses. For museums, this discussion reflects tensions in theory and in practice. This is in part because the invention of the modern public museum coincides with the era in which Habermas locates his concept of the public sphere. In order to make this connection between Habermas's public sphere and its visual and spatial aspects, let us turn to the *STPS* in detail.

Structural transformation of the public sphere

Emerging from the German intellectual tradition of critical theory, Habermas, like his colleagues in the Frankfurt School, was concerned with the theory and practice of democratic social systems. The Frankfurt School did not produce a unified critical theory of society, but engaged in extensive multidisciplinary approaches, and at times oppositional theoretical approaches to critical theory. It influenced many academic disciplines concerned with issues of social life and domination. The concept of the public sphere is said to be one of the most "significant contributions of the Critical Theory of the Frankfurt School" in recent decades (Koivisto and Valiverronen, 1996: 18).

In his preface to the *STPS*, Habermas states that "the category 'public sphere' must be investigated within the broad field formerly reflected in the perspective of the traditional science of 'politics'" and argues that the public sphere does not fall within the ambit of political sciences alone (1989: xvii). For Habermas, an analysis of the public sphere necessarily engages numerous disciplines; otherwise the object "disintegrates." In other words, the public sphere is fundamentally an interdisciplinary realm.

In the words of Thomas McCarthy, in his introduction to the 1989 edition of the *STPS*, Habermas presents a "historical-sociological account of the emergence, transformation and disintegration of the bourgeois public sphere" (McCarthy, 1989: xi). It is a sphere that he defines as being between "civil society and the state" (1989: xi). The bourgeois public sphere was "institutionally guaranteed" – it was officially recognized by the state and consulted accordingly as a sphere with a critical function in relation to the state. It was constituted by private people, who put reason to use in public discourse and it "publicly monitored" the state through such discussion (McCarthy, 1989: xi). To qualify for access, citizens needed to be educated and owners of property. Discussion occurred around matters regarding the state and so-called civil society. The right to freely express views critical of the state significantly altered the relationship between the state and private citizens.

Habermas writes:

> The French Revolution eventually triggered a movement toward a politicization of a public sphere that at first revolved around literature and art criticism. This is true not only of France, but holds for Germany as well. A "politicization of associational life," the rise of a partisan press, the fight against censorship and for freedom of opinion characterize the change in function of the expanding network of public communication up to the middle of the nineteenth century. The politics of censorship, with which the states of the German Federation fought against the institutionalization of a political public sphere and managed to delay its advent until 1848, only made it more inevitable that literature and criticism would be sucked into the whirlpool of politicizations. (1992a: 424)

The bourgeois public sphere was critical of the mechanisms and outcomes of the absolutist state as representing only the interests of the monarchy and the clergy. This critique enabled the development of a public sphere that, according to Habermas, was not only more democratic, but also itself became the site for the development of modern democracy. We should note here, the emergence of the modern "public" museum in this same era.

STPS [handwritten marginal note]

Habermas's account identifies the structures by which the bourgeois public sphere developed as a new tier of the representable public through publishing in the newsprint media. He identifies the public as distinct from the state, the marketplace and the intimate sphere of the family. According to McCarthy (1989: xi), Habermas traces the emergence of the bourgeois public sphere in relation to "the interdependent development of the literary and political self consciousness of the new class" in the mid-eighteenth century (through to the Revolution of 1789). A type of self-reflexivity was fostered through new cultural practices such as reading societies and political journalism. Developing alongside the political manifestation of the bourgeois public sphere were forms of communication that functioned as new and effective conduits for this self-representation. What emerged was a particular type of "representative publicness."

The groups functioning in Habermas's version of the bourgeois public sphere used the print media, conversation, reading groups and literary organizations, and rational debate in public spaces such as coffee houses, markets and town squares. Habermas's new representable public also created new expectations about the citizen's right to avenues through which to express their views, and the right to access domains in which a citizen's views could be communicated to other citizens. A new means of discussing and disseminating one's views became available and subsequently became politically powerful in articulating the concerns of the public.

Habermas's bourgeois public sphere essentially depended on a concept of normativity; on the idea that a developed practice of social and political actions would become regular and accepted in political life. These practices, such as using reason and rationality in personal conversation and public discussion, become institutionalized as norms.

The practices and contexts used to establish normative communication are a highly contentious aspect of Habermas's notion of the bourgeois public sphere. He claims that particular modes of communication and forms of behavior are necessary for communicating with others on public matters in the public sphere. An atmosphere conducive to consensus, compromise and rational discussion is, he states, paramount. It is a domain where private subjects are conscious of being "in public" and "acting for" the public good. The private sphere, in contrast, is particular or subjective. The historical and conceptual exclusion of the concerns of the private sphere from the public sphere, Habermas argues, is necessary to prevent the emergence of as many versions of the public sphere as there are private persons. How would consensus and agreement be reached on matters of public importance, he asks, if all matters were basically negotiated on the basis of private interests alone? The bourgeois public sphere is a model expressed in a historical moment, a real historical example of how democracy should work and how it could work effectively. As a real practice, it existed for a relatively short period of time, but it remains an ideal, yet workable, form of social organization.

Habermas's bourgeois public sphere cannot be understood outside of, or apart from, "the unique developmental history of the civil society" from which it originated (1989: 6). Habermas himself considers a sociological method too limited for understanding its emergence because it "proceeds on a level of generality at which unique processes and events can only be cited as examples – that is as cases that can be interpreted as instances of a more general social development" (Habermas, 1989: xv–xviii). It is important to use "equally strict criteria for the structural analysis of the interdependencies at the level of society as a whole" (1989: xv–xviii). Habermas's work, thus, uses "features of a historical constellation that attained dominance and leaves aside the plebeian public sphere as a variant that in a sense was suppressed in the historical process" (Habermas, 1989: xviii).

The *STPS* charts democracy as central to the experiences of modernity. However, like the project of democracy, Habermas sees the emancipatory capacity of the experience of modernity as incomplete, and remaining incomplete to this day. Habermas's later work, particularly his work on theories of communicative action, also considers forms of purposeful and rational interaction between individuals that enable them to participate effectively in public processes. Forms of communication, particularly the use of reasoned and rational argument in the process of negotiation in the public domain, preoccupy Habermas. In his later work, the notion of democracy is developed from the *STPS* and is significantly influenced by the combination of empirical (socio-historical) work and the theoretical development of the public sphere. The theory is based on empirical research on the late eighteenth century, and the way in which Habermas later modifies his thinking demonstrates his commitment to using these practices in his work.

Throughout Habermas's work, revolutionary mid-eighteenth century Europe forms a key point of reference, having both real and imagined potential for the full emancipation of the people. For a short period, the educated and uneducated strata, he notes, became committed to the function of the bourgeois public sphere: the bourgeoisie and the working classes joined forces to constitute the liberal bourgeois public sphere.

The writings of John Stuart Mill and Alexis de Tocqueville, Habermas notes, raise a fear of the majority, a specter of the dominant opinions or "unreconciled interests," becoming a coercive force overwhelming the "compulsion of reason" in the public sphere (1989: 132). Public opinion, understood in this sense, becomes "the reign of the many and the mediocre"; this in turn is understood as characterizing the unruly masses (Habermas, 1989: 133). The outcome, according to Habermas's critique of de Tocqueville, was *conformity* of public opinion rather than consensus through critical debate, or the considered form of deliberation, favored by Habermas.

This critique may suggest that the possibility of more than one type of public sphere, indeed of competing public spheres, is not part of Habermas's thinking. However, in writings following the publication of the *STPS*, including engagement with critiques of *STPS*, he outlines the kinds of differences that may be tolerated within his model of the public sphere (Habermas, 1992a). However, these differences are not unlimited. Despite acknowledging that at least "[e]mpirically, [he] has learned most from the criticisms that point to the exclusionary mechanism of the public sphere," Habermas still argues for the centrality of consensus and the use of reason and rationality in the public sphere.[3] In privileging this form of public engagement, Habermas overlooks (as do his critics) the significance of space as an alternative – in a non-exclusionary way – in which the public sphere operates and the public itself is constituted. For museums it suggests we consider how discussion contributes to understanding how exclusion is produced, *and* how processes of deliberation in the formation of consensus, or a limited version of it, are determined and performed, and by whom.

Public Sphere/Private Sphere

Habermas's conception of privateness encompasses not only the private individual in the context of the market economy and commodity exchange, but also the private person in the home or the familial context. For Habermas, such separation is necessary to maintain the distinct functions of each sphere. The private sphere tends to be linked to the public sphere, though, when the market economy affects the economy of the private sphere:

> The line between state and society, fundamental in our context, divided the public sphere from the private realm. The public sphere was coextensive with public authority, and we consider the court part of it. Included in the private realm was the authentic "public sphere," for it was a public sphere constituted by private people. Within the realm that was the preserve of private people we therefore distinguish again between private and public spheres. The private sphere comprised of civil society in the narrower sense, that is to say, the realm of commodity exchange and of social labor; imbedded in it was the family

within its interior domain (Intimsphäre). The public sphere in the political realm evolved from the public sphere in the world of letters; through the vehicle of public opinion it put the state in touch with the needs of society. (Habermas, 1989: 30)

The private and public spheres were distinguishable on the basis of the private interest lying outside the public realm, and ceasing to matter in the public sphere: "The public's understanding of the public use of reason was guided specifically by such private experiences," which developed from the "subjectivity of the conjugal family's intimate domain (*Imtimsphäre*)" (Habermas, 1989: 28). The concept of private, however, is also entwined with the private market economy:

> The status of the private man combined the role of owner of commodities with that of head of the family, that of property owner with that of "human being" per se. The doubling of the private sphere on the higher plane of the intimate sphere . . . furnished the foundation for an identification of these two roles under the common title of the "private" . . . the political self-understanding of the bourgeois public originated there as well. (Habermas, 1989: 28–29)

According to Habermas, blurring the distinction between the private and public spheres weakens the political possibilities for reforming a "truly liberal democracy," the central project of his model. When the boundaries between public and private become significantly obscured, what could be termed a "pseudo" public sphere is created:

> The downfall of the public sphere, demonstrated by its changing political functions, had its source in the structural transformation of the relationship between the public sphere and the private realm in general. (Habermas, 1989: 142–143)

As outlined above, the public sphere sits between the state and the premodern court on one hand and between civil society and the private intimacy of the newly constituted conjugal family on the other. This new sphere developed via new literary, cultural and political debates. As we have seen, new forms of social life in cafés, and in literary and debating salons, employed reasoned and rational critique. Public opinion forming and the development of publicity ensued, as literary journals and print media flourished, and in academies and galleries and salons. New public spaces emerged. The public museum was one of the most significant.

Habermas on Art and the Public Sphere

Art – its appreciation and practice – is considered by Habermas as more appropriately understood within the private sphere than the public. Released from its functions in the service of social representation, art became an object of free choice and of changing preference. "The 'taste' to which art was oriented from then on became manifest in the assessments of lay people who claimed no prerogative, since within a public everyone was entitled to judge" (Habermas, 1989: 40).

Like the concert and the theatre, museums institutionalized the lay judgment on art: discussion became the medium through which people appropriated art. Innumerable pamphlets criticizing or defending the leading theories of art built on the discussions in the salons and reacted to them: art criticism became conversation (Habermas, 1989: 40). Amateurs were the most immediate audience for art in the first half of the eighteenth century. Art critics played a significant function in relation to the production of art, as the publication of criticism helped distribute information about the arts generally, and about the relative value of different works. The art critic then went on to function as a public educator:

> The art critics could see themselves as spokesmen for the public – and in their battle with the artists this was the central slogan – because they knew of no authority beside that of the better argument and because they felt themselves at one with all who were willing to let themselves be convinced by arguments. At the same time they could turn against the public itself when, as experts combating "dogma" and "fashion," they appealed to the ill-informed person's native capacity for judgment. (Habermas, 1989: 41)

Salons and coffee houses also became sites for audiences of art criticism. Criticism appeared in journals. While some "tastes" were still recognized as connoisseurship, the individuals who constituted the public were "not to be obligated by any judgment except their own" (Habermas, 1989: 41). Here Habermas seems to suggest that artwork only reached the public via criticism in journals distributed in coffee houses and salons; he does not see art as intrinsically communicating and debating issues of public concern. This will emerge as an important gap in his work.

Habermas's essay on "Modernity: An unfinished project," first written in 1980 and later published in an edited volume, set outs his view on the nature of art in relation to the everyday practice of life. It elaborates on aesthetic modernity, which was "begin[ning] to take shape clearly with Baudelaire and with his theory of art." Modernity is:

[a] consciousness . . . that expresses itself in the spatial metaphor of the avant-garde – that is, an avant-garde that explores hitherto unknown territory exposes itself to the risk of sudden and shocking encounters, conquers an as yet undetermined future, and must therefore find a path for itself in previously uncharted domains. (Habermas, 1996: 40)

Habermas's call for a non-aesthetic assessment of modernity and the public sphere is cause for concern if we are to consider the museum and its practices as central to both. It is the transgressive and the interconnected aspects of art and the public sphere that I will now focus on.

The mobility of the avant-garde (which included artists) is problematic for Habermas's theory, because of its contingent, unknowable nature. The avant-garde's "anarchistic" intentions are to be subversive and to rebel "against the norm-giving achievements of tradition" from the Enlightenment (Habermas, 1996: 41). But for Habermas, the use of reason and rationality are necessary for such unsettling times: precisely what the avant-garde lacks is the necessary respect for reason and rationality. The "elite counter-cultures" from which artists ("bohemia") emerge are misguided, according to Habermas, because their primarily focus is on lifestyle, and their concerns are too subjective and too particular. He writes of the avant-garde, that "the idea that the mission of art is to fulfill its implicit promise of happiness by introducing into society as a whole that artistic lifestyle that was defined precisely as its opposite" (1996: 44). The project of modernity, he says, "only comes into clear view when we abandon the usual concentration on art" (1996: 45), and the focus on art is "too particular" a discourse, requiring specialist knowledge, setting itself apart, creating "expert cultures," from the general everyday lifeworld experience of the public. Art and institutions of culture are deemed autonomous rather than part of a broader context of social life, despite the new relationship of the museum to the state and public affairs more broadly.

Immanuel Kant's writing on the public sphere strongly influenced Habermas. Following Kant (1952), Habermas argues that "[t]he quality of a work [of art] is . . . determined quite independently of any connections it might have with our practical relation to life" (Habermas, 1996: 47). Rather than being understood as a vital part of political discourse offering representations and articulations of the critique of modernity, art and visual representations of the public sphere are considered outside public discourse unless they are understandable to the "expert in the field of everyday life" (Habermas, 1996: 51). Provided that one's experience of art can be seen to relate, or be relevant, to the "problems of life . . . [art can then enter] a language game that is no longer that of art criticism proper" (Habermas, 1996: 51). It is only then that aesthetic experience can be open to reason in the discourse of modernity or even democracy, where:

> aesthetic experience not only revitalizes those who need interpretations [of everyday life] in the light of which we perceive our world, but also influences our cognitive interpretations and our normative expectations, and thus alters the way in which all these moments refer back and forth to one another. (Habermas, 1996: 51)

As I outline below, the inclusion of aesthetic experience as a legitimate part of the public sphere is also significant for understanding the museum as a public sphere. Spaces of the city are both the symbolic and real spaces of modern life/spectacle. The aesthetic, represented in the museum, comes to

Image 1.3   Hubert Robert, *Projet d'aménagement de la Grande Galerie du Louvre en 1796*, 1796. Paris, musée du Louvre/© Photo RMN/Jean-Gilles Berizz

be a form of simultaneous normative/avant-garde discourse in the public sphere: the interaction of the aesthetic dimension (private) and the institutional (state) enter public discourse and thus the public sphere.

Encountering modernity, I argue, was as much a spatial experience in eighteenth-century European social, private and public life as it was an intellectual experience. In France in particular, promenading, or walking, in public spaces in the city and surrounds was a significant aspect of public life, and is represented in Western art and socio-historical accounts of the period. The city became the obvious site for the new bourgeois public to *see* itself, but residents of Paris also made their presence apparent in Sunday sojourns to the nearby provinces. Noting these trends, many writers and critics in the late eighteenth and early nineteenth centuries concerned themselves with the extraordinary development of leisure and cultural activity that was specific to the experience of modernity. The spectacle and experience of world fairs, museums, the new glass-covered arcades, and department stores came to represent modern life and a different type of democratic potential. This kind of activity demonstrated one way in which modernity was articulated, and coincided with the development of new forms of social behavior and organization.[4] As represented in art of the period, it was a time when the newly formed bourgeoisie could see themselves and *be seen* as a public.

Historical coherence

The historical coherence of Habermas's bourgeois public sphere has attracted significant criticism. Critics ask, for example, whether the public sphere actually existed, as he describes it, in the period. His account is also contested on the grounds that it excludes different cultural communities, and therefore excludes the history of non-bourgeois sectors of social life. It is noted that Habermas openly privileges literary discourses because of their prevalence in representing the public sphere.

According to Geoff Eley, "[i]t is important to acknowledge the existence of competing publics not just in the nineteenth century, when Habermas sees a fragmentation of the classical liberal model of *Öffentlichkeit*, but at every stage of the public sphere and, indeed, from the very beginning" (1992: 306). In popular, peasant, working-class movements and nationalistic movements, Eley argues, we see such subaltern publics being constituted. Benjamin Nathans (1990) suggests that from its very inception, the bourgeois public sphere was heterogeneous, and identifies the existence of this differentiated and contested public and social life in late eighteenth-century Europe. Historical research, Mary Ryan (1992) suggests, reveals that the bourgeois public was never "the public." All three critics argue that, contrary to Habermas's account, a host of competing counter-publics arose, virtually contemporaneous with the bourgeois public. These included nationalist publics, peasant publics, elite women's publics, and working-class publics. If, then, there never was an actual "Habermasian" public sphere, is it possible to produce one based on an idealized concept?

Alternative views: counter-publics

Other critiques of Habermas's work can be found in critical theory, philosophical and cultural critiques of communication theory and practice, and the history of women's systematic exclusion from the public sphere. Despite criticism, however, Habermas's concept of the public sphere is still considered valuable. It is commonly used as a springboard for a wider range of speculations on the concepts and practices of democracy and the social structures that underpin it. Habermas's public sphere, according to Miriam Hansen, "continues to provide an objective standard for political critique" (1993: xxvii) for a variety of disciplines, and for a large number of theorists concerned with democracy.

Theorists of the same period, including Geoff Eley (1992), Joan B. Landes (1992), Oskar Negt and Alexander Kluge (1993), and Michel Foucault (1965, 1973, 1977), have engaged significantly with Habermas's use of reason in thinking about democracy. They cast public life and the public sphere in a different light: as being contested and contestable; as producing alternative publics; as producing a democracy that is forever in transition, potential and incomplete. Are spatial and visual discourses not significant cultural and aesthetic discourses on democracy and public life in the late eighteenth century, they ask? It is in such aesthetic discourses that we find a more fragmented and diverse notion of modernity, offering a significant challenge to Habermas's view.

Building on this work, I seek to understand how the historical specificity of Habermas's model might have an impact on the concept of the public sphere as it relates specifically to the idea of the museum and to its practices. The *STPS*, according to Peter Hohendahl, is Habermas's response to the political pessimism of Theodor Adorno and Max Horkheimer's *Dialectic of Enlightenment* (Hohendahl, 1992; Horkheimer and Adorno, 1972). In contrast to these theorists, Habermas makes a positive assessment of the European Enlightenment; he does so also in his account of the (incomplete) project of modernity. For Habermas, the emancipatory potential of a bourgeois public sphere lies in its capacity to allow the "individual" subject to be free within the institution of democracy.[5]

The provocative tension and potential in Habermas's work, for Hohendahl, lie in the difficulty of distinguishing between the public sphere as a theoretical concept and as an "actual" model of the public sphere. Hohendahl views Habermas's later work as an attempt to deal with some of these issues, which were unresolved in the *STPS*.

Critical limits and situated reason

Thomas McCarthy considers the way in which the subjects" social, historical and political context affects their understanding of argumentation in the public sphere. McCarthy's critique of the public sphere focuses on the dependence on the use of reason in accessing the public sphere. Subjects, he argues, may be unable to access or develop the type of reason required for use in the public sphere. In response, I ask: If access to the public sphere is contingent upon the use of reasoned and rational discourse, how is the public sphere accessible to all?

Seyla Benhabib, Thomas McCarthy, and Nancy Fraser raise concerns about how the norms and forms of communication of the public sphere are actually negotiated and understood. Benhabib notes the absence of any discussion of negotiation and development of the public sphere in Habermas's work. Habermas claims that the avant-garde as a transgressionary movement did not "speak for the public sphere, nor did [it] constitute a public sphere" (1992a: 421). However, as Hohendahl points out, Benhabib's critique tends to rely on Habermas's more recent writing rather than his *STPS* (which does acknowledge some contestation). The empirical character of the *STPS*, with, for instance, Habermas's identification of "actual" sites where public discourse occurred, is different from his later, more abstract concept of communicative action.

It is apparent in Habermas's *STPS* that a certain decorum and protocol were required (or at least preferred) for the people to participate in public discourse; indeed it was considered necessary in public spaces, such as cafés or town squares, and in contributions to newspapers (Benhabib, 1992a). We will see in the representations of how the new public museums were imagined that this was also the case.

The insistence on particular procedures – the use of rationality and reason – established through the process of citizens *observing* democracy becomes the inflexible aspect of Habermas's public sphere. While such procedures were meant to guarantee the nature or form of the public discourse, ways of interpreting so-called normative practices of being in public could also be misinterpreted. In this sense, although people may have observed and then imitated what they observed, that did not necessarily guarantee access to a

Image 1.4   Honore Daumier, *Free Admission Day – Twenty-Five Degrees of Heat*, 1852. Acc. no. 920048 – Research Library, The Getty Research Institute, Los Angeles, California (920048)

forum for public discourse or the power to influence discourse. Using these practices could become the basis of exclusion – and the basis of the moralizing role that the museum would take.

Building on the above critiques, I consider below the possibility of a non-universal public, and the role of vision and visuality when deciphering the public sphere. I discuss the way in which the cultural sphere, in general, offers viable, alternative discourses through which to consider the public sphere.

The central problem is whether or not Habermas's public sphere takes account of different cultural values and needs. Habermas (1992a) acknowledges both that there are many different communities and that they need some way to communicate with each other. He recognizes that generalized points of communication are necessarily made on an abstract level, and that these are required for reason and rationality. He argues that such a level of abstraction is required for understanding the public sphere. This, however, does not necessarily negate the need for (non-abstract) norms and consensus as the fundamental tenets of the public sphere.

According to Hohendahl, in McCarthy's critique of the public sphere "the debaters and the sites are not stable and have to be negotiated in accord with specificity and its needs and values" in a pluralistic society (1992: 106). There are many forms of engagement with the public sphere which produce a more divergent notion than Habermas's, McCarthy argues. This conclusion is supported by the work of others such as Mary Ryan (1990, 1992, 1997), who critiques the public sphere on the basis of history, presenting a counter-narrative based on her research on the eighteenth and nineteenth centuries and the ascension of women (as citizens) into the political field in the United States.

Inclusion in the public sphere, particularly in Habermas's model, requires reasoned and rational discourse on matters of public concern, but inclusion does not assure equality; it often merely brackets difference. By bracketing I mean tolerating, or including, yet presuming that the difference seen should be modified to comply with the apparently normative conditions of the public sphere – this implies that the counter-public must surrender its difference.

As Fraser argues:

> [I]f social inequalities in deliberation means proceeding as if they don't exist when they do, this does not foster participatory parity. On the contrary, such bracketing usually works to the advantage of dominant groups in society and to the disadvantage of subordinates . . . But this assumption is counterfactual, and not for reasons that are merely accidental. In stratified societies, unequally empowered social groups tend to develop unequally valued cultural styles. (1990: 64)

The point is that democracy of a Habermassian kind has not yet been achieved. Fraser is more interested in the type of democracy that does "actually exist," imperfect as it may be. The forms of communication between publics, the public sphere and the state need to be decipherable and flexible, she suggests, so that negotiation between them can occur. In a Habermassian sense, such modification should take into account the essential notions of communication in the public sphere. However, accommodating the existence of competing publics involves not only modifying the form of discourse of the public sphere to reflect "actually existing democracy," but also needs to take into account the multiple ways in which different publics articulate their "publicness" and the spaces in which they present themselves. In particular, I argue the importance of visual and spatial discourses as crucial elements of the public sphere, offering viable alternatives to the centrality of the literary public sphere.

Alternative public spheres

One of the central figures of modernity recognized in literature, history, geography and sociology is Charles Baudelaire's nineteenth-century *flâneur*, walking the street, experiencing the modern life ([1863]1986). The *flâneur* existed in a time and space experienced differently than in previous centuries. Baudelaire's dandy – voyeur, commentator and man of the street – came to signify the urban experience during the period post-1848 Revolution (Clarke, 1985). This relationship indicated a belief that aesthetics were key to the experience of modernity. It also generated anxiety. In 1903, Georg Simmel wrote of his concern of the impact of the modern city on individual subjectivity. In a similar vein, Sennett (1992) argued that modernity required a new attitude toward others in social life. Janet Wolff, Griselda Pollock, and Carol Duncan argue specifically that the domain of modernity, as it is discussed in literature and art history, "describes the experience of men," with an emphasis on "the public world of work, politics and city life." "[D]espite the presence of some women in certain contained areas," Wolff argues, "it was a masculine domain" (Wolff, 1985: 37). The discourses of modernity here reflect similar concerns noted above in the work of Ryan, Landes and Fraser, that the defining characteristics of the public sphere do not acknowledge the structural boundaries that prevented greater participation from women.[6]

Landes (1988, 1995) uses paintings as a basis to critique Habermas's universalist public sphere and to demonstrate its exclusive nature. The importance of vision to modernity is its relationship to space illuminating an important connection with public life. Visuality in the form of paintings communicated particular discourses of modernity and the social position of women: "the socio-political implications of spatial organization of the painting itself" can indicate details about social relations (Massey, 1994: 232).[7]

Vision and visuality are important aspects of imagining both the public sphere and the public space. Vision and visuality refer not only to the physical act of seeing, but also to its social and historical contexts. Both vision and visuality are historical and social. Yet, as Hal Foster outlines:

> neither are they identical: here the difference between the terms signals a difference within the visual – between the mechanism of sight and its historical techniques, between the datum of vision and its discursive determinations – a difference, many differences, among how we see, and how we see this seeing or the unseen herein. (1988: ix)

Nevertheless, the importance of vision and visuality as a mode of discourse has not been examined in most accounts of the public sphere. Visual representations of publicness and the emergence of the bourgeois public sphere were, according to Joan Landes, potentially prophetic of the role women play in democratic societies (Landes, 1988). The speculative or subjective character of interpretations of "the visual" (like the spatial) could in part be responsible for this neglect. The (uncertain) science of the senses – aesthetics – in relation to the public sphere has been overlooked. This may explain why museums have been overlooked in Habermas's model.

Contested Boundaries and Cultural Spheres

The traditional distinction between public and private, as it affects women in the public sphere, remains a vital point of contestation in Habermas's concept of the public sphere for Benhabib (1992a) and others, including Ryan (1992, 1997), Landes (1988, 1995), and Fraser (1989, 1990). The common concern expressed by these theorists is that the private, domestic and familial spheres are treated by Habermas as lying outside the public sphere. They argue that the private realm is also of a political nature. The two spheres are inextricably intertwined. Different forms of participation in the public sphere, as I discuss later, may, however, reveal alternative forms of discourse and thereby alternative publics. As I discuss in Chapters Four and Five, the move within the museum context to seek engagement with communities in new ways signals the recognition by some museums of formations of discourse other than the more general notions of public and audience.

Despite this, for Benhabib, Habermas's theory of the public sphere emerges as superior to other models of "public space." Benhabib (1992a: 73) identifies Habermas's "discursive public space" as a model "which envisages a democratic-socialist restructuring of late capitalistic societies." She indicates the importance of the domain where public discourse occurs and is legitimated. According to Benhabib, the articulation of public discourse as it occurs in public space is central to the public sphere as a model of democracy. The domain where public discourses occur is thus spatialized.

For Benhabib there is a need for a more complete theory of the public sphere, one that encompasses those who are excluded. Such a theory would necessarily consider the normative character of the public sphere and its development to date. The conceptual basis of Habermas's writing about the public sphere, especially his notion of the normative forms of discourse, is more useful, Benhabib suggests, than his focus on the historical emergence of the bourgeois public sphere.

It appears that one implication of Habermas's argument is that the post-bourgeois public sphere of the late twentieth century is rendered politically less effective if the inclusion of the private sphere is as rapid and extensive as that which weakened the short-lived bourgeois public sphere of late eighteenth century Europe. As Habermas traces tensions arising from this liberal rhetoric of being accessible to all (which was not the case in practice), we see that, according to McCarthy, with:

> the further developments of capitalism, the public body expanded beyond the bourgeoisie to include groups that were systematically disadvantaged by the workings of the free market and sought state regulation and compensation. The consequent intertwining of state and society in the late nineteenth and twentieth centuries meant the end of the liberal public sphere. (1989: xii)

In other words, although Habermas's bourgeois public sphere is no longer feasible or "real," it has been influential in current critical thinking, in attempts to "salvage that arena's critical function and to institutionalise democracy" (Fraser, 1990: 58). By understanding the conditions that allowed the public sphere to emerge, it is possible to comprehend whether the "public sphere can be effectively reconstituted under radically different socio-economic, political and cultural traditions" (McCarthy, 1989: xii).

The insistence on a normative mode of behavior and communication certainly limits the potential of the public sphere to be accessible to all.

Cultural differences, for instance, not only challenge the premise of the public sphere but also require the content and focus of deliberations in that sphere to change. Despite the centrality of the cultural and historical specificity of Habermas's public sphere, the importance of the cultural is not fully acknowledged. Acknowledging cultural differences has the potential to undermine Habermas's universalizing principles. How might these different cultural values be part of the public sphere? Were they indeed part of the historically specific model he devised? A consideration of the links between late eighteenth-century modernity and particular discourses on the public sphere may indicate the potential for a more pluralistic or combative public sphere.

Unlike Habermas, McCarthy and Benhabib argue that the public sphere is inherently cultural and that it is expressed and shaped through the cultural interaction of those who participate in it. Unlike Habermas, though, they do not explore this empirically. They argue that acknowledgement of the existence of different cultural values introduces a challenge to the normative aspect of Habermas's public sphere. It is important to remember that Habermas's public sphere, as outlined in the *STPS*, is cultural – that is, literary – in a general sense. This is crucial. It appears that Habermas excludes other forms of the cultural as residing in the private domain, yet the literary is considered generalizable and essentially public. Specifying any other particular cultural form or practice dedicates it to the private intimate domain, not to the public sphere. In effect, a tension between the content and form of the public sphere develops. This is also where the aesthetic is implicated in cultural forms or practices. Because, following Habermas's interpretation of Kant, the aesthetic is considered to be based on subjective judgments – and for Habermas it is considered too particular for public discourse – such judgments are personal and not generalizable or rational.

The Role of Space and Vision in the Public Sphere

Public discourse is inherently spatial and visual and within that context it positions the role of institutions such as museums as central to the discussion of the public sphere. Space and vision are part of the working processes of the public sphere. The public sphere does not exist *a priori*.

The function of public discourse is to "hold the state accountable to 'society' via 'publicity'" (Fraser, 1990: 58). The recognition of the public sphere and public opinion, in the form of publicity, therefore requires familiarity with the means of representation of the public sphere. On this point Habermas acknowledges that publicity is a necessary function and practice of the public sphere, but he does not fully acknowledge its frequently visual character. For instance, in "earlier varieties of the public sphere it was important that images of the body not figure importantly in discourse" (Warner, 1992: 385). Emerging here is a paradoxical, unacknowledged reliance on the visibility of the public sphere in the forms of publicity needed to produce the public sphere. The appearance of public buildings housing public authorities, the spectacle of "official" state receptions, the published public opinion seen in print, all rely on being seen to produce and reproduce the appearance of democracy. The visual character of Habermas's bourgeois public sphere emerges in both the metaphorical use of things visual and in the reliance on visual signs of the public sphere, such as cultural material produced in response to contemporary life. Art and architecture, and representations of public space in the museum context are, I argue, visual signs of the public sphere and articulate the museum as a cultural public sphere.

The (unacknowledged) importance of vision to Habermas's public sphere also appears in his concerns with a place, or a site, where the public find representations of public opinion. The designation of places as "public," and hence visible, relies on linguistic distinctions. Habermas traces the etymology of the term "public" to its German root "*öffentlich*," which was used during the eighteenth century to mean the same as the French term "*publicité*" (publicity). He suggests that "the public sphere did not require a name of its own before this period" (Habermas, 1989: 3). A distinguishing feature of the term "public" in Habermas's account of its etymology is the difference between the common and the particular (1989: 6). The common is synonymous with the term "public" (*publicus*) and the particular with the term "private" (*privitus*).[8] The word "public" is more often defined in terms of the word "private":

> In the fully developed Greek city-state the sphere of the polis, which was common (koine) to the free citizens, was strictly separated from the sphere of the oikos; in the sphere of the oikos, each individual is in his own realm (idia). (Habermas, 1989: 3)

Habermas's model of the public sphere is also paradoxically spatial, in that the discourse that characterizes the liberal bourgeois public sphere actually occurs somewhere – as we have seen, in a *place*: a coffee house, a public square or in reading groups. In identifying these sites, he also marks the development of a public space, a space in which the public congregated freely to discuss matters of importance.

In defining the German history of the term "public sphere," in her Foreword to *Public Sphere and Experience*, Hansen refers to Habermas's influence on Negt and Kluge (Hansen, 1993). A footnote at this juncture acknowledges that the term "the public sphere" has strong spatial overtones. Public sphere "implies … the social sites or arenas where meanings are articulated, distributed, and negotiated, as well as the collective body constituted by and through this process, 'the public'" (Hansen, 1993: ix). It also implies a spatial concept of "openness … [which is] produced both within these sites and in larger, de-territorialized contexts."[9] It is also recognizes the possibility to conceive of a public space that is not simply a fixed site. This, I would argue, is not inconsistent with Habermas's framing of a public sphere:

> The public life, bios politikos, went on in the market place (agora), but of course this did not mean that it occurred necessarily in this specific locale. The public sphere was constituted in discussion (lexis). (Habermas, 1989: 3)

Public life was decipherable in places where people gathered, and if these citizens also came to engage in discussion of matters considered "public," the places became part of a public sphere. Habermas's notion of a public sphere is less about location, however, than about the presence of discourse between people on matters public, but, as we have seen, his historical and theoretical account of the emergence of the bourgeois public sphere also identifies material places where public discourse occurred. Material sites are an implicit condition for Habermas's model of the bourgeois public sphere to exist, even if the existence of public space did not necessarily ensure public discourse.

As discussed above, for Habermas, inclusion of the aesthetic makes the public sphere too context-bound, susceptible to value judgments, and too particular. Culture is interpreted as not being generalizable beyond a specific cultural community. But what else might this particularity reveal, especially as it is cultural minorities" communities in pluralistic societies that question norms, precisely because of their exclusion from the public sphere? Indeed, have there been other cultural or aesthetic discourses of the public sphere? Do they corroborate Habermas's account?

It has already been said that the term and concept "public sphere" "implies a spatial concept, the social site or arenas where meanings are articulated, distributed and negotiated, as well as the collective body constituted by this process, 'the public'" (Hansen, 1993: ix). Rather than pursue this "implication" in terms of what is often understood as a kind of "openness to all," Hohendahl produces perhaps the most convincing and productive argument around the contemporary relevance of Habermas's public sphere. He states that:

> there is no single model of the public sphere, rather different societies have developed a variety of models with specific institutional and formal (procedural) features . . . The boundaries and the structure of the spaces where public debates of political and social issues take place are not stable; they have to be negotiated in accordance with the needs and values of the community. (Hohendahl, 1992: 107)

In an essay entitled "Further reflections on the public sphere," published in 1992, Habermas responds to criticisms of his bourgeois public sphere. He also discusses whether the public sphere model is "capable of, or can accommodate the notion of a bourgeois public sphere which has competing public spheres" (1992a: 425). While acknowledging a need to amend some areas of his analysis in respect of the normative basis of the public sphere, he raises the question "What else could stand in its place?" One response is suggested in this book.

Conclusion

As important institutions of the public sphere, museums need to engage in complex negotiations with funding bodies, interest groups, benefactors and their profession if they are to be effective and relevant. Assumptions are often made, however, about what is meant by the term "public" in this context. Its meaning is often assumed, and it is also often assumed that this meaning is shared. In the mid-1980s, Benedict Anderson's work on the term "nation" identified a similar problem, leading him to argue that the philosophical poverty of the term would underpin conflict on a new scale within nations. So it did: the very meaning of a term that has created conflicts in the world has itself been subject to deep debate. In turn, I argue that the term "public" in the museum context also suffers from a kind of philosophical poverty, rendering it at times almost meaningless. The term is vexed, often bearing expectations that are impossible to meet. In the so-called "history wars" in the United States and Australia, questions about what constitutes the public, public culture and public history were central to the discussion about the identity of the nation. How, then, does the public participate in public culture; with what histories do the people identify; and what constitutes cultural institutions as public? This chapter has examined the notion of the public sphere and its historical, empirical and philosophical underpinnings. It has outlined the different ways in which "the public" is invoked, empirically and conceptually, often in contradictory ways. It has also identified how the aesthetic and cultural contribute significantly to the public sphere. As I discuss in subsequent chapters, this multiplicity of meanings is reflected in the museum context. I ask: can the public sphere and the museum be genuinely *public*, "open to all," even democratic?

Notes

1 Until the translation of the *STPS*, the two volumes on theories of communicative action were seen as Habermas's most significant work (1984, 1987).
2 This counterposes his own view to that of Rousseau, who, Habermas claims, "wanted democracy without public debate" (1989: 99). Habermas argued that in Rousseau's approach reason and rational discussion would be sacrificed to popular sentiment.
3 He cites Ryan (1992) and Eley (1992) as being particularly compelling, despite some theoretical problems (Habermas, 1992a: 466).
4 "Modernity is . . . a matter of representations and major myths – of a new Paris for recreation, leisure and pleasure, of nature to be enjoyed at weekends in suburbia, of the prostitute taking over and of fluidity of class in the popular spaces of entertainment" (Pollock, 1988: 52).
5 Michel Foucault makes a significantly different assessment of the Enlightenment, producing different possibilities for the subject in the public sphere and in public space (see Foucault, 1984a). Foucault and Habermas share similar goals – to emancipate the subject – but via different (yet related) means.
6 Women are among the alternative, competing publics that have been historically under-represented in public discourse. Landes and Massey recognize that visual discourses of modernity revealed women as significantly marginalized from public life.
7 Edouard Manet's painting *Olympia* (1863, musée d'Orsay) is often cited as an example of this.
8 Also see the different ideas of "community" as outlined by Jean-Luc Nancy in *The Inoperative Community* (1991a) and in his article "Of being-in-common" (1991b). The term "community" is described by Nancy as either being in common through choice, or being in common through no choice. The word harbors contradictory meanings, as I discuss in Chapters Four and Five.
9 Hansen (1993) opens her Foreword with a quote of Kluge's, referring to "[t]he public sphere [as] the site where struggles are decided," which is a distinctly spatial reference. While Hansen acknowledges the spatial dimension of the term "public sphere," she does not explore this any further in her Foreword. This is surprising given the insightful nature of this comment and the tendency of Negt and Kluge to consider cultural discourses of the public sphere that are non-literary, and how diverse cultural communities contribute significantly to discourses of the public sphere and democracy.

2

Historical Discourses of the Museum

The use of "public" in the context of the museum is not new to the twenty-first century. Debates about the public nature of the museum – in terms of audience, public space, and public discourse – have occurred since the late eighteenth century. This chapter charts how the museum has been constituted as a public space, the transition from the princely collection to the eighteenth-century cultural institution with an important role: democratizing culture. I use key authors engaged in identifying and theorizing the history of the modern museum to illustrate different ways in which the museum has been historically understood in terms of its relationship to the public, public culture, and its democratic function. It is not a history of museums per se, but a tracing of that history as it relates to the term "public." It situates the development of modern museums in the late eighteenth century as part of the experience of modernity – a significant disjuncture from earlier periods of change in the relationships between the state and cultural institutions such as museums, but also a more widespread and profound change in the everyday life of citizens.

To commence the chapter, I summarize the development of museums, demonstrating how the public museum differed from private collections of royalty and merchants and explain what this meant for relationships between the museum, the state, the intended audiences and the methods of display. I then focus on the late eighteenth century and consider an important link between the development of the public museum and Habermas's public sphere. This connects to the established history of the birth of the modern museum and its relationship to the public sphere. The works of two important artists, Louis-Léopold Boilly and Jacques-Louis David, are explored to highlight the importance of visual discourses in the emergence of the "public." This development is vital for understanding how museums moved from the private collections of princes to being understood as representations of the discourse of the public sphere.

The Development of Museums

The word "museum" is Latin from the Greek word "*mouseoin*" (Alexander, 1979). The term initially meant "the abode of the muses; these abodes were groves on Mounts Parnassus and Helicon," which later became temples, then universities with many colleges (Dixson, 1919: 3). Some of the earliest museums were in cities such as Alexandria, Athens, and Rome. They were associated with knowledge creation and dissemination (similar to the role of modern universities), or were devoted to displaying captured treasures. With the destruction of the city of Alexandria, the term "museum" almost disappeared, "and was only revived with the arts and sciences about the middle of the seventeenth century" (Dixson, 1919: 3). While the art collections of royalty and wealthy buyers were the forerunners of public art galleries, and the royal menageries became the predecessors of modern zoological gardens, the museum emerged from the private "cabinet of curiosities" to become the public collection of history, anthropology, geography and technology. Debate about the birth of the "public museum," and which was the first, has wavered between the British Museum (which developed from the will of Sir Hans Sloane, who died in 1753 and left his massive private collection as the basis for the establishment of the British Museum) and the musée du Louvre.

The fifteenth-century Medici Palace in Florence is often considered the precursor, with its select invitations to visit, its acquisition and collection practices, displays and philanthropy. The Medici's use of its collections and its granting of access to them shifted from the private realm and signaled the way in which museums would become signifiers of knowledge and power in new ways for centuries onwards (Alexander, 1979). There are other important developments in the history of museums that are worth acknowledging: notably the first university museum, which was opened in Basel in 1671, and the Ashmolean Museum in Oxford, which was established in 1683 as the first public natural history museum (Barrett and McManus, 2007).

The modern museum, from which our contemporary museums have emerged, was an important part of changing social values and practices in the nineteenth century. It was also part of the experience of modernity. Not only did the numbers of cultural institutions increase, but access to museums and other cultural institutions was more widespread and the displays were more likely to reflect the world of the new merchant classes and the everyday experience of the city, rather than the world of royalty.

Prior to the late eighteenth century, "museums" were generally "collections of valued objects [that] formed a part of the cultural accessories of power in contexts in which it was the organisation and transmission of power within and between ruling strata rather than the display of power before the populace that was the point at issue" (Bennett, 1995: 27). The opening of the Louvre in Paris as the first public museum in 1793 was a significant departure from the curiosity cabinets inside palaces, the collections of the clergy and the collections of the merchants, which imitated the collections of royalty (see Hooper-Greenhill, 1992). The idea of the Louvre palace being a royal art gallery was advocated much earlier by Lafont de Saint-Yenne in 1747, largely because the royal collection was in storage and was inaccessible and a royal art gallery would be a monument to the king and the glory of France should it be opened for the display of great works of art (Duncan and Wallach, 1980).

It is important not to mistake the eighteenth century art museum for the fully formed public, national institution of the nineteenth century. According to Prior, the state was yet to play a formative role in the eighteenth century, and the nation was yet to be brought into line with the state. Furthermore "culture was yet to be subsumed under the latter's socio-political remit" (Prior, 2002: 35). He adds that:

> museums in the eighteenth century were not usually owned by the state on behalf of the people as a corollary to citizenship, governance and democracy. Visitors were subjects not citizens and power was represented 'before' them rather than 'for' them. (Prior, 2002: 35)

The change from the princely collections of the late eighteenth century to the public museum of the twentieth century was a journey replete with debate about what is a museum, what role should a museum have in society, who attended museums and what benefit was gained by doing so, and how should museum practice accommodate intended visitors. Many of these concerns, and some of the answers, pre-date the "new museology" that was packaged and presented by Peter Vergo (1989).

By the middle of the nineteenth century, the emerging modern public museums were a vital part of the industrialization and colonial processes. Museums catalogued and presented socioeconomic and technological change to their audiences. The major imperial museums in London, Paris, and, later, Berlin displayed the wealth and curiosities of each country's dominions to the central cities of those empires – this often had significant environmental and cultural impact on those colonies and territories (Barrett and McManus, 2007). The majority of today's great art museums of the Anglo-Saxon world were created in the Victorian Age and this influenced cultural development in the main metropolitan centers and the development of museum culture all over the world (Barringer, 2006).

The nineteenth century saw a rapid and unprecedented growth in the number of museums. While the study of natural history is much older than the nineteenth century (see Barrett and McManus, 2007), I will use the growth of natural history museums in the nineteenth century to illustrate my point. By 1900, there were 150 museums of natural history in Germany, 250 in Britain and 300 in France (Sheets-Pyenson, 1988). The growth in these museums was not confined to the imperial powers: Sheets-Pyenson (1988) noted that in 1900 there were 250 natural history museums in the United States and, speaking at the Australian Museum in 1919, Thomas Storie Dixson noted that in 1903 there were 31 natural history museums in New York state (population 7 million) and 10 in California (population 1.5 million).

The growth in the number of museums resulted from the confluence of technological progress and ideas about civilized societies. The technological progress of the eighteenth and nineteenth centuries enabled various countries in Western Europe to explore and colonize distant lands. The display of objects from these colonies in the largest cities of the imperial powers not only showed the citizens of the imperial country what they possessed and how they were changing it, but also aimed to fulfill the earlier goals of leading scientists, such as Francis Bacon, to broaden knowledge and challenge the intellect. The orderly display of objects, their perusal and the resultant education of the viewer, were intended to engender a fascination with the world, and a respect for authority, particularly from the working classes.

In addition to the large public museums in the most powerful cities, private museums existed where individuals, such as Sir John Soane, collected objects of personal interest. Many of these private museums have not survived, thereby making the Sir John Soane Museum in London a modern-day rarity. The Sir John Soane Museum, like the Pitt-Rivers Museum in Oxford, is of interest partly because it is a museum of a museum. Preziosi (2003: 79) asked of the objects in this museum, "how are we to construe them in a meaningful manner? What, if anything, are they supposed to mean? And for whom (apart from Soane) would they be meaningful?" That is precisely the point – this museum continues the tradition of collecting large groups of objects for personal possession. Dana (1917, reprinted in Anderson, 2004: 17) claimed that "these collectors were usually entirely selfish in their acquisition . . . they collected that they might possess, not that they might use, or that others might use, the things collected for the pleasure and advancement of the world at large."

The idea that museums and collections had a purpose and value other than as private collections for the personal interest of their owner was the foundation for the public museum. The governments of different countries began to acquire by various means the collected treasures of individuals, and established collections that would be open for the public. The buildings in which these collections were housed were often unsuitable for the "reception and proper display of works of art and archeology," restricting the ability of museums to display the objects appropriately, and "made both casual observation and careful study of most of the objects a burden instead of a pleasure" (Dana, 1917, reprinted in Anderson, 2004: 17).

The critique of museums as being "gloomy" and "dull" (Wood, 1887: 384) highlighted some of the concerns in the nineteenth century about the buildings that museum collections were housed in, and the role of the museum. Wood (1887: 384) wrote that: "full of interest to the expert, there is no concealing the fact that to the general public a museum, of whatever nature, is most intolerably dull . . . ." Wood (1887: 390) also proposed to create separate museums for the education of pupils and for "those who had passed the stage of pupilage and wanted the museum for the purpose of study."

This concern about the level at which to pitch the museum also connects with the debates about who the "public" was that the public museum should be attempting to attract. Various accounts of the late nineteenth-century museums highlight the challenges that some of these museums faced in being public, while observations about the use of museums by various social classes questioned the value of claims about the civilizing and educating role of museums for "the masses."

Much was made of the importance of educating the working man and his family. This involved both the education and the entertainment of the working classes, often to lure them away from the public houses. In the mid-nineteenth century, Henry Cole contrasted the public museum with the home life of the working man:

> The working man comes to this Museum from his one or two dimly lighted, cheerless dwelling-rooms, in his fustian jacket, with his shirt collars a little trimmed up, accompanied by his threes, and fours, and fives of little fustian jackets, a wife, in her best bonnet, and a baby, of course, under her shawl. The looks of surprise and pleasure of the whole party when they first observe the brilliant lighting inside the Museum show what a new, acceptable, and

wholesome excitement this evening entertainment affords to them all. (Cole, 1857, reprinted in Siegel, 2008: 246)

Did not read

In a related vein, John Wood wrote of the educational value of museums. He desired to "construct a museum especially adapted to the despised Tom, Dick and Harry, which would amuse them, should be of such a nature as to compel them to take an interest in the subject, and perchance to transform them into the Thomas. H. Huxleys, Richard Owens, and P. Henry Gosses of the next generation" (Wood, 1887: 391). Although the importance of entertainment and education were realized by some museum curators and boards in the nineteenth century, these functions continued into the twentieth century, well before the rise of the "new museology."

The counter-argument to this perspective, and one that is sometimes raised about the educational value of contemporary approaches to museum practice, is found in the writings of Stanley Jevons in the late nineteenth century. Jevons was not against the educational value of museums, but he argued that it varied significantly and should not be assumed. According to Jevons, the "advantage which an individual gets from the visit may vary from nil up to something extremely great" and "the degree of instruction derived is quite incapable of statistical determination" (Jevons, 1883: 55). Importantly, Jevons critiqued the notion of visitor studies, which became even more popular in the twentieth century, by noting that:

> There seems to be a prevalent idea that if the populace can only be got to walk about a great building filled with tall glass-cases, full of beautiful objects, especially when illuminated by the electric light, they will become civilized. At the South Kensington Art Museum they make a great point of setting up turnstiles to record the precise number of visitors, and they can tell you to a unit the exact amount of civilizing effect produced in any day, week, month, or year. But these turnstiles hardly take account of the fact that the neighboring wealthy residents are in the habit, on a wet day, of packing their children off in a cab to the so-called Brompton Boilers, in order that they may have a good run through the galleries. (Jevons, 1883: 55)

While Jevons highlights the limitations of counting visitors and associating this with education, it was apparent that museums were a form of entertainment as well as supposedly being educational. Concerns about the entertainment value of the museums overriding their educational value have continued to this day. By the early twentieth century, museums were supposed to be promoting "rational amusement" (Lucas, 1908, reprinted in Genoways and Andrei, 2008: 59). The proliferation of "hands-on" exhibits in the late twentieth century has raised further questions about the entertainment and educational functions and performance of various types of museums.

The growth of museums in the nineteenth and twentieth centuries can be partly attributed to the notions of educating and civilizing societies, particularly the lower classes. Museums were an integral part of the colonial project during the nineteenth century. Henare (2005: 15), writing about New Zealand in 1840, noted that ". . . the establishment of a learned society with its ubiquitous museum was among the earliest tasks of founding a new settlement." This notion of civilization also operated in rapidly growing cities in the United States. The development of a major public museum announced that the city had "arrived." As Duncan (1995: 54) observed, "a big, showy art museum could announce to both national and international business and banking communities the arrival of a city financially and politically." The same author recognized that museums "conferred social power" and that they reinforced class boundaries while they simultaneously "appear as unifying and even democratizing forces in a culturally diverse society" (Duncan, 1995: 54). Following from the ideas discussed above about the working man and his family visiting the museum, it is evident that "while late nineteenth century museums were thus intended *for* the people, they were certainly not *of* the people in the sense of displaying any interest in the lives, habits, and customs of either the contemporary working classes or the labouring classes of pre-industrial societies" (Bennett, 1988: 64, emphasis in original). Other authors, such as Bourdieu and Darbel (originally 1969) argued that museums, particularly art museums, purport to be accessible to all, but are not accessible to the working classes. According to these authors, even if there is no admission charge to enter, attendance is voluntary and working-class people do not have the cultural capital to feel comfortable in these spaces and to understand how to decode the objects.

Bennett's sharp observation about museums being *for* the working class, but not *of* the working class, extended to the display of objects in museums. One function of museums was to impress upon visitors the power of the state. Initially, this meant that following on from the private collections of wealthy collectors, in the cabinet of curiosities, displays were comprehensive: virtually everything collected was displayed. The criteria for collection and display of material were often uniqueness, distance between the location of the material and its display, and the individual (sometimes aesthetic) properties of the object. In the late nineteenth century, as collections expanded rapidly due to colonization, displays in many major museums became selective. Sir William Flower, Director of the Natural History Museum in London, advocated displaying fewer objects in the public exhibition so that lay visitors had space to view the objects and could gain a general understanding and appreciation of nature (Flower, 1898; Sheets-Pyenson, 1988). The full collection was available to specialist researchers to conduct scientific inquiry.

The museums, along with various organizations, such as the Royal Society in London, were responsible for promoting scientific and cultural advancement, and were influential in the promulgation of ideas about nature. Museum curators taught at universities, and museums were involved in research activity (Yanni, 1999). The modern museum was a product of the late eighteenth- and nineteenth-century conceptions of "the public" and of citizenship. Tony Bennett's identification of the modern museum as part of a new relationship between the public and the state via public cultural institutions mirrors my concerns in this book. He notes that the museum's formation "cannot be adequately understood unless viewed in the light of a more general set of developments through which culture, in coming to be thought of as useful for governing, was fashioned as a vehicle for the exercise of new forms of power" (Bennett, 1995: 19).

Before considering power in more detail, it is useful to position the museum relative to developments in other fields in the nineteenth century. Bennett himself offers the examples of what would now be called urban planning (principally the writings of James Silk Buckingham in 1849 and Benjamin Ward Richardson in 1876) as evidence of a change in thinking regarding the influence of the environment (here understood as surroundings, and including cultural institutions such as museums and libraries) in the nineteenth century. In summary, it was seen as being possible to produce morally upstanding citizens if those people had been exposed to "desirable" cultural institutions such as museums and libraries, rather than the tavern or public house (Taylor, 1999). Dipesh Chakrabarty (2002) expands this concept of "desirable institutions" to include zoological gardens and universities, in what he labeled, drawing on the use of the term by Homi Bhabha (1994), an example of "pedagogic democracy." Institutions such as schools, universities, libraries, and museums, "produced" a citizen; this was in contrast to the "performative" model of democracy, which involved debate within institutional structures such as museums and universities.

The contrast between the "civilizing" influence of institutions such as museums, libraries, and universities and the damaging influence of the pub or tavern on "the masses" was expressed eloquently by Henry Cole reporting on the Paris Exhibition of 1867. For Cole, it was imperative "to try and get these people out of the public-house, and I know of no better mode of doing it than to open museums freely to them" (Cole, 1857, in Bennett, 1998: 126). If the museum was no longer a place of exclusion, but instead a place open to the public without entrance fees (primarily to tempt them away from public houses and taverns), what were the implications for museum practice? Bennett (1998: 126) claims that "the public comes to be imagined and addressed . . . as an object of programs of social management aimed at lifting the cultural level of the population by exposing the public . . . to the improving influence of art [and culture] in the public museum."

The nineteenth-century public museum represents a new power relationship, not one in which power was shared and transmitted within and between ruling strata. Now the state and the museum were engaged in displaying power to the populace. This changed relationship coincided with colonial expansion, itself a product of, and an exercise of, power, which usually led to the accumulation of objects and the creation of new power networks. The nineteenth-century public museum, therefore, was often reorganized to "house" the expanding collections and display some of these objects (and the connotations of power) to a growing constituency. The public character of the museum was moving from a private collection of objects acquired mainly for their exotic worth to a publicly accessible institution housing an array of material arranged for the educational benefit of different classes in society.

The early part of the twentieth century saw the continuation of many of the trends established in the latter part of the nineteenth century. This included the development of new museums and adding to the collections of established museums. These processes were not without their critics. During the twentieth century, museums continued to increase in numbers throughout the world, with the United States alone having an estimated 17,500 museums in 1995 (American Association of Museums, 1999). Robinson (2006) noted that most American museums have been established since 1970. Visitor numbers have also increased substantially, but perhaps more importantly than quantifying the number of museums and their visitors, it is necessary to discuss the significant changes to museums during the twentieth century.

In terms of museum collections, Theodore Low pre-empted the latter debates about the role of the curator and the idea of popularizing the museum by commenting on the conservative nature of curators, whom he saw as focusing on the arrangement of exhibitions without sufficient consideration of the needs of the public and how they would understand the arrangement. Low also critiqued the directors of the museums, who he said, following tradition, "have been much more interested in the building up of collections and in the scholarly prestige of the institution than in making it useful" (Low, 1942, reprinted in Anderson, 2004: 33).

Other authors saw a major change between the museums of the nineteenth and twentieth centuries. Lucas (1908, reprinted in Genoways and Andrei, 2008: 59) wrote about the changes in public museums in the 25 years prior to this time: "one of the great differences between the old museum and the new is that the one displayed objects while the other aims to illustrate ideas." In other words, the culture of collecting was being maintained, but in many museums the culture of display was changing. Lucas cites the example of displaying birds. Rather than having many birds on display, which would have little meaning for the average museum visitor, the new museum would display "a single group showing one of these birds at home, the purpose of which is to show the conditions under which birds live and to interest the beholder in the study of bird life" (Lucas, 1908, reprinted in Genoways and Andrei, 2008: 59).

As new cities emerged, they generally developed new museums. This process accelerated later in the twentieth century, partly as a result of increased leisure time, greater awareness of the importance of history and the ongoing desire of cities and towns to gain recognition and status. Among the museums, the presence of highly visible universal survey museums, such as the Metropolitan Museum in New York and the National Gallery in Washington, DC, remained particularly noteworthy and sometimes controversial.

The universal survey museum, an idea derived from the Louvre and nineteenth-century thought about collecting, displaying, and the role of museums in countries that were politically and economically powerful, reached its zenith in the United States in the twentieth century. According to Duncan and Wallach (1980: 466), the National Gallery in Washington DC, which was completed in 1941, is "perhaps the most complete realization of the universal survey idea in America." It is a museum "which could be anywhere in the Western world" and "claims the heritage of Greco-Roman civilization as an abstract and universal value" (Duncan and Wallach, 1980: 466).

The proliferation of museums in recent times is partly linked to the demise of the universal survey museum idea. Museums in the twentieth century became more specialized, and began to focus on the needs of particular audiences and to represent cultures that were absent from the great universal survey museums. One important development was the emergence of museums for children, either specifically dedicated museums or the instigation of programmes and the refurbishment of existing spaces by established museums. The Brooklyn's Children Museum, which opened in December, 1899, was the world's first museum designed specifically for children. By 1908, the curator of this museum could claim that "the average annual attendance for the past five years has exceeded 94,000 visitors" (Gallup, 1908: 374). The urbanization of America and the civilizing effects of museums were both cited as important reasons for the establishment and support of such a museum in Brooklyn, "whose population is boxed in apartments or brown stone blocks of such vast extent as to place the country beyond the experience of many children" (Gallup, 1908: 374). The creation of a child-friendly museum was considered crucial when we "consider the influence for good or evil of habits acquired in leisure hours, and of the demoralizing influence of crowded streets and back alleys . . ." (Gallup, 1908: 374).

The development of children's programs, traveling exhibitions to visit schools and rural settlements, and the hosting of school holiday activities were a feature of many museums in the twentieth century. The Australian Museum in Sydney initiated a number of such programs, and, like the Brooklyn Children's Museum, compiled detailed statistics about the number of users of these programs (Barrett and McManus, 2007). The link between the existence, use, and benefit derived from such programs is, following Jevons (1883), open to debate, but it is apparent that many museums in the twentieth century were engaging with new audiences and moving beyond merely adding to existing collections and displaying all, or increasingly only part, of the collection for the benefit of the learned scholar.

The history of the Brooklyn Children's Museum (see Duitz, 1992) is particularly interesting as it highlights a number of important concerns for museums in the twentieth century. First was the changing demographics of Crown Heights, the neighborhood in which the museum was situated. The transition from a neighborhood dominated by white, middle-class immigrants (mainly Jewish, Italian and Irish) to a mainly Caribbean population raised challenges about who was the museum's "public." This eventually led to more engagement with the new community of the neighborhood, and considering the racial mix of the staff at the museum and the board of directors (Duitz, 1992). Second, the program decisions needed to cater for "multiple and overlapping audiences that range from neighborhood residents to international visitors" (Duitz, 1992: 253). Similar to many other museums in the late twentieth century, the Brooklyn Children's Museum designed programs to "meet the needs of special audiences [which] reflect[ed] the museum's commitment to serving a diverse constituency" (Duitz, 1992: 253).

In addition to the recognition of diverse constituencies (which could be seen as a postmodern approach to what had formerly been called "the public'), many museums in the late twentieth century engaged with visitors to the museum as consumers and customers. This development arose in part because of the attitude of some governments to the funding of museums, which, along with other public institutions such as libraries, were expected to be more self-sufficient and to work within the opportunities and constraints of market forces. One response to this situation was the creation of the "blockbuster" exhibition, for which visitors would pay and would then consume the accompanying merchandise being sold in the museum shop, now expanded and easily accessible as visitors left the museum building. Barker (1999a: 127) noted that, "although large-scale, highly publicized art exhibitions drawing several thousand visitors took place as early as the mid-nineteenth century, the blockbuster show as we know it is a relatively recent phenomenon." She suggests that the main characteristics of the blockbuster are that it is shown in two or three cities, that it is almost always sponsored by the corporate world, that it has advance booking and should attract a minimum of 250,000 visitors (Barker, 1999a). Barker (1999a) gives Thomas Hoving, the Director of the Metropolitan Museum of Art in New York from 1967 to 1977, the credit for conceiving the blockbuster format as a way of popularizing the museum and countering claims of elitism, although Prior (2005: endnote 2) dates it earlier to the Fourth Plan (1962–1965) and André Malraux in Charles de Gaulle's government in France. The continued existence of the blockbuster is, according to Barker (1999a), likely because of the combined impact of potentially high financial returns and the ability of the museum to avoid charges of elitism. The blockbuster approach has its downsides (including long queues, financial risk if it is not well attended, possible closure of other exhibitions, the potential syphoning of visitors away from smaller, less central museums), as Zolberg (1995) and Barker (1999a) recognized. The blockbuster exhibition is a particular form of exhibition – it can bring in large audiences but the character of the museum experience may be impaired. James Cuno (2004: 73) goes further, writing that museum professionals need to be "weaning ourselves off our reliance on temporary exhibitions and all of their attendant hype."

Despite, and in some cases because of, these developments in many museums throughout the twentieth century, it is apparent that by the late twentieth century not everybody was happy with museum practice. Many of the critics were coming from outside of the museum sector. One major compilation of these critiques and a response to them was the emergence of the "New Museology" (Vergo, 1989). We explore this particular idea in more detail later in this book. At this point, it is helpful to consider the above history of museums in relation to the notion of the public sphere.

Museums were, and remain, an important part of the public sphere, but this relationship is complex and open to debate.

Museums and the Public Sphere

In addition to the display of colonial wealth and the educating of citizens about the power of the state, during the late eighteenth and early nineteenth centuries the museum also had another important function: to display the public to itself, so that it was possible to see what it meant to be a model citizen. In other words, as well as being a model of what citizenship involved, the museum was also a disciplinary space in the lived experience of citizenship and democracy.

The intended audience, and the nature of the relationship between museums and the state, left little room for museum practices that questioned the authority of the museum. The public was to be educated; they were not to challenge the unidirectional transmission of knowledge and values. Chakrabarty (2002: 9) reminds the reader that a Native American man could not have walked into a museum in the nineteenth century and challenged the representation or the provenance of material objects, even if he demonstrated an intimate knowledge of those objects. This refusal to allow questioning and debate of knowledge and values was not confined to colonial subjects – it extended to working-class men and women, and others, in the imperialist country. It was not until near the end of the twentieth century that postcolonial and identity politics emerged from other contexts, and academic disciplines, and were imported into museum studies and the museums themselves.

The nineteenth-century museum demonstrates Habermas's concept of public space and its articulation with the public sphere. The birth of the public museum is a significant symbol of the French Revolution and of the promises of modern democracy emerging at this time. Initially, it is the collections and houses of the aristocracy that are turned over to the public. In the following century, particularly in the case of the Louvre, artworks that symbolized the new republic were commissioned, to reinforce the significant transaction that had occurred. The publics were primarily constituted as the visitors to these new institutions. In effect, their presence in the museum, watching each other and being seen, learning the codes of public comportment, developing knowledge of the visual, encountering different social strata, is generally what it could mean to be public, as subject and object. I emphasize "generally" because these are the ways in which the public interacted with places such as the musée du Louvre, as described in accounts of visits to museums (McClellan, 1994). This kind of engagement then comes to symbolize the museum as a public institution. One's engagements with the functions of the institution were generally trans-mitted through associated salons and reading groups. "Public" is invoked in a number of ways here: as public cultural institution, managed by repre-sentatives of the public, presenting public culture to the visiting public, or the populace in general, and in the museum as public forum.

Many authors have made claims about the modern museum becoming a site for the state to further its capacity to discipline and educate its citizens (Bennett, 1995; Hooper-Greenhill, 1992). The museum is well recognized as a place that people visit, where they meet, look at objects, learn, and look at others looking at objects. It is a place managed for the public by the state, a cultural institution of the state and a public place. The public is articulated within and by the museum, but it is not equivalent to, nor represented by, the state. It is about a more specific relationship with a public sphere situated between the state and the private realm.

An interesting and important function of the nineteenth-century public museum, in addition to education and discipline, was as a space of leisure. A number of commentators have noted the move from museums being primarily educationally focused to being places of entertainment, in com-petition with other forms of entertainment to attract visitors and sell products. The museum as a space of leisure is not a new phenomenon (van Aalst and Boogaarts, 2002). People used to picnic in the galleries of the Louvre and the British Museum – which would be an interesting sight and sound to behold today. While the publics emerging from these new nation-states did not quite measure up to what museum curators and directors had in mind for these public museums, the picnicking does illustrate the way in which the museum was perceived as a place of leisure for the citizens of Paris and London (also see Bennett, 1995; Taylor, 1999). It is amusing to think of the experience of museums as being "pass the salt, mind the pictures," but this phrase does highlight the multiple and conflicting relationships between museums and "the public" in the nineteenth century.

Images with similar messages as Daumier's *Free Admission Day*, 1852 (Image 1.4) and *The Sunday Question*, 1869 (Image 2.1) appear within dominant accounts of the history of the museum as examples of how particular sectors of the public sphere of the period were unfamiliar with the practice of being in a public space or institution such as a gallery or museum. While the museum as a public space may have been equated with the public garden or park, accounts of the incorrect way to be in public have contributed to the discourses of the museum as a disciplinary space: where the public were educated about how to behave and about what

THE SUNDAY QUESTION.

THE PUBLIC-HOUSE;   OR,   THE HOUSE FOR THE PUBLIC?

Image 2.1 John Tenniel, *The Sunday Question. The Public-House; or, The House For The Public?*, 1869. Reproduced with permission of Punch Ltd, www.punch.co.uk

culture mattered, as seen in the accounts of the spatial practices within the museum by Tony Bennett (1995) and Eilean Hooper-Greenhill (1992). The emergence of this aspect of the museum coincides with other institutions learning to manage the growing populations and newly designed public services. As Bennett (1995) explains, the state and the museum form an alliance that sees culture on the agenda of government in ways not previously imagined. In this sense, museums, like hospitals, asylums, and prisons, involved spatial practices that were about educating the public, and about teaching preferred cultural practices and associated knowledge.

 This is a very familiar discourse, not only because it is influential, but because it has been, apart from chronological accounts of the history of the museum (Bazin, 1967; Alexander, 1979), the predominant discourse since the 1990s. I am identifying discourses used to develop a history of the museum as a site of "publicness" because I want to suggest another history of the museum as a space of the public sphere that also warrants consideration. Rather than seeing the museum as a site of leisure versus culture, popular versus elite, or educational versus curatorial, we might see the interrelated aspects of the museum in new ways. In order to see the history of museums, and its relationship to contemporary museum practice and debates, we need to consider the persistent role of vision, particularly in relation to the public sphere. The significance of vision in the context of modernity further supports its potential as discourse of the public sphere.

As we shall see below, in many accounts of the history of museums the role of vision or aesthetics is declared anti-democratic or too elitist and coincides with Habermas's view of the role of vision in identifying and interpreting the public sphere, past and present.

Aesthetics, Vision, and the Public Sphere

Writing about modernism and aesthetics in Habermas's work, Martin Jay (1985) identified where Habermas's idea of communicative action engaged with aesthetics: "art has found a modest place in his elaborate theoretical system" (Jay, 1985: 126). For Habermas:

> The idea of modernity is intimately tied to the development of European art; but what I call "the project of modernity" comes only into focus when we dispense with the usual concentration upon art. (Habermas, 1981: 8)

By this, Habermas is referring to how art is normally about individual reflection as distinct from being involved in any process of emancipation. There is also a recognition of the emancipatory capacity of art to take up the cause of the bourgeois project. Art at the time of the emergence of the bourgeois public sphere was on the whole, for Habermas in the bourgeois public sphere, too specialized to be integrated sufficiently into the lifeworld, or everyday practices, of those outside the art world. Philosophers of the Enlightenment envisaged a new function for art, according to Habermas: "Enlightenment philosophers wanted to utilize this accumulation of specialized culture for the enrichment of everyday life, that is to say, for the rational organization of everyday social life" (Habermas, 1981: 9). It is in Habermas's writing on modernity and postmodernity that he elaborates on the role of art. Art, he says, became too specialized with the advent of the private market economy. It was too autonomous, according to Habermas, as the "artist [was encouraged] to produce his work according to the distinct consciousness of art for art's sake" (1981: 9). The project of bringing art and everyday life together was doomed, as:

the attempt to declare everything to be art and everyone to be [an] artist, to retract all criteria and to equate aesthetic judgement with the expression of subjective experiences – all these undertakings have proved themselves to be sort of nonsense experiments. (Habermas, 1981: 10)

Despite attempts by various art movements, such as the Surrealists, "an emancipatory effect does not follow," according to Habermas (1981: 10). Art as a cultural tradition requires knowledge that is too specialized for it to have such an effect (Habermas, 1981: 12). He states that:

> Bourgeois art had two expectations at once from its audiences. On the one hand, the layman who enjoyed art should educate himself to become an expert. On the other hand, he should also behave as a competent consumer who uses art and relates aesthetic experiences to his own life problems. The second, and seemingly harmless, manner of experiencing art has lost its radical implication, exactly because it had a confused relation to the attitude of being expert and professional. (Habermas, 1981: 11–12)

One concession Habermas makes is when art is "reappropriated" for political purposes in the everyday lifeworld. In such an instance, groups such as workers "went back and forth between the edifice of European art and their own milieu until they were able to illuminate both" (Habermas, 1981: 12). In such a situation, the workers reappropriate the expert's culture, a process that Habermas (1981) considered commendable. The expert's culture is then no longer autonomous but is inextricably connected to the everyday lifeworld. Thus the education and disciplining of the workers to appreciate art and culture as presented in museums and galleries, and to emerge as good citizens, had the potential to influence the lifeworld of the workers. It was not something that remained separate from their everyday existence, but something that was reappropriated and could have shared meanings, or mean different things, in the expert's culture and the worker's culture.

However, overall Habermas (1981: 13) believes that the failure of attempts "that called for the negation of art" (as represented in movements such as the Surrealists) is due to the way in which they positioned themselves outside of the generalizable world, preferring the "spontaneous powers of the imagination." He proceeds to identify this aspect as giving rise to conservative positions, in particular the postmodernism of neoconservatives. According to Habermas (1981: 13–14), neoconservatives argue "that politics must be kept as far aloof as possible from the demands of moral-practical justification," and assert that "the pure immanence of art disputes that it has utopian content, and points to its illusory character in order to limit the aesthetic experience to privacy."

But what do these arguments mean when we consider the visual or cultural politics emerging in Habermas's *Structural Transformation of the Public Sphere*? What are the ramifications of his argument on historical interpretations of the art produced during the revolutionary decades of the bourgeois public sphere? Does Habermas give due consideration to the role of culture, vision, and visuality in relation to the development of the public sphere and public institutions? Furthermore, does he give it due consideration given that it is mutually constitutive with space? As noted in Chapter One, for Habermas:

> The "town" was the center of civil society not only economically; in cultural-political contrast to the court, it designated especially an early public sphere in the world of letters whose institutions were the coffee houses, the salons, and the Tischgesellschaften (table societies). (Habermas, 1989: 30)

Habermas tends to use visual and spatial metaphors to substantiate, or elucidate, his theoretical propositions on the public sphere. Even within his focus on the aesthetics of modernity, aesthetics are polarized as either too subjective, or too much like mass culture (Habermas, 1989). Instead, he privileges "the new domain of the public sphere whose decisive mark was the published word" and thereby also privileges the "reading public" (1989: 16). He does this without sufficiently explaining the significance of vision and visuality in relation to public life or the experience of modernity. Yet space and vision are mutually constitutive. Significantly, non-literary discourses also articulate a differentiated public sphere historically, at least in terms of Habermas's model (Landes, 1988; Calhoun, 1992). It is on this basis that we may question Habermas's reliance on literary discourses as constitutive of democracy, modernity, and the public sphere. I suggest that this focus limits the democratic potential of the public sphere.

Vision is not privileged by Habermas in the way that literary discourses are because he believes the visual to be about vision as a medium – either a potential conduit to mass culture, or too particular. Vision, as spectacle, becomes conflated with mass culture, "disdainful and unlettered," symbolic of the burgeoning masses (Jay, 1994: 590). Unlike accounts that privilege literary discourses, the primacy of vision and space in modernity reveals the museum as a crucial space of the public sphere.

Art History and the Public Sphere

Art historian and urbanist Rosalyn Deutsche "question[s] [Habermas's] homogenising tendency ... [the] singular, unified public sphere that transcends concrete particularities and reaches a rational – noncoercive – consensus" (1996: 287). She swiftly dismisses Habermas's public sphere on the grounds that it does not take into account different conceptions of "public" and critiques of modernity which question the use of reason in the public sphere. Deutsche (1996) states that she is more skeptical than Habermas of reason and modernity. She prefers to engage with critiques of reason and modernity in relation to the public sphere.

Other art historians, such as Thomas Crow and Virginia Spate, consider the role of art during the emergence of the bourgeois public sphere and the revolutionary decades. Spate (1980) considers the manner in which art from the revolutionary decades corresponds with political changes of the period. She traces the historical narrative of the period through the development of artists who, according to Spate, felt the "necessity for making the Revolution visible."[1] In a more detailed account, Crow (1985) examines the relationship between the works of art and the revolutionary decades. He closely examines the relationship between the public interest in art and the development of salons and public galleries such as the Louvre. He identifies the way in which painting was employed for varying political agendas. However, this analysis remains primarily within the disciplines of art history and history more broadly. Within art history, there is little engagement with the critical theory that deals with the same period and theme. One interesting example is Stephen Eisenman's "The Generation of 1830 and the Crisis in the Public Sphere" (1994). Eisenman makes reference to Habermas's definition of the public sphere, its characteristic of being open to all, and its bourgeois nature. He does not acknowledge, however, Habermas's avoidance of the aesthetic in relation to the bourgeois public sphere. Eisenman states:

> Ideally suited – by virtue of its simultaneously empirical and commodity character – to its role within the bourgeois public sphere, painting played a pivotal cultural part in the unfolding of world historical events in the eighteenth century. That elevated cultural status, however, could not outlive the public sphere itself. (1994: 189)

Indeed, Eisenman proceeds to discuss the public sphere assuming that the aesthetic, in particular the visual art of painting, is a significant component. The socially engaged artist, according to Eisenman, became affected by the collapse of the bourgeois public sphere. This collapse gave rise to the artist taking on "official" commissions from a variety of sources once more, or embracing the politics of a counter-public sphere, such as the "avant-garde," or otherwise "pursu[ing] the chimera of autonomy" as a modernist artist (1994: 190). The different affiliations of the artists identified by Eisenman are useful here. While I would argue that it is possible that all artists are now affected by some form of relation to the state and the public sphere, we may also see how, in the eighteenth century, "avant-garde artists" and the "official artists" were particularly affiliated to the bourgeois public sphere. Habermas does not make any real distinction between the different types of practice and affiliations of artists during the period of the bourgeois public sphere, apart from polarizing them as either too populist or too subjective. The "type" of artist that Habermas identifies as being too individualistic for the public sphere resembles the autonomous artist – the artist who is "free," or set apart from political, social, or economic realms. But is it the autonomous individual who is most freely able to associate with the public sphere? While generally Habermas sees creativity per se as having positive repercussions socially, he does not see creativity as contributing to the communication of reasoned argument. However, some artists chose to engage with the public sphere by depicting everyday life in cafés and market places – such as Louis-Léopold Boilly (1761–1845) in *Interior of a Parisian Café, c. 1815* – and political events, both real and imagined. Some used their creative skills to assist with the staging of street pageants. Others reflected on, and created images symbolizing, the emergence of the bourgeois public sphere.

We might note again that for Habermas it is perhaps overly simplistic to equate images of people promenading in places deemed public, or sitting playing draughts in cafés, with the public sphere, unless this form of recreation can be interpreted as rational discourse. However, as I have discussed above, the role of vision and visuality that developed during the eighteenth century gave rise to new forms of expression for the public sphere. The public sphere was, and one could argue to a degree still is, restricted in terms of entry, as Griselda Pollock identified:

> These territories of the bourgeois city were not only gendered on a male/ female polarity. They became the sites for the negotiation of gendered class identities and class gender positions. The spaces of modernity are where class and gender interface in critical ways, in that they are the spaces of sexual exchange. The significant spaces of modernity are neither simply those of masculinity, nor ... those of femininity, which are as much the spaces of modernity for being the negative of the streets and bars. They are, as the canonical works [of art] indicate, the marginal or interstitial spaces where the

fields of the masculine and feminine intersect and structure sexuality within
the classed order. (1988: 70)

For Pollock, vision and space are particularly important in modernity.
She describes the way a demarcation between private and public spaces is
represented in the works of artists. She points out that the types of subject
matter painted by women artists of the nineteenth century, such as Berthe
Morisot (1841–1895) and Mary Cassatt (1844–1925), were restricted to
the domestic and familial spheres. Their access to "public spaces" was
limited to parks and gardens. The artworks that Pollock focuses on are not
only spatial representations of these parameters, but show women's
"apparent" marginalization from a particular Habermassian form of public
sphere. These representations, similar to the representations of authors,
politicians, and civic leaders, are informed by their positionality and intentions. In this sense, no single form of discourse such as literature should be
prioritized as part of the public sphere, nor should discourses such as art be
excluded from the public sphere.

The work of artists is an important part of the visual discourse of social life
in the eighteenth and nineteenth centuries in Europe (Crow, 1985, 1995;
Eisenman, 1994). It revealed the separate spheres of social life, and, in this
sense, laid bare the structures of the public sphere. As I discuss below in
relation to the work of Jacques-Louis David, art played an active part in the
public sphere – as a mode of "performative democracy" where democracy
did not just exist, but was performed. Paintings, while subjective representations, were vital to the performance of democracy in this time period.

Art history offers insights into the formation and development of the
public sphere that are not addressed in Habermas's work. This limitation –
the absence of visual discourses – is important because it has, to date, limited
the engagement between museum studies and notions of the public sphere
and public space.

Representing the public sphere

Art history adds an important dimension to our understanding of the public
sphere because it enables us to learn from historical representations of the
public sphere. In this section of the book I consider images that show the
historical development of the public sphere. Image 2.2 is Louis-Léopold
Boilly's *Interior of a Parisian Café, c.1815* and it is indicative of everyday
scenes of the period identified by Habermas. Subsequent images are discussed
because of their significance to the late eighteenth-century art historically, and
their contribution to issues of the public sphere outlined in the first chapter.

Image 2.2   Louis-Léopold Boilly, *Interior of a Parisian Café, c.1815*. Musée de la Ville de Paris © Musée Carnavalet/Roger-Viollet

These images have also come to form the collections of the newly invented public museum, considered representative of the emerging public sphere.

A Parisian Café

In *Interior of a Parisian Café* (which hangs in the musée Carnavalet, Paris), we see the kind of space where the public sphere materialized. Cafés, as Habermas recognized, had an important place in Parisian life during this period. Here men could meet to discuss politics and other serious matters. As the drawing shows, women were not included, unless they were employed to serve the men.

In this drawing we see a differentiated public sphere: those represented in the image appear to be from distinctly different sectors of society. These differences are represented by the use of well-established codes of dress to indicate class differences and by the placement of these sectors in spatial arrangements, which are also indicative of political hierarchies of the period (Spate, 1980; Crow, 1985).

The foreground focuses on groups of men playing draughts, a game often played in cafés at the time. At first glance the scene is divided into two parts:

on the right-hand side are men dressed in the style of the "Old Regime," with powdered wigs and silk stockings. On the left-hand side, working men in their caps, and bourgeois men in their particular style of trousers intermingle without incident. The atmosphere is convivial, illustrating the way in which the liberal bourgeoisie performed in the public sphere:

> Boilly provides an image of the division in French political life between the "ultras," and the old "emigrés" to whom Louis XVIII had restored lost privileges, and the liberal faction that was born of the ideas and principles of the Revolution. (Spate, 1980: 29)

It would be overly simplistic to interpret this image as merely illustrative of social divisions, real or imagined, resolved or ongoing. The left-hand side of the scene is more populated than the right. Both the left-hand side and the middle of the scene show a game in progress. Conversation on the left-hand side seems more "engaged" than in the center or on the right. The "side" representing the "old regime" shows two figures in the foreground engaged in separate activities, although they are seated side by side; the figure in the front appears to be reading a newspaper. The right-hand side of the image is far less populated. At the far right-hand corner of the image, women serve men from behind the counter. It is the game of draughts, however, that occupies the central focus of the scene because it is the place where the different sectors of the public sphere actually meet. The playing of draughts seems to function as a form of communication, something that can be played upon mutual ground within the differentiated public sphere. It is perhaps in the act of playing, seeing others "play" and being willing to "play," that the different groups within the public sphere (in the café) have developed a form of trust being suggested and represented here.

Imagining the political potential of the public sphere involved creating images, including art, that demonstrated the public sphere being possible, being "real." The visual may be used with caution in the same way that literary sources are used as a historical record and as representation of the political space of the public sphere – "real" and imagined. The visual is constitutive here as it simultaneously influences the way the subject shapes the space of the public sphere and is shaped by it.

In *Interior of a Parisian Café*, the artist and viewer are positioned as if on a lectern, looking out at the people, forming part of the congregation merely in the act of looking. The viewer's eye is directed towards the central table in the foreground of the composition. The main column supporting the ceiling is positioned behind them – as if to suggest that it is these kinds of groupings, in front of the column, that symbolize the pillars of modern public life. The invitation to take a seat is apparent. Several seats are vacant, for those who are free, willing, and available to participate in the public sphere.

These conclusions do not contradict the kind of public spaces that Habermas suggested. The Boilly drawing is a good example of the simultaneity of visual and spatial discourses of the public sphere. This image, and others by the same artist, depict people congregating in public spaces or piazzas, museums, and in the streets. Other artists, such as Jacques-Louis David, as I discuss below, used different themes to represent their interest in the bourgeois public sphere and its politics.

Before considering other images, I want to emphasize the apparently simple way in which the public sphere is represented in material and abstract form. The scene discussed above is probably fictional or an amalgam of different café environs and events. However, such spaces actually existed in any number of cafés in Paris (Spate, 1980). Architects such as Étienne-Louis Boullée, in his project for a memorial to Isaac Newton (*Cénotaphe de Newton*, 1784: see Image 1.2), even argued that there was an actual building shape synonymous with the period. Boullée's cenotaph, although never built, was a space particular to the period and the ideal of democratic forms for the public sphere (Von Falkenhausen, 1997).[2] Like Boullée's cenotaph, the image of the Paris café also illustrates particular spatial aspects of the public sphere. The space of the café indicates another source for understanding spatial relations in the public sphere. These spaces were important, in a material and abstract sense, and this importance is significant for contemporary understandings of the public sphere and public space.

Visions of the public sphere

In France, in particular, a significant expression of publicness emerged in the eighteenth century and flourished into the nineteenth century. It was represented in Western art and socio-historical accounts of the period between the late eighteenth and the late nineteenth century as promenading, or walking, in public spaces in the city and surrounds. While the city became a more obvious site for the new bourgeois public to see itself, residents of Paris also made their presence apparent in Sunday sojourns to the nearby provinces. Many writers and critics of the period concerned themselves with the extraordinary development of leisure and cultural activity that was specific to the experience of modernity.

A sense of how the public sphere developed in the nineteenth century to accommodate, or illuminate, a diverse public is apparent in T.J. Clarke's (1985) writing, which examines Paris and its surrounding

Image 2.3 Edgar Degas, *Mary Cassatt at the Louvre: The Etruscan Gallery*, 1879–80. Katherine E Bullard Fund in memory of Francis Bullard, by exchange, 1983.310. Photograph © 2009 Museum of Fine Arts, Boston

suburbs in this period. Clarke discusses the burgeoning leisure activities of the bourgeoisie in nineteenth-century Paris. The expanding rail network enabled people to journey from the city to the country on Sundays as transportation technology improved. Leisure activity, such as walking in parks and gardens, promenading along the Champs Elysées, visiting the Louvre (see Image 2.3) and strolling along the boulevards designed by Haussmann became generally accepted social behavior in Paris among the bourgeoisie, the petit bourgeois and the working classes.

The most significant forms of spatial and visual changes in the nineteenth century in Paris were designed by Baron Georges-Eugene Haussmann, who was appointed by Napoleon III in 1853 to the post of Prefect of the Seine Department of France. Haussmann, a lawyer and civil servant, became powerful by transforming Paris into a modern city. His job was to improve the city's planning. For two decades Haussmann oversaw the clearance of rambling medieval streets and substituted his own concept of a modern city: wide, straight boulevards with imposing façades, converging at major junctions marked by monuments, public buildings and points of importance such as city gates or railway stations. "Haussmannization" is now often seen as a type of urban "vandalism," and foreshadows the devastations of the twentieth century in the name of progress; it can appear as an imposition by an authority eager to control and police its population and to suppress revolution. It was also a type of renewal, or "beautification" process, informed by the utopian rhetoric of modernity that had emerged during the late eighteenth century. Haussmann cleared the city of what he saw as eyesores, especially the slums, and created a system of public parks and pleasure grounds which:

> provided the illusion of social equality, while behind the scenes his building project initiated a boom of real estate speculation whereby the government expanded the private coffers of the capitalists with public funds. (Buck-Morss, 1989: 88–89)

Social coherence was signalled by the opening up of the city not just for pedestrians and new forms of transport, but also to the light of which it had been deprived due to its medieval skyline. This "opening up" was a visual and spatial indication of how democracy was supposed to work – the city was reformed so that the public could see itself and be seen by the state. It became a generalizable space in the way that Habermas writes of the public sphere. The Haussmann spatialized public sphere was a space visually open to all. In that space, all individuals could more easily see each other forming the public. Haussmann's urban plans and futures were tied to the political possibilities of urbanism and everyday social life, intended to encompass the previously disenfranchised sectors of Paris, namely the working class. However, commentators such as Walter Benjamin saw it differently:

The true purpose of Haussmann's work was to secure the city against civil war. He wanted to make the erection of barricades in Paris impossible for all time. ...The breadth of the street is intended to make the erection impossible, and new thorough-fares are to open the shortest routes between the barracks and the working class districts. Contemporaries christened the enterprise "strategic embellishment." (Benjamin, 1978: 160)

Haussmann's "strategic embellishment" forms the basis of what Buck-Morss (1989) refers to as modern statism. The power of the state, as opposed to the public sphere of the late eighteenth century, was increased by this spatial organization of Paris. The state was omnipresent in the spatial organization in the city and its surrounds. What was designed for the city became a model, influencing the visual form and content of space for the public.

While "Haussmannization" is recognized as a state program that affected people's experiences of being-in-public, and public-being, it also provided new spaces for state authorities to observe and supervise social life. People (and their behavior) became more visible to each other and the state. Hence it can be argued that this vision, this organization of space, promoted regulation of one's self and others for the "greater social good."

This kind of activity demonstrated one way in which modernity developed from the eighteenth century, and it coincided with the development of new forms of social behavior and organization.[3] The bourgeois public could increasingly see themselves as a public in public spaces. We might note again that for Habermas it is perhaps overly simplistic to equate images of people promenading in places deemed public, or sitting playing draughts in cafés, with the public sphere, unless this form of recreation can be interpreted somehow as rational discourse. However, as I have discussed above, the new roles of vision and visuality during the eighteenth century gave rise to new forms of expression for the public sphere. It is useful to consider the importance of visuality to modernity.

Artists' accounts are an important part of the visual discourses of social life in the eighteenth and nineteenth centuries in Europe (Clarke, 1985; Crow, 1985, 1995; Eisenman, 1994). Vision figured as a discourse of the public sphere in paintings, revealing the various spheres of social life and the lifeworld of its citizens, as we have seen in Boilly's *Interior of a Parisian Café, c.1815*. I turn again to consider the way in which specific eighteenth-century paintings contribute to our understanding of the emergence of the public sphere.

In her interdisciplinary critique of Habermas's public sphere, Joan Landes considers art history very useful. Art history accounts of the period, particularly Thomas Crow's account, employ political and social history to discuss the stylistic development as well as the content of paintings. These accounts may produce differing understandings of the role of art, particularly as the subject matter of the paintings intersect, and may challenge some aspects of Habermas's account.

Habermas argued that the bourgeois public sphere was a central element of the experience of modernity. Landes and Doreen Massey both argue that visual discourses of modernity revealed women as significantly marginalized from public life. Visuality in the form of paintings, for both writers, communicated particular discourses of modernity and the social position of women: Edouard Manet's painting *Olympia* (1863, musée d'Orsay) is often cited as an example.

Landes and Massey both concern themselves with the visual arts. Landes uses paintings to demonstrate what she considers the exclusive nature of the public sphere. Massey is primarily engaged with debates on space and place in (cultural) geography and with issues of democracy and feminism.

Landes's *Women and the Public Sphere in the Age of the French Revolution* (1988) considers the status of women in social life in France prior to, and during, the emergence of the bourgeois public sphere. She challenges Habermas's argument that the bourgeois public sphere was "open to all," arguing that prior to its emergence women were relatively influential in the public life of elite classes, and that with the emergence of the bourgeois public sphere they were systematically marginalized. The evidence for this, she argues, lies in the representations of women relegated to the home and the domestic sphere. She considers the visual representations of public sphere as essentially male dominated.

Landes articulates conflicting cultural discourses of the public sphere. In her account, these discourses illustrate how the public sphere was not "open to all" (although she does not address the socially constitutive nature of the interaction between the visual and the space of the public sphere). It is her account of Jacques-Louis David's (1748–1825) *Le Serment des Horaces*, 1784 (commonly known in English as "The Oath of the Horatii between the Hands of their Father": see Image 2.4) that is of relevance here. Jacques-Louis David was an active and powerful artist of the French Revolution. Many examples of his work function as public memorials of the period and he is often cited as the most significant artist of the time (Spate, 1980; Crow, 1995).

Image 2.4   Jacques-Louis David, *Le Serment des Horaces,* 1784. Musée du Louvre, Paris/© Photo RMN/Gérard Blot/Christian Jean

A visual discourse of the public sphere

Le Serment des Horaces, 1784

Before considering the way in which Landes engages with The Oath of the Horatii, I will outline the importance of this image. David's *Le Serment des Horaces* was a royal commission and was painted five years before the revolution. In art history accounts there have been many debates about the political significance of the work, regardless of David's intentions. The subject of the work, according to Spate, "complied with the official policy of using antique heroes to express elevating sentiments" (1980: 10). However, "it was seen to be a radical statement not only because of its subject, but because of its style" (Spate, 1980: 9–10). The style proved to be very popular among anti-government pamphleteers. The painting was shown to the Parisian public – "to great public acclaim at the Biennial Salon exhibition of the Royal Academy of Painting and Sculpture" (Landes, 1988: 152).

David's style was considered "unadorned" and "austere" and less "refined than the older generation of officially sanctioned artists" (Spate, 1980: 10). According to Spate, his work was interpreted by critics as symbolic of the moral situation of the time and as a sign of political and social change. The significance of the work was magnified by the public exposure of the work in the Salon, and "as the Revolution approached, political ferment was reflected in the Salons" (Spate, 1980: 10).[4] For these reasons, this work can be interpreted as "more symbolic than illustrative" of the period and "thus more demanding" (Spate, 1980: 9).

According to Landes, "David's visual rhetoric symbolizes the oppositions between family and state, private and public life, characteristics of the new republic" (1988: 13). Analyzing the painting, which uses a Roman myth of three sons pledging their faith and the strength of their will to their father for the "common good" of society, Landes argues that the "simplicity and power" of the image "foreshadows the gender outcomes of the political revolution" (1988: 13). The "open to all" rhetoric of the public sphere is challenged successfully by Landes as she considers the systematic manner in which the public presence and power of women was diminished in the bourgeois public sphere.[5] A multifarious and conflictual public sphere is revealed by Landes's account of the historical public sphere.

The Tennis Court Oath, 20th June 1798
David's work often engaged directly with public matters, and was known to incite public discussion (Crow, 1985; Eisenman, 1994). There are many examples of visual discourse of the public sphere in David's work. One such image, less "symbolic" but more illustrative than The Oath of the Horatii, is his later print *The Tennis Court Oath* (Image 2.5). This image also provides a useful guide to the types of material space considered conducive to public discourse. Both images are representative of public discourses. *The Tennis Court Oath* is a similar composition – using a one-point perspective – to Boilly's *Interior of a Parisian Café*, yet they differ in content, as the café scene does not depict identifiable civic leaders. More overt, however, is the way that David recalls his Oath of the Horatii. In *The Tennis Court Oath*, we see the Horatii-type stance: arms are outstretched and saluting. The multiple figures form a unified body, filling a tennis court in Versailles, conveying the burgeoning bourgeois public in dramatic form.[6]

David's *Tennis Court Oath* foreshadowed a new kind of history painting. The image celebrates "the moment during the Estates General of 1789 when delegates of the Third Estate pledged to remain in permanent assembly until they had achieved a constitution: they would 'die rather than disperse, until France was free'" (Crow, 1985: 255). In the period

Image 2.5   Jacques-Louis David, *The Tennis Court Oath, 20th June 1789,* 1791. Château de Versailles et de Trianon, France/© Photo RMN/Gérard Blot

immediately before David's work, the most prestigious form of painting was history painting, where events were depicted using religious, historical, and mythological themes that had endured in history. David ushered in a new role for painting. Rather than painting for the church or monarchs, David communicated directly with the public, a largely illiterate body, about their own history (Spate, 1980). This is clearly an example of an artist consciously attempting to influence the public and thereby supporting the emergence of the democratic process. Emerging from this period was a new role for the artist in social life. The Louvre and salons were opened up to the new audiences for art. "There the ordinary man or woman was encouraged to rehearse before works of art the kinds of pleasure and discrimination that once had been the exclusive prerogative of the patron and his intimates" (Crow, 1985: 3). There were also new patrons – the state, or sectors of the bourgeois public sphere – commissioning works celebrating the themes of the Revolution: the modernizing project of new democratic institutions and political practices was not only political but also cultural. The visual became central to the shaping of social relations and constitutive of the public sphere and the spaces where it was articulated.

The Tennis Court Oath was commissioned by the Society of the Friends of the Constitution (commonly known as the Jacobin Club after their meeting place) and was never fully realized in its intended form – as a history painting of conventional proportions. The image we see is an etching made from a finished drawing. The painting depicts individual members of the Society who contributed financially to the commission. Some members were to be represented by life-size figures, which also gives an idea of the intended scale of the painting. Prints of the working drawing were widely distributed.

The composition of *The Tennis Court Oath*, like that of the Horatii, has a single-point perspective that sets up the didactic function of the picture. Other parts of the composition work to support this. Many of the individuals represented in the image stand in a pose similar to that in the Horatii. Most figures raise an arm and direct it towards a central focus of the image, the point where the constitution is meant to be finalized. This focal point is reinforced by the grid on the floor tiles in the foreground. According to Wolfgang Kemp, this focal point also coincides with the eyes of the central figure in the painting, President Bailly, head of the provisional parliament: this "vanishing point focuses the composition on the point at which two systems of communication merge: one within the painting and one between the painting and the viewer" (Kemp, 1994: 208). The all-seeing, intensely focused eyes of Bailly are at the central point of the image.

Kemp (1994) makes a useful link here between the theatricality of the image, the theatrical nature of political activity and new designs for theatres of the period: it was now essential for all patrons, regardless of social status, to be able to see the performance. "[U]nobstructed vision and hearing," and being seen by all, were two important criteria for the new democratic theatre spaces. The amphitheatrical structure of the floor, the specific site for *The Tennis Court Oath*, ideologically (visually and spatially) reflected the concept of a theatre for democracy.

Like the Horatii, the image in *The Tennis Court Oath* is structured in a very theatrical, stage-like way. Within the space, many compositions function independently, yet reinforce the central event depicted. The lighting highlights the many previously competing wills combining to form the new republic. A meeting in the foreground appears to represent consensus and agreement between the church and the bourgeoisie. A woman, symbolic of the institution of the family, binds the agreement with her arms around institutional representatives of the church and the bourgeoisie. The message here is ultimate unity and strength. Behind them is the public sphere, whose members declare their allegiance to the newly formed state with their sea of outstretched arms, representing strength and virility. On both sides of the drawing we see that this unity is perhaps only momentary. The winds of change are evident in the billowing curtains; civil unrest and uncertainty seem to be waiting in the wings.

Indeed, the painting was intended to express the force of the will of the people and was to be exhibited in the hall of the National Assembly. However, it was abandoned in 1792 due to insufficient finances and debates about which public figures should be used to represent the public. On this point, Crow comments that "when the painter identifies his work completely with the contemporary public sphere, forsaking the distance of metaphor, that sphere will perpetually escape representation" (1985: 258). Crow believes that resolving issues of representation of "the" public sphere requires "a stable political consensus" (1985: 258).

Crow's argument misses the mark: the public sphere is by necessity forever in formation and contestation, and this is clearly represented in these images. The visual strategies employed to depict the public sphere in both these images are similar, yet the images are markedly different. The artist has played a very powerful role in both: David was representing the public sphere to itself, as interpreted by the artist. This process of interpretation is unavoidable in all literary and visual discourses. What is crucial here is that David developed a visually recognizable way of representing the public sphere to itself. This was central to a public, many of whom were illiterate, learning how to become a "public."

This issue of visual representation mirrors the problem of representation of the public sphere more generally in the revolutionary project of democracy. On closer inspection of *The Tennis Court Oath*, David seems to convey both the potency and fragility of the period. While the necessity of unity may have been his intended message, he is also foreseeing the contingent nature of democracy. David successfully manipulated pictorial devices of perspective and lighting to engage with and depict the many competing spheres of influence in the formation of a new democracy. This kind of staging strategy was consistent with David's other activities, which included organizing festivals involving the "orchestration of mass symbolic behaviour in the streets" (Crow, 1985: 258). This staging does not simply suggest that people merely assembled in such places; his work was a direct engagement with the institution of the public sphere. This engagement also extended to the site-specific nature of the image. *The Tennis Court Oath* was commissioned for the floor of a new French parliament building. The design was intended to allow anyone entering the building to see themselves as re-enacting, or performing a role in, the forming of the constitution of the bourgeois state.

Artists either reveled in the newness of modern life or dwelt upon what had been lost. They were generally concerned with an appropriate way of expressing their vision of modern life, or expressing their chosen subject matter through the eyes of modern life. While vision was important in developing the public sphere, and representing it to itself in the imperial countries, it was also crucial in representing the colonies to themselves and to European nations. In the absence of photography, artists were crucial in the exploration of the South Pacific and the ensuing process of colonization. While Habermas overlooked visual discourses when considering this time period, it is apparent from historical material that others recognized the centrality of visual discourses in conveying ideas, information, and expectations about life in this time period.

Conclusion

One of several questions that arise from this realization that the public sphere had a material, spatial dimension concerns the marginal status of spatial discourses in Habermas's interdisciplinary framework. An examination of the actual places where public discourse occurs suggests that an investigation of spatiality in the public sphere would further an understanding of how the public sphere functions and acknowledge the significance of the visual in the bourgeois public sphere.

We might note, however, that it is perhaps overly simplistic to equate images of people promenading in places deemed public, or sitting playing draughts in cafés, with Habermas's theory. To do so would require these forms of recreation be interpreted as a form of rational discourse on public matters. But how can images of people in public places be considered a discourse?

The irony is that literary discourses are apparently capable of being seen this way. Habermas privileges the literary as a more developed form of communication than the visual; the visual seems on one level too subjective and on another more of a (mass) spectacle, overly simplified and commodified. There is a significant contradiction here, I argue: Habermas sees modern society as sufficiently sophisticated to comprehend and engage with literary discourses of the public sphere, but not with visual art. Even in his later work, Habermas maintains that while the so-called "cultural" societies (mainly those urban bourgeoisie who could, and did, read) gave rise to the bourgeois public sphere and "certainly remained an exclusively bourgeois affair, they did provide the training ground for what were to become a future society's norms of political equality" (1992a: 423–424).

The "social nodes of a literary culture revolv[ed] around novels," which were read increasingly widely (Habermas, 1992a: 423). According to Habermas, "cultural society" consisted mainly of the urban bourgeoisie, who willingly read new publications and thus became part of a "dense network of public communication" (1992a: 423). Habermas argues that the greatest potential for emancipation was through the use of literary discourses of the public sphere. Participation in this discourse was dependent upon the suspension of personal interest and the exclusion of the market from the public sphere. The centrality of the literary for Habermas (1989) is emphasized in his argument that commodification of the literary domain signals the downfall of the bourgeois public sphere because, as this occurs, public opinion is made and formed directly by the media. Habermas dismisses the visual, but as we have seen through an examination of the work of artists such as Louis-Léopold Boilly and Jacques-Louis David, visuality was crucial in the development of the public sphere. Museums were an important part of this new public sphere, and it is apposite that the significant paintings discussed in this chapter now hang in museums.

Among other things, this chapter has demonstrated the importance of vision in the development of the public sphere. One of my main arguments is that the importance of the visual has contemporary relevance in museum practice. This can be seen in the following chapter, when we consider the contemporary museum as public space.

Notes

1 Spate (1980: 11) also states that "There was an urgent need to create a new imagery, to make the principles of the Republic such as Liberty and Equality visible to a largely illiterate population." Spate mentions the way in which artists were directly involved in creating outdoor spaces, gardens in particular, in the form of spaces for festivals, such as the Festival of Federation or 1790, where "20,000 people of all classes helped prepare the ceremony at which the National Guard swore loyalty, with the gesture of the Horatii, to the nation and to liberty" (1980: 11). She continues: "Many artists, above all David, worked on the design of these great festivals, and if these forms of artistic involvement are overlooked, our understanding of the art of the Revolution is grossly simplified" (1980: 11).

2 Susan von Falkenhausen states that:

the sphere thus derives the metaphor for totality, a totality that is rooted in nothing, without above or below, without hierarchy or focus. It is a disembodied, immaterial body, the image of an abstraction and, as such, the image of transcendence that needs neither gender nor heavenly authority; but it is nevertheless not without gender. (1997: 249)

For von Falkenhausen this achieves two things "for the masculine" – the masculine is "the centre of discourses without being named" and "it is imagined as perfect" (1997: 249). "The metaphor of the pure sphere had scarcely become established . . . when it appeared in architectural visions of the Revolution, above all in the Academy competitions of Year II for the temple to the revolutionary cult of unity, and the spaces in which the 'Souveraineté du Peuple' was to be cultivated, whether by the National Assembly or local bodies" (1997: 249).

3 According to Pollock:

Modernity is presented as far more then [sic] a sense of being 'up to date' – modernity is a matter of representations and major myths – of a new Paris for recreation, leisure and pleasure, of nature to be enjoyed at weekends in suburbia, of the prostitute taking over and of fluidity of class in the popular spaces of entertainment. (1988: 52)

4 The painting was exhibited in the Salon, six weeks after the fall of Bastille, when there was a euphoric belief in the King's willingness to acquiesce in reform and in the realization of the "social contract"; it was, however, conceived in 1787, when few would have believed in the possibility of a French republic, and should be seen as a reminder of the stern obligation of the social contract rather than as an incitement to revolution (Spate, 1980: 10).

5 It is important to note that Landes's *Women and the Public Sphere* considers the cultural representation of women in writing of the period as well as in the visual arts. I have mainly focused on her chapter on David's *The Oath of the Horatii*. Landes also acknowledges that other forms of visual discourses, such as cartoons, prints and illustrations, were circulated in this period.

6 Kemp identifies the court as representing one in Versailles:

After celebrating the first anniversary on twentieth June 1790, deputy Dubois-Crancé entered a threefold motion at the Jacobin club: that the tennis court of Versailles should be preserved as a landmark of national interest . . . "The Theater of Revolution." (1994: 203)

Jacques-Louis David stated that:

The place a work of art occupies, the distance which you have to overcome in order to see it, these factors contribute in a special way to the work's aesthetic value. In particular the paintings which previously served as church ornament lose much of their attraction and power when they do not remain at the place for which they were made. (cited in Kemp, 1994: 202)

3

The Museum as Public Space

Assumptions about the public nature of museum space are often made because of the democratic basis (historically, politically, and ideologically) upon which museums were formed. Yet the relationship between the materiality of democratic public space and discourses about democracy is little understood in museology. This chapter discusses the limitations and potential of these discourses and outlines the relationship between space and democracy in the museum context.

The chapter outlines the spatial aspect of the public sphere and the key characteristics of public space. It works from the premise that many museums claim to be public spaces without realizing what makes them distinctively public, or accessible as places of public address. According to Paul Williams, "the importance of space and spatial effects in the museum experience is a topic routinely neglected within museum studies" (2007: 77). The chapter begins with the relationship between the concept of the public sphere and (material) public space. As discussed in the previous chapter, visual discourses are important in the accounts of Habermas and his critics of the public sphere. I suggest here, however, that spatial discourses also indicate the potential for a differentiated notion of the public sphere.

The links between museums and the state in Europe emerged at the same time as the museum was identified as an important institution of and for the public. The fact that museums are often institutions of the state seems to exclude them from being spaces of the public sphere. In other words, if the museum is to be understood as a space of the public sphere, between the state and the people, then it needs to be a site where the people are able to determine and address matters of public importance. As I argue, this distinction goes largely unrecognized within the museum sector. The desire to be truly democratic, or to produce and manage a space that is truly of the public sphere, is desired by many working in the museum sector throughout the world. My point is that knowledge of the distinctions and differences allows museums to engage in an informed way about the

Museums and the Public Sphere   by Jennifer Barrett
© 2010 Jennifer Barrett

implications of the many uses of the term "public." This chapter explores how the idea of public space is much contested in other disciplines and these contestations reveal interesting tensions in the museum context, which I explore in the latter part of the chapter by looking at the "museum without walls" and the "post-museum."

Public Space

Defining public space has preoccupied many in the social and political sciences and geography. Public space can mean many things (see Fyfe, 1988; Oakes, 1997; Ryan, 1997; Harvey, 2006; Message, 2006; Iveson, 2008). A place to meet, a park, a marketplace, a place to protest, a place to celebrate – all can be understood as spaces of public address.

What designates a space "public" in a Habermassian sense are the types of activity and subject matter that are initiated and played out within it. To qualify for inclusion in "the public," the subject of discourse in public space must be of public importance (such as processes of democracy). For Habermas, this is an essential criterion of what constitutes the public sphere. Habermas's concept of public space therefore is primarily abstract. However, in his historical account he cites cafés and piazzas as "material" public spaces because these are key sites where people tended to meet and to congregate. The extent of his empirical research primarily identifies public spaces where matters of rational discourse occur. Furthermore, this space is "inclusive" to all who abide by the normative form of initiation and exchange of discourse.

It is this idea of public space, as "all inclusive," that is often overlooked in discussions of Habermassian notions of the public sphere that also attempt to address public space and museums. In effect, the public space is often conflated with the public sphere. Qualifications of this kind are rare in discussions on public space. Throughout his *Structural Transformation of the Public Sphere* (*STPS*), Habermas (1989) argues that public discourse constitutes the public sphere, yet his public sphere is frequently used interchangeably with public space in disciplines such as cultural studies, museum studies, urban studies, and geography.

Public space has maintained a central symbolic role in the production and reproduction of democratic societies. But how important is public space in a material sense? What does it mean for space to be "public"? In what senses are museums "public"? The characteristics of public space often are reminiscent of the Greek agora in form and purpose: an open space where citizens can meet as equals to deliberate over public matters. These notions are then treated as the fundamental characteristics of what it is to be in public and a part of the public sphere.

The specific instance of democracy that has been the basis for the "traditional" concept of public space – the first democracy, the agora in ancient Athens – is often raised as an exemplary model of democratic space. Habermas (1989: 3), amongst others, cites the agora in the Greek city state of the polis as where public life occurred, but qualifies this by stating that "of course this did not mean that it occurred necessarily only in this specific locale." Urban and architectural historians, for instance, remind us that the central themes being derived from study of the agora are that public space was open to all citizens, and it was the space for the citizens to congregate as a public to express itself freely. It was a space where citizens considered and debated matters publicly and attempted to influence the state (Euban et al., 1994; Hansen and Raaflaub, 1995). The public in this sense was distinct from the state. It was the body between the state and the private individual. Ideas of public space and citizenship are mutually constitutive in this context.

It is understood that within the Greek agora (and Roman forums), access to these spaces and political agency was conditional and connected to citizens' rights. Despite physical access to public space, some sectors of the so-called public would be denied access to the political activities that took place within it. Public space in this sense is never really free. According to Don Mitchell, "[i]n Greek democracy, for example, citizenship was a right that was awarded to free, non-foreign men and denied slaves, and women, and foreigners" (Mitchell, 1995: 116). However, he argues:

> [p]ublic space occupies an important ideological position in democratic societies. The notion of urban public space can be traced back at least to the Greek agora and its function. (1995: 116)

The agora was the symbolic as well as the geographical node of the Athenian polis. Some authors, such as Paul Cartledge (1998: 12), even claim its success lies in "its multiple forums, and determined practice of, creative political and social adaptation." According to Cartledge, the Athenian polis was "a large, complex and heterogeneous Greek society," "the most radically democratic Greek polity," but it was confined to citizens (1998: 12). However, women and slaves were excluded from this space and hence excluded from the public life of the polis. This process of exclusion is perhaps the most significant problem in using this model as an ideal for democracy, as we see later in the reference to the polis in late eighteenth-century France, something Habermas (1989) defined as a problem. This book is not about the theory of democracy as such. Whilst the ideal of democracy is important here, it is concerned with what the ideal implies in relation to the public sphere and public space.

A form of public space had been "a practised place" for centuries (following de Certeau, 1984: 117; see also Latour, 2005). People came together freely in places such as streets and town squares to exchange views and opinions on matters of relevance to the public body. These concerns included cultural, political, and economic issues. Alternatively, people could come together to participate in activities such as festivals, executions, and markets, to view regal processions, and to hear proclamations of government. These spaces also educated people physically and visually about the power of dominant institutions, such as the monarchy, aristocracy and clergy, by the architectural presence of the palaces, castles, and cathedrals that dominated the city and townscapes.

Construction of specific state-engineered public space emerged with the maturing of democratic societies. Modern democracy began to take shape in the West during the age of democratic revolutions around the end of the eighteenth century, largely as a result of the French Revolution and the American War of Independence. Habermas (1989) noted the political repercussions of the French Revolution in England and in Germany, and identified how leading authors such as Edmund Burke, John Locke, and Jeremy Bentham commented on the French Revolution. The translation of the Revolution's ideas into English was influential in the concept of democracy developed prior to, and during, the American War of Independence. In this war, the American cause was aided by the French.

Public spaces developed most clearly with the constitution of democratic republicanism in the nineteenth century in Europe and America (Moore et al., 1988; Francis and Hester, 1990; Mosser and Teyssot, 1990; Hunt, 1992). Public space and public utilities, comprising modern transportation systems, hospitals, libraries, universities and schools, museums and parks, were deliberately designed to end a fifteenth-century tradition of a space where state and society met at the street (Çelik et al., 1994). Such meetings were haphazard and, in Paris, the construction of public space was designed to effect public order: to raise health standards, provide education, and prevent the likelihood of mass riots (Rabinow, 1989). The reshaping of Paris by Baron Eugene von Haussman in the late nineteenth century, for instance, has been considered one of the more radical processes to effect such change. The development of boulevards throughout Paris has been interpreted as both a beautification plan, for opening up the city for the public, and as "strategic beautification" of a military kind, with the widening of the streets for easy passage for military vehicles and troops (Buck-Morss, 1989). This linking of public space to public authorities presents challenging issues when we consider the role of public space and its relation to the public sphere.

As discussed, public space functioned as a platform or stage to educate the emerging bourgeois public on how the public sphere functioned in generating democratic societies. Education of how to "be" in public, and what to expect of one's fellow citizens in public, was discernible on the public stage. The public stage took the form of both formal and informal spaces where people met and discussed issues of public concern. Habermas (1989: 3) particularly identifies cafés and piazzas as the types of sites where people congregated, although he argues that an actual physical space was not considered essential for public discussion to occur.[1] He also identifies the formative role of the church and courtly life in relation to the conception and development of the bourgeois public sphere and the significance of its public institutions.

Public space became important for the bourgeois public to see itself, and to see how to conduct itself publicly. Consequently such "looking" and "seeing" in public spaces formed an important social function. Public space, I argue, is therefore both abstract and material; by this I mean conceptual and concrete. But how does the material site of public discourses influence the public sphere? If we are to understand Habermas's account correctly, for Habermas an actual site is immaterial. The public sphere is constituted by discussion of public matters.

The museum is one such public space where public discourse takes place (or at least is said to take place). Claims about the public nature of museums can be found in museology and professional accounts analyzing and describing the significance of the museum (Bennett, 1995; McClellan, 1994, 2008; Weil, 2002; Heumann Gurian, 2005).[2] The public, as audience, automatically assumes that the space of the museum is then public space. The exhibitions are conceived for the public, and it is therefore considered that the subject matter is of public importance. The term "public" is used in very different ways in each of these contexts, with a general intention of being relevant to the people as symbolic of democratic societies.

Many theorists consider that public space "represents the material location where the social interactions and political activities of all members of the 'the public' occur" (Mitchell, 1995: 116).[3] All sectors of social life would be expected to be seen in a public space on these terms. However, Mitchell argues that such an expectation is characteristic of an idealized notion of public space (and ultimately the public sphere) and this is not democratic space as it is "actually" practiced or realized (see Mitchell and Staeheli, 2006; Iveson, 2008). According to Mitchell, "[t]he ideal of a public sphere is normative, Habermas (1989) theorizes, because it is in this sphere that all manner of social formations *should* find access to the structures of power within a society" (Mitchell, 1995: 116, emphasis in original).

In his case study about "The People's Park" in Berkeley, California, Mitchell identifies two opposing notions of public space as "more or less corresponding with Lefebvre's" *Production of Space*:

> public space was an unconstrained space within which political movements can organize and expand into wider arena … [as distinct from] one of open space for recreation and entertainment, subject to usage by an appropriate public that is *allowed* in. Public space thus constituted a controlled and orderly *retreat* where a properly behaved public might experience the spectacle of the city. (Mitchell, 1995: 115, emphasis in original)

In this context, Mitchell identifies Henri Lefebvre's "*representational space* (appropriated, lived space; space-in-use) and *representations of space*, (planned controlled, ordered space)" as demonstrating the distinctions between these two types of public space (Mitchell, 1995: 115, emphasis in original; see also Williams, 2007). Mitchell (1995: 115) adds to Lefebvre's model the importance of "space for representation" because, by "claiming space in public, by creating public space, social groups themselves become public." For instance, Mitchell argues that public space is the only space where groups such as homeless people can be public. In his case study he refers to this process – of making disenfranchised sectors of society such as homeless people visible – as being essential for democratic societies. What emerges as central to his discussion about political struggles is the importance of "the distinction between the public sphere and public space" (Mitchell, 1995: 117). It is at this point in his argument that Mitchell states that:

> The public sphere in Habermas's sense is a universal, abstract realm in which democracy occurs. The materiality of this sphere is, so to speak, immaterial to its functioning. Public space, meanwhile, is material. It constitutes an actual site, a place, a ground on which political activity flows. (1995: 117)

For Mitchell, real public spaces are essential for social and political issues to be contested: "Politics are impossible without the simultaneous creation and control of *material public space*" (Mitchell, 1995: 123, emphasis in original). Mitchell's interests in the distinctions between the public sphere and public space are useful. He directs us to Howell's (1993) essay on public space and the public sphere as Howell compares Habermas's concept of the public sphere with Hannah Arendt's "historical geography of modernity." Howell (1993: 314) prefers Arendt's model (with some amendments) because "public space, [is] distinct from the public sphere, has not lost its geographical significance." Arendt emphasizes the importance of particularity and locality in her concept of public space and argues that this is the scale at which political action can be freely initiated.

In summary, Arendt (1958) argues that human activity falls within three categories: labor, work, and action. Labor and work refer to survival and human productivity respectively; however, action lies outside of these categories. Arendt draws out the distinctions between the social and political using these categories. The "social" for Arendt is grounded in the realm of human activity, issues, or concerns that intersect with the world of economics and the social. The social is the category in which citizens could pursue materialistic ends. It was the category that could "devour" the spheres of the public and private realms (Arendt, 1958: 45). Issues such as poverty, social justice, equity, and homelessness, are considered "social" by Arendt, but they do not belong to the political realm. She identifies the political realm as the place of action – of individual action. Individual action is articulated through speech, where "men show who they are, reveal their unique personal identities and thus make their appearance in the human world" (Arendt, 1958: 179). According to Arendt, human action is a basic need and the basic need of the citizen is to be free. Freedom can only be assured if the public sphere is maintained. In being free, citizens fulfill their potential. Freedom is not attained through coercion but through the diversity of opinions of citizens. Arendt's notion of private and public were also based on the idea of the Greek polis, where the private sphere of the home was distinguished from the public polis. While the home, the private sphere, falls in the realm of necessity, the public is in the realm of freedom, the space of action. In other words, the private existed for the public, the polis. This is the opposite of Habermas's distinction between the private and public spheres. For Habermas, the people become "individuals" before entering the public realm. For Arendt, loss of the public sphere is the loss of freedom.

Howell argues that Habermas's normative model of political theory does not consider "modernity's historical geography" when the normative aspect is so central to modernity (1993: 310). Howell notes the absence of "space" in Habermas's work and claims that "this transhistorical work lacks an effective geography" (1993: 311).

In contrast, Craig Calhoun does not view Arendt's concept of public space as useful because she:

> does not tie her idea of public space to the state in the way Habermas does his notion of the public sphere, she does not stress any singular point of coming together. ... What is most "comprehensive" is not any such space among concrete contemporaries, but the space of memory, in which the identities of individuals are disclosed in the stories told about them. Such identities require a field of common knowledge within which to be comprehensible ... (Calhoun, 1997: 251)

The distinction Calhoun makes about different notions of space is useful because museums which claim publicness are invariably supported in some way by the state. It does seem that working from Habermas's notion is more productive for considering the potential of museums. Museums can be such a field, such spaces of memory where stories could be told. In Australia, for instance, the National Museum of Australia examines themes of land, nation, and people, "revealing the stories of ordinary and extraordinary Australians, promoting the exploration of knowledge and ideas and providing a dynamic forum for discussion and reflection."[4] Many museums identify personal stories as a significant component of what they do. The Imperial War Museums in Britain (in London, Manchester and elsewhere) focus on such material for their collections. Indeed, the Australian War Memorial and many other museums also acknowledge and explore the Holocaust and its legacy. The Lower East Side Tenement Museum in New York "tells the stories of 97 Orchard St.," of the spaces and time when immigrants and working people resided in the tenements.

Mitchell identifies the conundrum, that "[t]he materiality of this [public] sphere is, so to speak, immaterial to its functioning. Public space, meanwhile, is material" (1995: 117). He then uses the terms interchangeably and assumes public space as the public sphere. In this form, Mitchell's analysis therefore argues for a return to a more "traditional" public space reminiscent of the agora, albeit in a modified form. Mitchell's account of public space has much to commend it, such as the way that public space is a central form of visually representing contestations within civil society. However, Mitchell's account does not discuss in a detailed manner the way in which public space is central to the concept of the public sphere. Significant too are the types of material public space identified by Mitchell. These primarily seem to be spaces that are outside, such as in parks or public squares, spaces of protest and contestation. Cultural spaces of the museum for instance are not recognized in much of the literature on public space in either political sciences or geography. Yet many museums continue to be sites of contestation. The British Museum is a well-known site of conflict. The Elgin Marbles/Parthenon Sculptures, including their acquisition and the debate around repatriation to the Acropolis Museum, are well documented. The British Museum states that it is "[a] museum of the world, for the world."[5] The Smithsonian Museum of American History is also the site of a well-known debate about the Enola Gay (the plane that dropped the first atomic bomb on Hiroshima) and representations of war. This contestation occurs within the parameters of the Smithsonian, which is celebrating its re-opening, where they have, according to Director Brent Glass:

> transformed the building with a light-filled atrium, open vistas, and a grand staircase, all of which contribute to the feeling of the Museum as a public square – a place where ideas and information are exchanged amongst community members …[6]

The Museum of New Zealand, Te Papa Tongarewa (Te Papa), also uses spatiality to signal that it is inclusive and accessible. Like many museums, it uses the idea of "a forum for the nation," a communal meeting place (*marae*), to indicate how it is a place of encountering other visitors and the cultures represented within Te Papa. The Museum of World Culture in Sweden states as its goal that it is an "arena for discussion" and a place in "which many and different voices will be heard, where the controversial and conflict-filled topics can be heard and addressed," "a place where people can feel at home across borders."[7]

Many museums state that their institutional spaces resemble the idea of the agora or forum, yet this has tended to escape the notice of authors interested in public space. The literature produced in geography and the social sciences generally locates public space outdoors and in relation to contested uses of material space – the examples often cited are parks and gardens, the impact of urban development, housing issues, and so on. These specific spaces are often used perhaps because they are overtly political *and* material in character (see Staeheli and Mitchell, 2007). In their survey of literature about the notion of public space in geography discourse, Staeheli and Mitchell found that the dominant questions were about "what characterizes space as public?" and "who are the public?" (2007: 792–793). The term generally referred to physical space and sociability is a defining element of the notion. Public space tended to be understood as normative and political. Museums, however, are rarely cited as public space or spaces of public address, despite the area's central concerns being space, its representation, history, and use.

Sharon Zukin (1995) outlines how important public space is to the culture of cities. As distinct from new public spaces ("transactional public space") of "telecommunications and computer technology," like Mitchell, she is interested in "public spaces as places that are physically there, as geographical and symbolic centres, as points of assembly where strangers mingle" (1995: 45).[8] For Zukin, the numbers of prisons are increasing, and are a type of public space. This is in contrast to authors such as Message (2006), Williams (2007) and McLellan (2008), who note the growth in numbers of museums as an "anchor" for a public cultural space. Museums have become a significant part of urban revitalization strategy (van Aalst and Boogaarts, 2002), as seen in cities such as Liverpool, England, where the Albert Dock has used a museum as the foundation for revitalizing the area. Tate Liverpool – "Tate of the North" – has contributed to the once-industrial city of Liverpool "beginning to emerge as a bustling cultural centre."[9] Similarly, the industrial center of Bilbao in the north of Spain was transformed by the spatial reorganization required for the development of the Guggenheim Museum, Bilbao.

Zukin (1995) argues that private sector interests drive changes in how public space is used. This argument has also been advanced by Harvey (2006), Blackmar (2006) and Mitchell and Staeheli (2006). Zukin (1995) likens the surveillance function of prisons to older, more symbolic and "pleasant" public spaces such as parks and this surveillance of the public space, she argues, is due to increasing concern about private interests: personal safety or the protection of private property. Places such as parks are thereby rendered "symbolic public spaces" as their use in a "truly" public way becomes history. Using New York City as her central example, Zukin identifies a direct relationship between the use of public space and public culture: "Creating a public culture involves both shaping public space for social interaction and constructing a visual representation of the city" (1995: 24).

Zukin further identifies the interdependency between public culture and public space:

> If monuments of culture – great public spaces, statues, buildings – were supposed to inspire, they were shaped, in turn, by material civilization that conceived and constructed them. (1995: 11)

Zukin, however, is ambivalent towards the role of culture, in particular artists, art, and museums, as they are increasingly manipulated to represent the interests of the city. Cultural institutions, such as museums, are entwined with the economics of the city, "as if to emphasize their prominence in the city's symbolic economy" (Zukin, 1995: 23). Perhaps it is for this reason that museums – as symbolizing art or culture in the general sense – do not feature in many of the discourses about public space in the urban context, particularly cities. Echoing Habermas, Zukin asserts that artists are generally "co-opted into private property redevelopment projects as beneficiaries, both developers of an aesthetic mode of producing space (in public art, for example) and investors in a symbolic economy" (1995: 23). Designers and video artists fare no better in Zukin's account because they visually re-present the city through the support, financial and cultural, of "business and real estate elites" (1995: 23). Visuality is interpreted as particularly potent and hence dangerous to the social and public life of the city. By contrast, authors such as Tony Bennett (2006) advocate multiplicity in "civic seeing" within museums and go further to advocate museum engagements with the visually impaired, citing initiatives by the Tate Modern and the British Museum as significant in encouraging a broader range of museum visitors who engage museums with a broader range of senses. Visuality figures significantly in the culture of cities.

Every attempt "to rearrange space in the city is also an attempt at visual re-representation" (Zukin, 1995: 24). In Zukin's view, the commercialization of culture limits the potential of public culture to effect democracy in a positive way:

> Culture can also be used to frame and humanize the space of real estate development. Cultural producers who supply art (and sell "interpretation") are sought because they legitimize the appropriation of space. (1995: 22, citing Deutsche, 1988)

Zukin laments how "culture" has become the domain of competing interests ranging from the role of culture in social change to being a saleable commodity for both public and private interests. She identifies the significance of the way public space changes in relation to public culture generally; the past uses of public space, which are now symbolic spaces, were, she suggests, more conducive to democracy. They become a barometer of social life. Places such as parks and gardens are identified as more compelling forms of public spaces.

The importance of art and culture in influencing a city's material life is viewed from many perspectives. For example, influential museums theorist Stephen Weil has noted that "[b]ecause art museums became one of our most important occasions for public architecture . . . to be institutions that embody some of society's highest aspirations, it has become commonplace in recent years to speak of them as successors in some sense to the great

Image 3.1   *Forecourt, British Museum,* Jennifer Barrett, 2005

churches and cathedrals of earlier centuries" (Weil, 2002: 181). An example of such claims can be seen with the Frank Gehry-designed Guggenheim Museum, Bilbao. When it opened in 1997, it was described as "a spectacular structure made of titanium, glass, and limestone – was hailed as the most important building of its time."[10] Similarly, the Guggenheim Museum, New York, claims that its building is a significant architectural icon of the twentieth century while simultaneously being an educational and cultural center for the people. Weil outlines the contradictions inherent in claiming that museums are "palaces for the people" as identified in Nathaniel Burt's (1977) book of the same title. Weil's account also reveals his frustration with the aesthetic, hence inaccessible, nature of art museums (Weil, 2002: 183). The solution is to reorient the focus to the social, cultural, or historical for redemption.

Absent from these discussions, however, is acknowledgment that the aesthetic dimension (or art) has the capacity to reflect upon or affect

Image 3.2   *Turbine Hall, Tate Modern,* Jennifer Barrett, 2004

public opinion. Indeed this absence reflects a view that artists (and art curators) do not necessarily seek to create consensus or comply with a norm and instead reflect diverse or personal views or an alternative discourse of the public sphere. Such alternative views may not seek to create consensus but instead seek to bring a matter of importance to the attention of the public in the form of art and exhibition. Ward, for instance, argues that it is, in effect, a form of publicity in a Habermassian sense (Ward, 1995).

While Zukin does not use Habermas explicitly, her consideration of the relationship between culture (in particular the visual arts), the potential of public culture, and the role of public space in relation to democracy, is similar to Habermas's and Weil's view of art and the culture industry in relation to the public sphere. In particular, culture is perceived by Zukin (and perhaps by geographers concerned with public space) and Habermas as weakening the public sphere because it is equated with individualism and elitism, whilst they also acknowledge that it once had political potential: for Zukin, in the 1960s, for Habermas (1989), in the late eighteenth century.

Another author who considers what makes space "public" is Rosalyn Deutsche. Deustche's work is generally concerned with "art, architecture and urban design, on the one hand, with theories of the city, social space, and the public sphere on the other" (1996: xi). She is concerned with strategies used to dominate social and public space and the way in which images of unified public spaces mask structured inequalities in social life. Her interest in art and public spaces focuses on the performative aspect of art in relation to democracy in such space. Public parks and homelessness are one example she also uses to discuss this discourse of power in public space (1996). Conflict in public space, Deutsche argues, "far from the ruin of democratic public space, is the condition of its existence" (1996: xiii). Taking her cue from Lefebvre's *Production of Space*, Deutsche sees space, and consequently public space, not as "neutral," but "rather, political, inseparable from the conflictual and uneven social relations that structure specific societies at specific historical moments" (1996: xiv). Elsewhere, she defines public space as "intimately connected with ideas about what it means to be human, the nature of society, and the kind of political community we want... [S]upporting things that are public promotes the survival and extension of democratic culture" (1996: 269). Whilst acknowledging that, like democracy, public space is contested space, she elaborates, drawing on French political philosopher Claude Lefort's account of public space: "The public space, in Lefort's account, is the social space where, in the absence of a foundation, the meaning and unity of the social is negotiated – at once constituted and put to risk. What is recognized in public space is the legitimacy of debate about what is legitimate" (1996: 273). Deutsche also points out that Lefort's (1988) theory of radical democracy is drawn from:

> the French bourgeois revolution of the eighteenth century [which] inaugurated a radical mutation in the form of a society, a mutation he calls, following Alexis de Tocqueville, "the democratic invention". The democratic invention was one and the same event with the Declaration of the Rights of Man, an event that shifted the location of power. (1996: 272)

For Deutsche, public space thereby becomes an institutionalized space of contestation. Following her interpretation of Lefort, this is a participatory notion of public space. I want to draw attention more specifically to her influential discussion of public space. The significant point for Deustche is that public space should not be the site of a positivist, unifying, and universalizing rhetoric about its relation with democracy. Moreover, she is interested in a distinctive form of art that engages with, or is intrinsic to, an issue of public importance. Art that is politically engaged in this way is then effectively a form of publicity, of public discussion. It echoes very much Habermas's notion of publicity. This distinction also has implications for debates about the museum as public space: should the museum be a voice of authority resolving debates and conflicts, or should it be facilitating debates amongst heterogeneous publics? Message (2006) highlights the universalizing tendencies around public space, using the example of the site where the former World Trade Center in New York City once stood, a site that involved proposals for a memorial museum and debates about democracy, freedom, and the threat of terrorism.

Such contestation over the form and content of museums is not unusual. The Mission Statement of the United States Holocaust Memorial Museum in Washington also makes clear that it is about public discourse and debates about democracy:

> The Museum's primary mission is to advance and disseminate knowledge about this unprecedented tragedy; to preserve the memory of those who suffered; and to encourage its visitors to reflect upon the moral and spiritual questions raised by the events of the Holocaust as well as their own responsibilities as citizens of a democracy.[11]

Although Deutsche does not discuss it, her influences draw on many of the same events and theoretical concerns as Habermas, particularly her use of Lefort in relation to the French Revolution and the role of discourse in formation of the public sphere. She does refer obliquely to Habermas as she considers how the term "public" is "unproblematized" when it is invoked to connote a "real–real people, real space, real social problems," or a more "traditional space of left political projects" (Deutsche, 1996: 318–319). Deutsche interprets Habermas cursorily, dismissing his work on the basis of its reliance on consensus reached through use of rational discourse and his failure to consider critiques of the universalizing tendencies of modernity "that are less hostile to differences or conflict" (Deutsche, 1996: 287). She emphasizes that there are other conceptions of "the public sphere" (1996: 287). For Deutsche, "inclusiveness and accessibility [of the public sphere] has always been illusory" (1996: 319). Ultimately, Deutsche believes she is arguing for a more radical public space, resulting in a more radical concept and practice of democracy. Her argument also appears similar to discussions in the discipline of geography and urban studies outlined above. Like those authors, she interprets contestation as signifier of publicness in relation to space. Public space appears more radical, more democratic. She does not acknowledge the spatial potential of Habermas's public sphere. What is useful, however, is the sense that the democratic potential of public space, while idealistic in many instances, is elusive yet the process of trying to achieve its potential is perhaps what makes it real, less idealized and imaginary.

These debates about public space, whether actually existing public space or imagined public space, should be considered in conjunction with the historical connections linking institutions and the use of space, as identified by Habermas. According to Habermas (1989: 8–9), only the church had "a specific locale for their representation of publicness: the church," where the "'surroundings' were part and parcel of the publicity of representation." The church, as a representative space, also functioned simultaneously to include and exclude people through processes of staging religious and courtly ceremonies. Habermas illustrates the forma-tive way that the church and its symbolic functions come to influence new institutions of public authority and corresponding decorum. The formative role of the church and the court, for Habermas, merely demonstrates the symbolic function of representation in the public sphere as having no specific locale.

The importance of space in learning, in that learning is situated within space rather than being enveloped by space, is recognized by a limited number of museum authors (Falk and Dierking, 2000; Williams, 2007). Museums, churches, educational institutions, and so on, have particular forms of space that mean many things are likely to be learned, including, as has been noted in the previous chapter, whether an institution such as a museum is creating a disciplinary or participatory space. Williams (2007: 77) commented that this lack of attention to the spatial effects of museums is surprising, given that "museums are partly distinguished from other forms of historical representation by their 'sited-ness'; by the non-verbal nature of their messages that resides not just in material culture, but also in the museum's particularly visible sense of spatial orchestration." It is the "non-verbal nature of their messages" that conflicts with Habermas's account of the public sphere. Museums (of art), Habermas argued, inter-preted and organized the lay judgment of art that was expressed in criticism (Habermas, 1989: 40–41). It organized the public's experience of this in the museum. Museums can, and do, promote rational debate, but the non-verbal messages that are often not recognized, and hence not debated, are vital in influencing the public sphere.

It is important to recall here that Habermas argued that the locale was not significant because it is the discourse generated, the representative function of the institutions, that constitutes the public sphere. However, I would argue that these emerging "institutions of the public sphere," these formative spaces, provided the basis for developing appropriate forms of communication and representation as the power of the court and clergy lessened. Therefore, the spaces of these new public institutions, such as the museum, are spaces central to the emergence of Habermas's bourgeois public sphere in the eighteenth century. The spaces of new public institutions, such as memorial museums (Williams, 2007), are also central to contemporary debates about the character of the public sphere.

As I discussed in the previous chapter, spaces where the public congregated were also represented in images from the period. An example of an image that typifies the space of cafés, for instance, is Louis-Léopold Boilly's image of a Paris café (see Image 2.2). In this image we see a differentiated public sphere in an interior of a café. Other images, such as Hubert Robert's paintings of his exhibition plans for the Louvre (Image 1.3), also function as representations of the developments of this period historically and politically. These images demonstrate the links between the way in which public space of the time was used and the discourse of the public sphere (about how to be in public), what occurred in public, and the representation of the public in the form of visual images, which were subsequently exhibited.

The public spaces Habermas identifies are far more central to the production of the public sphere, and to our understanding of democracy, than he or his critics imagine. Competency in deciphering public space becomes a necessary skill for participating in (or challenging) democracy. I suggest that the location of "actual" public space (i.e., space where the public sphere materializes, rather than simply officially sanctioned public space) is more than accidental to Habermas's method in revealing the public sphere. Might the ability to identify the forms or types of public spaces also be relevant to understanding democracy in the early twenty-first century? The insufficient regard Habermas gives to the questions of space which emerge from his own analyses of the public sphere is significant. Understanding the representations of the public sphere in non-literary discourses can assist in revealing how the culture of democracy works. The historically situated bourgeois public sphere emerges as part of the experience of modernity, of which spatial and visual discourses also feature, albeit primarily as aesthetic discourses. As I discussed in the previous chapter, in his writings on modernity as an incomplete project of the Enlightenment, Habermas elaborates on the role of aesthetics in modern life, and we considered how he interprets space within an aesthetic realm. This is useful because it gives us tools to locate public space within the overarching concept of modernity.

Locating Public Space in Modernity

The articulation of the experience of modernity is first evident in the work of European artists in the late eighteenth century who dealt with the subject of modern life. Visual representations of this subject illuminated an awareness of change in their surroundings. Thus, artists expressed the need to formulate new ways to represent what they saw. Some artists worked with the individual's relationship to the experience of modernity, while others considered the broader social implications of social change in their work.

The public sphere, according to Habermas, is central to democracy and to the formation of modernity. As discussed in the previous chapter, he argues convincingly that the public sphere is an "institution" central to modernity. I will consider several accounts of modernity that coincide with the period of Habermas's influential public sphere that also link the history of museums to a spatial practice of being public, as limited as it may have been. The legacy of this history shows how many museums have attempted to be public – inclusive, accessible – since their modern invention. They have been products of their time, interpreting what it means to be "public," in accordance with the site, practices and discourses of the period, demonstrating how the idea of accessibility also changes over time and space. Most notably we see how attempts to be democratic in the museum context are inextricably linked to the emergence of the public museum in the late eighteenth century.

Modernity is the experience of the new, "the character of life under changed circumstances" which emerged in the late eighteenth century (Harrison and Wood, 1993: 126; see also Berman, 1983; Frisbee, 1985; Harvey, 2003). This experience was felt by individuals at all levels of social life, although inevitably not in the same manner nor to the same degree. The public sphere emerged as an important part of social life where changes brought about by modernization and modern life were experienced. Habermas argues that the use of reason in public life was necessary for the citizens in this "new age" to communicate and interact, to be somehow united in their experience of accelerated change. It was also the means by which they could convey matters of public import, using reason, in a world where the experience of time sped up and became pressured, and once-familiar ways of life became known as history.

Accounts of the experience of modernity in social and political life range widely, from a focus on the personal experience of the period to the broader issues and to what Habermas refers to as a generalized experience. The latter includes political revolutions, changes in transportation, the experiences of developing colonial Empires and the development of public institutions such as hospitals, prisons, and schools. Habermas's interest in modernity focused on the generalized and generalizable experience. He considers a non-subject-centered use of reason, which he calls "communicative action" – the practice of everyday communications and of everyday speech. As outlined in the previous chapter, questions about how these rules and regulations of communication are set – what counts as rational – are central issues surrounding Habermas's focus on "communicative action." Subjects, or individuals, are necessarily part of social life and social relations with others. Subject-centered reason is likened to aesthetic judgments that are considered to be based on individual taste and value judgments, and therefore not generalizable as required in Habermas's public sphere. It therefore follows that he advocates an account of modernity that is concrete or material due to his skepticism concerning aesthetic discourses of modernity. Habermas attempts to deal with a non-subject-centered use of reason by rejecting the possibility of an individuated notion of reason. But how can aesthetic discourses of modernity be avoided if modernity is so central to the public sphere and vice versa? How could individuals experience modernity in a "generalized" way? This would require individuals to suspend their subjective interests for the interests of the common good. This would require, however, an individuated "judgment," where individuals must use their "senses" to assess what the common good may mean. Habermas does not account for the aesthetic at this point in his formation of the public sphere, of deciding to suspend one's own interests for the common good (Eagleton, 1990). I would argue, however, that to act in the interests of others relies upon subjective judgment of some kind. This is considered further in the discussion below.

Space for the Public – The Public Museum

A study of the history, present, and future of museums would be inadequate without a rigorous consideration of space. McClellan (2008) notes that the earliest spaces of museums were not actual space, but idealized designs of museums on paper. These designs were the medium to transfer the perceived space of the heavens into human architectural form. There was usually an absence of actual objects and specimens in these designs, as if "their flawed contingency would compromise the expression of the ideal" (McClellan, 2008: 56).

Contemporary museums are, however, entwined in debates about the relationships between the material objects and the people, the material objects and the architecture, the museum and the city economy. In various ways, space becomes central to enabling different spheres – of social life, the public sphere and the state – to interact. This is present in contemporary museums, but also in other forms of contemporary spatial organization such as parks, gardens, city malls, and in the quasi-public spaces of shopping malls. The organization of space in the public arena is not new, however, as demonstrated by Michel Foucault. In the eighteenth century, the organization of space became central to the developing technologies of the state. As Foucault points out:

> If one opens a police report of the time (eighteenth century) – the treatises that are devoted to the techniques of government – one finds that architecture and urbanism occupy a place of considerable importance. (1989: 1–2)

The spatial is inextricably linked to government, which inevitably played a central role in affecting the everyday lives of citizens. Unlike Habermas, Foucault tends to interpret space as being a formative influence on the life of individuals. Similarly, he examines the pervasive spectacle of vision, the panopticon in social life. Below is a discussion of Foucault's work as it bears upon my central argument.

Two influential texts, by Tony Bennett (1995) and Eilean Hooper-Greenhill (1992), have used the work of Foucault to consider the museum as an institution that shapes knowledge and the subsequent impact of the museum on social, political, and cultural functions in social life. The museum's role in the development of cultural life was a significant link in the state's new relationship with the culture of its citizens. In particular, both Hooper-Greenhill and Bennett consider Foucault's argument that public institutions were designed with particular functions in mind. In effect, these spaces become disciplinary spaces of social life, with a direct impact on social life and the development of subjectivity and, in turn, the public sphere. They also become spaces – heterotopias – capable of encompassing contradictions.

Following Habermas, Bennett states that:

> the formation of the public sphere was closely bound up with the development of new institutions and practices which detached art and culture from that [courtly/religious] function and enlisted it for the cause of social and political critique. (Bennett, 1995: 25)

In the eighteenth century, the museum was still a space that glorified the power, culture, and traditions of the aristocracy, and the church. This was to change in the nineteenth century in Europe and much of the United States

of America as the museum became a site of instruction. In newly indus-
trializing countries such as Taiwan, the time period for the stages of
museum development are much more recent (Chang, 2006). In the
European context of the eighteenth century, discussions in museums and
salons about the works of art differed from the role of the works from the
point of view of the court or church. In the early formation of the public
sphere, art and literature showed more potential to be critical of civil society
and the state but, Habermas argues, became corrupted by commodification, as we saw in the previous chapter (Sherman, 1987, 1989).

Museums were spaces where public discourse, public decorum, politics
and culture were produced, observed and reproduced. The role of vision
was instrumental to this new public role of the museum and its new relation
with the state (see Bennett, 2006). Once spaces for the court, the public
museum became a space where public discourses were promoted. The
public museum therefore functioned as a disciplinary site for the public
sphere.

The modern public museum was given a new rationality distinct from the
private use of the building by the king and the church. The museum became
crucial for promoting a new set of values for, and of, the republic in France
(see Hooper-Greenhill, 1992; Bennett, 1995). The new public function for
the museum was to educate the public *en masse*, producing "civilized"
citizens for the republic. A new relationship was also forged between the
state and the public museum. Behind the scenes in the museum, a
"knowledgeable subject," known as a curator, produced knowledge for
consumption by the public in the public space of the museum. This role of
curator, however, was modeled on the monarch form of presentation of
objects and artworks. The "newness" of this function was relative to the
previous practices of those once-royal institutions. As the private galleries of
the monarchs had done, the collections functioned to display the culture of
civility and nobility. Liberating collections from the monarch, rendering
them "accessible to all" and thereby "public," meant that the "public
museum" was invented. This process, however, merely assumed that the
contents of the museum were "appropriate" for the new public sphere.
These new practices of the museum produced two contradictory functions –
an elite temple for the arts but also a utilitarian instrument for democratic
education and emancipation (Hooper-Greenhill, 1992).

The function of the public museum was not only to make the possessions
of royalty physically accessible to all in this new democracy, but also to assist
in the emancipation of the plebiscitary through education about the
civilized cultural life of the bourgeoisie. The works displayed in the museum
took on a new significance, in a new sphere. The appearance of the public in

the museum also took on significance as people observed each other being public. As more sectors of liberal public sphere accessed the museum, the museum provided potentially a new role for art in public discourse (Foucault, 1970).[12] Ironically, the art works which had often been commissioned by royalty and nobility were now being viewed by the bourgeoisie. However, the art that was viewed was intended to be representative of a new social system – of the bourgeois public sphere. This social system was not immediately visible; the bourgeois public was required to imagine it. The Louvre was not changed significantly following the Revolution (Hooper-Greenhill, 1992; Bennett, 1995). In time, new works of art would be commissioned by the bourgeois constituency.

The museum is also a useful model for understanding the dual role of space and vision (Hooper-Greenhill, 1992; Bennett, 1995; Perry and Cunningham, 1999). The museum was not simply for the visual representation of images and paintings, nor simply for seeing people and being in public. Vision was also important for understanding what was not immediately apparent: that the bourgeois public sphere was an institution, in that it was a socially recognized grouping of individuals and it was an institution that related to public institutions of the state. Placing public space within a disciplinary model of space demonstrates how public space can function as a site for the surveillance of, and a stage for, public discourse. In this sense, the public museum that emerged at the time of Habermas's bourgeois public sphere was also subject to interaction with new institutions that performed a disciplinary function for both the state and the public sphere. This is where Foucault's interests might usefully intersect with those of Habermas. It is also where we can extend current thinking in museum studies in the twenty-first century.

Space and Institutions of the Public Sphere: Habermas and Foucault

At this point, to further the spatial aspect of the idea of the bourgeois public sphere left unnoticed by Habermas, I consider the role of space in public life. As discussed above, for space to be a discourse of the public sphere for Habermas, it must be central to the "lifeworld," the everyday. Space, in conjunction with visual forms, becomes communicative. Considering Foucault's interests with regard to space and vision can further enhance this perception.[13]

In *Discipline and Punish*, Foucault identifies technologies of power used by "institutions" such as monasteries and armies, which become general formulae for the management of social life in the eighteenth and nineteenth centuries. Technologies of power are methods for controlling and managing social life. Some institutions, such as prisons or hospitals, are institutions of the state (although neoliberalism has seen that many of these functions are privatized). Other technologies relate to influencing people's behavior (for example, psychologically) and have an impact on all aspects of an individual's life. Technologies of power divide and control social life in terms of time, space, and mobility. In *Discipline and Punish*, Foucault uses the prison to demonstrate how space and power work to shape the way in which a subject functions in society (Foucault, 1977).

Foucault also cites schools, hospitals, and military barracks as "specialized spaces" that confine and control the inhabitants, separating them from the "mass" of population. In the context of confinement each individual has space and each space has an individual. The design of these spaces permitted constant surveillance. The organization of individuals into "cells" or "places" "orders" people in a way that renders space hierarchical, architectural, and functional. The spaces are disciplinary and simultaneously fix individuals' positions, mark places, limit their mobility and assign value to them. Disciplinary societies operate through technologies that survey, classify, and control time, space, and people. As the individuals are surveyed, classified and exposed to this system, they become their own "self-regulators," modifying their behavior in accordance with the demands of social norms. They also observe others. According to Foucault, there is then no need for force. In these institutions, the ongoing process of normalization becomes self-perpetuating. In Foucault's disciplinary society, a new "regime" of truth, normativity, and rationality emerged in the late eighteenth century. This regime was very much about the organization of public space in particular ways specific to the experience of modernity.

What are the implications of Foucault's accounts of Europe in the eighteenth and nineteenth centuries on Habermas's public sphere and its characteristics? As discussed above, Habermas's concept of the public sphere and how to practice it were conveyed, most importantly, in literary form. This account ignores the importance of space, the visual and non-rationality. How the bourgeois public sphere later influenced the reproduction and representation of itself in places and discourses such as the Paris Commune, or on Haussmann's boulevards, is not explored by Habermas in his later writing on modernity and the public sphere.

Both Habermas and Foucault distinguish between the actual physical spaces and the social practices of spaces, arguing that the practice of discourse (public or medical, for instance) is more important than the material existence of places where such discourse occurs. Foucault not only looks at public buildings, he also considers what is practiced by public institutions. He asks: how does what is practiced in the building affect the design of the building?

We have seen this relationship clearly in the emergence of the public museum. The original designs for public museums were drawings that represented the purity of the cosmos in architectural form (McClellan, 2008). The absence of material objects, or the engagement of visitors, was reflected in the spatial organization of these designs. Similarly, the opening of the palaces of royalty to the people made the museum "public" in the sense that museums moved from special invitations to being "open for all," but the spatial arrangement of the museums still conveyed the power of the state. The museum curator was an authority figure.

In recent times, the spatial organization of museums has been subject to various, often countervailing, influences. These have ranged from the commercialization of the museum interior (gift shops near entrances and exits), through to the debates about the architecture of the museum attracting visitors to see exhibits (as in the Guggenheim Museum in New York, the Pompidou Centre in Paris and the Guggenheim Museum in Bilbao) versus the importance of the exhibits relative to the architecture of the museum. The importance of public space is more readily acknowledged by museums as crucial to their publicness and, indeed, such recognition is entwined with how they state their goals, aims, and objectives. The National Museum of American History, the National Museum of Australia, Te Papa in New Zealand and the Museum of World Culture in Sweden, as outlined earlier, are examples. The relatively new, musée du quai Branly "is an innovative cultural institution – museum, educational and research center, and public living space all in one."[14] These examples are typical of museums of the twenty-first century which make explicit their intentions using a spatial indicator. They herald a new type of museum that is more intimate than its predecessor and more familiar with the source communities and visitors alike. While the lines between public and private (particularly in the form of commercial practices) have been blurred, it is critical to analyze the relationships between practices, design, and space, drawing on the work of authors such as Michel Foucault.

Foucault justifies his obsession with the spatial relations of modernity:

> I think through them I did come to what I had basically been looking for: the relations that are possible between power and knowledge. … Once knowledge can be analyzed in terms of a region, domain, implantation, displacement, transposition, one is able to capture the process by which knowledge

functions as a form of power and disseminates the effects of power. (Foucault, 1980: 69)

Foucault rejects the universalist project on empirical and logical grounds. The empirical objection is, he argues, that the universal subject is illusory for critical theory, in which the notion of power emanates from the state. One of Foucault's main concerns is the transition from the classical age to nineteenth-century culture. Foucault (1984) argued that Habermas's emancipatory goal of democracy and the public sphere was inherently flawed. This was because Habermas insisted on the use of reason (as influenced by the Enlightenment) and argued for the necessity of normative social practices for democracy to function (ideally) in order to free subjects (Ingram, 1994). For Foucault, this contradicts the Enlightenment notion of freedom because the "rational discourse of bourgeois science and morality ... only emancipate through domination" (Ingram, 1994: 218).

In modern life, for Foucault, technological and administrative means are used to solve many social problems. While the technologies may exist, what becomes more significant in understanding power is to identify who has the will to use such technologies and on what scale: local, regional, national, global. In this context, the power is not necessarily a one-way street, as is often presumed in relation to the state, nation, and its citizens: citizens can also "act upon" the state. This also assists in understanding how a more localized notion of the public sphere is conceivable, where the public sphere is acknowledged as situated, contingent, and limited.

Foucault's heterotopias – of different places – is useful to consider here. These are places that act as counter-sites, reflecting other "real" places in social life, similar to the case of the museum. In his essay "Of other spaces," Foucault argues that the space in which we live is heterogeneous:

> we do not live in a kind of void, inside of which we could place individuals and things ... we live inside a set of relations that delineates sites which are irreducible to one another and absolutely not superimposable on one another. (1986: 23)

Space is understood as relational. Foucault writes of two sites that are linked to all other sites, yet contradict all other sites: utopias and heterotopias. Utopias are essentially idealized and "fundamentally unreal spaces," yet they "have a general relation of direct or inverted analogy with the real space of Society" (Foucault, 1986: 24). Heterotopias, on the other hand, are similar to counter-sites (like alternative or counter-publics in the previous chapter), "a kind of effectively enacted utopia in which the real

sites, all other real sites that can be found within the culture, are simultaneously represented, contested and inverted" (Foucault, 1986: 24). They
"are absolutely different from all the sites that they reflect and speak about"
(1986: 24). Where the mirror reflects a placeless place of utopias, heterotopias reflect "a sort of simultaneously mythic and real contestation of the
space in which we live" (1986: 24).

Foucault considers the way which space reflects and comes to represent
reason as it extends far beyond the simple use of spatial metaphors. His
method is diagnostic, comparative, and divergent. Foucault's use of
Bentham's panopticon for theorizing power and knowledge, and norm of
surveillance, and the custodial nature of modern society, indicates the way
that the spatialization, or the space of reason, can be understood. Furthermore, it provides useful insights into how subjectivity, reason, and the
negotiation of differences, or contesting publics, are possible within a
modified Habermassian public sphere (Habermas and Levin, 1982: 28).

Public space is "utopian" if it remains in its Habermassian form.
Foucault's heterotopian public space, however, could accommodate the
contestable nature of lived democracy, where democracy is understood as
localized and situated, but not fixed. What does this mean for contemporary
museums? By now, it can be assumed that spatial organization is vital for
museums in many ways. Who organizes this space? How is it organized?
What opportunities are there to challenge this particular organization of
space? And, importantly, how do the answers to these questions help us to
define whether a museum is, or can be, "public"?

Foucault's work has the potential to complement Habermas's public sphere.
Indeed, it is possible that at this juncture the combination of both sets of
concerns more adequately reflects the practice of competing or counter-
publics in relation to the concept of the public sphere. A reminder of the
basis of these authors in understanding the spatial character of the
museum reveals the legacy of the project of the bourgeois public sphere and
how the concept of public is enmeshed with spatial metaphors. It also
magnifies what is at stake for museums in trying to realize the centuries-old
project of being democratic. It magnifies how the interpretation of the
ideology of this foundational term, and what it means for practice, changes
over time. The public sphere and subsequent concepts of public space are a
product of, and in turn shape, material space, not just discourse. This
process of shaping of material public space becomes situated, and potentially
it may become a place for particular individuals and communities. This is
evident in the recent reconsideration of how audiences are understood in
museums and how spatial practices need to reflect these newer relationships
with communities.

New Spatial Practices in Museums

As identified in Chapter Two, the museum in the twentieth century was critiqued for, among other things, the focus on the physical space and collections of the museum. This section of the chapter discusses two ideas that represented new spatial practices in museums: first, the museum without walls and, second, the post-museum.

Museum without walls

The idea of the "museum without walls," insofar as it is an idea that has had some impact on the rethinking of museums in recent years, originally came from Andre Malraux, a French art historian, theorist, and cultural minister in de Gaulle's government in the mid-twentieth century. Malraux played an active part in the cultural life of France (setting up and running various publishing houses) and was celebrated as a hero of the resistance. He actively attempted to broaden the appeal of art to a wider cross-section of the public and opened new cultural centers throughout France.

Malraux's wrote about the concept of what, in the French language, is *musée imaginaire*, or a museum that goes beyond the institutional framework of "the museum" of early modern museums. Instead, it appeals to the imagination. In the translation from French to English, however, *musée imaginaire* became "museum without walls," which actually changes the meaning significantly. In the original French text, Malraux's idea of *musée imaginaire* sought to establish a conceptual space of the human faculties: imagination, cognition, judgment within the museum – to make the museum more "humanist."

In the French version of the text, Malraux does not address matters of architecture, seeing the museum as a field of comparison – with a capacity to arrange and classify – stifling the potential of the *musée*. Along came corresponding disciplines that yielded to the English language's appetite for demonstration – for the "visualizable" example. The English translation renders the "museum without walls" as physical and takes the idea virtually as the transgression of a museum's walls – which was not Malraux's intention.

Malraux argues that museums these days (or at least in the late twentieth century) order objects into disciplined structures; consequently, they take away other *imaginary* possibilities for understanding them. He considers how this is primarily a Western phenomenon and one with a relatively short history (200 years). Before "the museum" existed as an idea – as a public institution of knowledge – we looked at collected objects and art works in an entirely different way.

> In China, the full enjoyment of works of art necessarily involved ownership, except where religious art was concerned; above all it demanded their isolation. A painting was not exhibited, but unfurled before an art lover in a fitting state of grace; its function was to deepen and enhance his [sic] communion with the universe. (Malraux, 1967: 10)

The idea of museum exhibition – public display, of objects *not* owned, shown fully "unfurled," amongst other objects – is quite alien to the way that these kinds of objects were *intended* to be seen. Museums extract objects from the realms of other types of experience and fit them into a structured public arena. Malraux speculated about the ways of moving beyond this structured and unimaginative way that museums operate. He suggested that the art book could be used as the model for "museum without walls" – or "museum of the imagination." When we look through an art book, we may choose to look randomly: we do not have a structure imposed upon us by the way in which, for Malraux, the museum orders and exhibits the art works. Malraux suggests that the "museum without walls" could be a way for the viewer to create his or her own narrative about the objects in collections; a public and structured experience instead becomes a private and highly subjective one.

Of course, one problem with Malraux's idea is that it is an abstract idea that has proved difficult to conceive of as an actual physical space – how do we actually make a real *museum of the imagination*? Since the mid-1990s, perhaps it could be argued that Malraux's "museum without walls" has been realized to some extent with the Internet and the availability of collections online. Digitized online collections allow us to make our own way through museums' objects. The "hypertext" capabilities of the Internet allow us to jump from point-to-point without sticking to prescribed avenues of movement between objects. For example, the Art Gallery of New South Wales in Sydney allows visitors onto their web site to search their objects based on different fields – producer, medium, department or date. We can pick our way through their collection without having a narrative imposed on the objects by the museum and the ways in which the museum physically arranges and organizes it. We may even construct our own online virtual exhibition of the works in the collection. The obvious problem, however, is that online museums are *virtual* environments. As much as they might realize, to some extent, Malraux's idea of the "museum without walls," we are disconnected from the physicality of the objects. The benefits of this approach are apparent when considering museums that work with people who own the cultural material, as in, for example, the New South Wales Migration Heritage Centre, where people can keep the material close to them in a personal context, but other people can view the material electronically.

The post-museum

For at least the past two centuries, museums have been based on what have become known as "modernist" assumptions. "These museum underpinnings included a focus on the museum building, an emphasis on display as the main means of communication, and a sense of knowledge as being unified. The artifacts and specimens were collected and classified, to produce an encyclopedic world-view, understood from a Western perspective" (Hooper-Greenhill, 2000: 151). The role of the curator was central in museum practice, because it was the curator who decided what was to be displayed, and how it was to be displayed. As noted elsewhere in this book, the role of the curator has been challenged intensely in recent years. This challenge stems from the questioning of modernist assumptions about what museums are and how they operate. Rather than this being the "death of the museum," a new type of museum has been advocated as "the rebirth of the museum" (Hooper-Greenhill, 2000: 151). This new concept of the museum is the post-museum.

The post-museum is based on notions of cultural diversity, accessibility, engagement and the use of objects, rather than the continued accumulation of objects. As characteristic of this process may be where de-accessioning has occurred, including where objects taken from indigenous people in colonial settings have been repatriated. Rather than being an object of curiosity to be viewed in a museum, the item may be returned to its original setting, where its meaning is linked to the cultures and the place of origin. Or the museum may remain the custodian of the material under the guidance of the source community (perhaps until the community feels it appropriate to receive the material). In some cases, such as with the Australian Museum, museums play an advisory role, assisting with the development of a "keeping place" to house the material in the community, for community use (Kelly and Gordon, 2002).

Recognition of cultural diversity and respect for various cultures extends beyond repatriation. Emphasis is placed on experience and process. The role of intangible cultural heritage also moves to center stage. It includes museum exhibitions that engage meaningfully with different cultures, in contrast to exhibitions and displays that commence from an assumption of the supremacy of Western knowledge, which is then universalized. The museum becomes more like a cultural center. Hooper-Greenhill's post-museum mirrors, in various ways, what James Clifford (1999) called a "contact zone." This term, which Clifford borrows from Mary Louise Pratt, is an attempt "to invoke the spatial and temporal copresence of subjects previously separated by geographic and historical disjunctures, and whose trajectories now intersect" (in Clifford, 1999: 192). Clifford identified how the organizing structures of museums, based on modernist practices, were like the "frontier," which was grounded in, and reflected, a Western expansionist perspective. Rather than the role of the curator being to care for the objects and display them from an authoritative position in relation to knowledge, post-museums have attempted to rethink and restructure the organization of the museum to engage different audiences in ways that are contact zones, while simultaneously recognizing the plurality of meanings and values inherent in the contact.

This involves moving from a visual culture of display to a wider concept of communication. According to Hooper-Greenhill, "the exhibition will form part of a nucleus of events which will take place both before and after the display is mounted" (2000: 152). She goes further to indicate what this may mean in terms of who is engaged, what they may produce, and how this new culture material may enter the collections. Hooper-Greenhill suggests that the events may involve:

> The establishments of community and organizational partnerships; the production of objects during educational programs which then enter the collections; periods of time when specific community groups use the museum spaces in their own way; writers, scientists and artists in residence; or satellite displays set up in pubs and shops. During these events, discussions, workshops, performances, dances, songs, and meals will be produced or enacted. (2000: 152)

The production of events and exhibitions as conjoint dynamic processes enables the incorporation into the museum of many voices and many perspectives.

This shift in the museum model has been facilitated by changing technologies that enable different ideas and practices to be implemented. The post-museum is not limited by its own walls, and through the use of technology can establish new relationships and communications outside the physical structure of the museum. Innovative examples of post-museum practice in this regard include the work of the New South Wales Migration and Heritage Centre in Sydney, a web-based museum, where the emphasis is on documenting the existence of important cultural objects, assisting to maintain their condition, and using technology to ensure that these objects remain in the cultural settings from where their meanings are derived. The stories that link people, events, and cultural beliefs and practices with the object are constructed conjointly.

Since the late-1990s, the post-museum has developed from an idea that emerged from postmodern and postcolonial critiques of museum practice to being something that is increasingly implemented in contemporary museums. The potential of this approach is far from exhausted. There exist numerous opportunities to engage with communities to conjointly pro- duce knowledge, challenge ideas and practices, and to preserve cultural material without resorting to processes of dispossession.

In order for these engagements to be successful, it is essential that we move from a modernist concern with "public participation" that envisages a homogenized "public," but do not succumb to romantic notions of "community." It is imperative that museum professionals avoid both romanticizing community as inherently "good" and unified, and resist the temptation to simply replace "society" with the term "community," because of the latter term's positive connotations, while all the time continuing to operate the same way as in the past. If one term simply replaces another, the potential for a rebirth of the museum, and hence the opportunities to (re)develop museums that are relevant for the twenty-first century, will be lost. In short, this is not a palatable option, because it means that museums will be increasingly perceived as mausoleums, as collections of dead objects, both literally and in terms of their meaning.

Post-museums, in order to engage in genuine participatory practices of knowledge creation and communication, must ensure that their practice is based on a concept of "diverse publics" that recognizes multiplicity, asymmetrical power-relations and fissions within "communities." Post-museums can be broad enough to accommodate many and diverse voices, sufficiently dynamic to include changes over time, and accessible such that they become safe and respected "contact zones." As Losche reminds us:

> Museums are often born with the nation state, and, so the usual story goes, reflect aspects of that state. At the same time not all aspects of history and culture are represented . . . Many cultural centres in the Pacific region seem to conform to a narrative that ignores the fact that some, at least, have emerged from ruins and violent pasts and thus cultural centres seem rather clean spaces, uncontaminated by history. (2009: 70)

The very nature of this process necessitates an emphasis on "becoming," of being dynamic and continually adapting to, and sometimes initiating, changes in society. In many ways, this nature equates to the expression of the ideal public sphere, which remains in a perpetual state of re-evaluation, self-reflexivity and modification, depending on the needs and content of publicly significant discourse at any given time. Post-museums should, over time, become what people think of when the word "museum" is used. If we are successful in this endeavor, the prefix "post" becomes redundant. We are creating, and to the extent that museums can and should be fixed, have created, museums for the twenty-first century.

Reconsidering the spatial practices of museums

What does this mean for the spatial practices of existing museums and new museums? At first glance it appears that new museums seem to have all the luck: an opportunity to have a new building, a renewed profile for museums and presumably new audiences. The world has seen an increasing number of new institutions built in the Pacific and in Europe. The expectations created for new museums are significant: new audiences, retention of core audiences, economic renewal, cultural revitalization, continued state support, and cultural affirmation for many. However, it is also the case that the universal museums have also renewed themselves in recent years. Examples of this renewal include the British Museum, Museum of Modern Art (MoMA), and the Louvre. These museums have developed new facilities for visitors and have been re-presenting some of the old collections anew. They, along with their newly designed siblings, also purport to be informed by "post"-practices of postcolonialism and postmodernism. What is it that makes these new forms of museums distinct from the museums of yesteryear?

As many museum commentators have advised, the museum will always carry with it the legacy of its origins, for better or worse (Hooper-Greenhill, 2000; Witcomb, 2003). Yet attempts to reconsider, re-present or redeem the museum are commonplace in museum studies and museum sector literature internationally (Message, 2006; Dibley, 2005). Indeed, many of the museums of the eighteenth century are undergoing renewal programs.

In 2003, the British Museum celebrated its 250th anniversary, making it one of the oldest public institutions in the world. The natural history collections were originally part of the collections of the British Museum but were given their own exhibition space in the 1880s (in South Kensington) in an effort to refine their collecting strengths (Wilson, 2003: 7). The British

Museum is of particular interest because it has, in recent times, actively sought to re-present both its collections and exhibition spaces. On 6 December 2000, the conversion of the forecourt of the British Museum, completed by architect Norman Foster, was opened by Her Majesty Queen Elizabeth II. The renovation enabled more of the vast collection to be shown and also provided many new public and education facilities. It involved the relocation of the British Library, once in the forecourt of the British Museum, to new premises. This, in turn, provides a space for the Museum to hold and display its own library material related to the collection. As part of the 250th anniversary, the British Museum opened a new permanent display: Enlightenment: Discovering the World in the Eighteenth Century. Intended as an examination of eighteenth century developments in the classification of knowledge, this exhibition displays objects produced in the Pacific, ironically, where many of the new museums are emerging.

One of the most significant areas of development in new museums and museums such as the British Museum and musée du quai Branly in France are new relationships established with communities. Communities of indigenous peoples have been effectively arguing for many years for the right to be consulted about the representation of their culture (Karp and Levine, 1991; Karp et al., 1992; Simpson, 2001). This is reflected in academic literature about the museum context since the late 1980s and is termed the "new museology" (Vergo, 1989). The idea is used to argue that museums should be accessible, intellectually and physically, to all peoples. To avoid universalizing accounts of the world in museums, new ways of working with indigenous communities have been developed. One strategy has been to rethink the performative aspect of the museum as "contact zone" (Clifford, 1999), a place of meeting for communities, particularly indigenous communities, and as a cultural center. Eilean Hooper-Greenhill's "post-museum" (2000) suggests that new ways of using the museum do not necessarily require the use of the collection. Both of these concepts are informed by the respective author's research in Canada and the Pacific region: Clifford in Canada (1999) and Hooper-Greenhill's visits to Australia and New Zealand (2000).

Museums as contact zones (Clifford), the post-museum (Hooper-Greenhill), museums as civic laboratories (Bennett) – all signal a particular shift in how museums are imagined. This is also signaled in the new museum – along the lines of Message (2006). The emphasis is on a relationship with communities as their publics, with communities producing meaning through cultural production of material and intangible practices, performances and so on. It mimics the form of community cultural centers, of which there are many around the world. In this sense, I argue that museums, as contact zones, post-museums or new museums, tread a fine line between breaking new ground and appropriating spaces and practices already situated elsewhere. The balance becomes one where we need to ask: who is invigorating who, and at what cost?

While I am generally supportive of the above museum practices, their potential dangers need to be made overt, if only to be avoided. The dangers are appropriation and duplication. These dangers emanate from a dissatisfaction with the concept of "public," and increasingly from the transferral of erroneous understandings of public to the term "community." These dangers may be avoided by developing and employing a more nuanced and respectful concept of "community," not as audience but as participants in the construction, communication, and management of museums and conservation of dynamic cultures. To this end, reciprocity is crucial because, without it, the danger of appropriation by well-intentioned museum professionals is real.

Conclusion

As discussed in the previous chapters, the manner in which individuals come to know how to be in public is pivotal to understanding how democracy works in its varying formations. In this historical model, Habermas argued that, in order for the subjects of democracy to participate in public discourse, they must possess the appropriate forms of communication – writing and speech. However, I have argued that, in order to develop and understand the forms of discourse possible in the public sphere, the subjects of democracy must be exposed to a place where democracy is performed, or acted out, so that they can understand it conceptually and materially. This occurs through spatial and visual practices. In other words, the spatial is an inherent part of Habermas's model of the public sphere. Space, as concept, and space as material or "real," cannot be considered oppositional; these are mutually constitutive, because such "approaches deter us from investigating the real political struggles inherent in the production of all spaces and from enlarging the field of struggles to make many different kinds of spaces public" (Deutsche, 1996: 375).

The latter section of this chapter explored the limitations of Habermas's bourgeois public sphere in the context of Foucault's parallel engagement with public life in the realm of public institutions of the state. In particular, I considered Foucault's interest in their spatial and surveillance functions, an examination which also indicated how space and vision were central to the formation of modern society and democracy. Space plays a pivotal role in the emergence of disciplinary technologies of power and the institutions of democracy, such as houses of parliament. It also plays a pivot role in contemporary public places, such as museums, where surveillance technology has changed the character of such spaces, and can be instrumental in excluding particular individuals or groups from a "public" space.

The concept of public institutions, as developed in the period of the bourgeois public sphere, still plays an important symbolic role in public spaces today. The inference about the public space of the monarch being inherited by the bourgeoisie is one example of how history is not simply disjointed between periods; it is continuous in some form, even in its rejection of past regimes. More recent incarnations of the museum as it attempts to be "public" have, to some extent, acknowledged the short-comings of the term "public" by looking towards the diversity of what constitutes "the public" and have arrived at new relationships with their audiences, sometimes referred to as community.

In the twenty-first century, museums exist within new political and cultural contexts. The museums are arguably more accessible, both intellectually and physically, to the public and to their communities of interest, than in previous centuries. In recent years, museums around the world have responded to critiques of their role in the process of colonization and appropriation of material culture. The responses are evident in a range of policy debates for museums and their related professions, and governments (Kelly and Gordon, 2002).

The following chapter takes up the discussion about the terminology and practices used to work with communities, audiences, viewers, the public. What goes on in the museum: how does the museum profession engage with audiences and make the space accessible and open to all? How does the museum function as a site within which public discourse can occur?

Notes

1 In his introduction to the *STPS*, Habermas outlines how the public sphere was constituted though *lexi* – discussion. The emphasis on the public sphere being formed through discourse of public matters is consistent throughout the *STPS*. The places where the public meets and appears go unnoticed by Habermas. See also Habermas (1964) and Hohendahl (1974). Habermas explains the concept of the public sphere and explicitly states that the public

sphere is a sphere that mediates between society and the state, through the formation of public discussion. Hohendahl clarifies the concept of the public sphere by stating:

> Habermas's concept of the public sphere is not to be equated with that of "the public," i.e. of the individuals who assemble. His concept is directed instead at the institution, which to be sure only assumes concrete form through the participation of people. It cannot be characterized simply as a crowd. (1974: 49)

2 For an interesting discussion about Heumann Gurian's book *Civilizing the Museum* (2005), go to the Museum 2.0 web site at: http://museumtwo. blogspot.com/2007_07_01_archive.html (accessed 31 May 2009). "Museum 2.0" is blog that explores how the web can be used in museums. The site is responsive to visitors: they determine what appears on the site as distinct from a museum providing the content. The site aims to increase community engagement with museums by providing ways for audiences and museum professionals to participate in discussion about all aspects of museums.
3 Mitchell also cites the following authors as concurring with his view: Fraser (1990), Hartley (1992), and Howell (1993).
4 See "About us" at: http://www.nma.gov.au/about_us/ (accessed 9 December 2008).
5 See: http://www.britishmuseum.org/the_museum/museum_in_the_world. aspx (accessed 9 December 2008).
6 See: http://americanhistory.si.edu/about/message.cfm (accessed 9 December 2008).
7 See: http://www.varldskulturmuseet.se/smvk/jsp/polopoly.jsp?d=126&l= en_US (accessed 17 December 2008).
8 In the same paragraph Zukin cites:

> A [relatively] recent decision by the New Jersey Supreme Court (*New York Times*, December 21, 1994), moreover, recognized that the great public space of modernity – "the parks, the squares, and the street ... have been substantially displaced by [shopping centers]," and consequently, that the private owners of these shopping centers could no longer prevent people from exercising their constitutional right to free speech. (Zukin, 1995: 45)

9 See: http://www.tate.org.uk/archivejourneys/historyhtml/bld_liv_site.htm (accessed 9 December 2008).
10 See: http://www.guggenheim.org/bilbao/about (accessed 9 December 2008).
11 See: http://www.ushmm.org/museum/press/kits/details.php?content=99-general &page=05-mission (accessed 9 December 2008).

12 Foucault becomes important for thinking about the public sphere for many reasons. His archaeologies could inspire the following questions: What is the impelling force that inspired the need for democracy, that in turn enabled democracy to become imaginable? What technologies enabled forms of modern democracy of the bourgeois public sphere to become possible? In particular, I am thinking of Foucault's discourse theory, where the actual originating site of an idea or "thing" is not what is sought as vital, but the discourse that articulates the needs for such a "thing" is articulated as more revealing, particularly of power relations. Hence, in thinking about the bourgeois public sphere, I would argue that evidence of the need for a meeting place for the people to discuss issues ought to be important for understanding the emerging bourgeoisie.

13 Foucault also has a tendency to use imagery, or the visual, to substantiate, or to further elucidate, his theoretical propositions without sufficiently explaining the significance of vision and visuality (i.e., how does one look and see). Foucault, in his work on Diego Velazquez's (1599–1660) painting, *Las Meninas* (*The Maids of Honour*), 1656, Museo del Prado, Madrid, considers the issues of representation and meaning. See Foucault (1991). He also makes a significant contribution to thinking about vision in his work on Bentham's panopticon, notions of surveillance and observation, and his technologies of power. Habermas and Foucault are both concerned with the formation and practices of power in the eighteenth century. The subject of reason proves to be a central concern for both Habermas and Foucault despite their differences. On this last point, see Ingram (1994).

14 See: http://www.quaibranly.fr/en/the-public-institution/index.html (accessed 15 December 2008).

4

Audience, Community, and Public

Introduction

Contemplating museums in the 1930s, Georges Bataille wrote:

> We must realize that the halls and art objects are but the container, whose content is formed by the visitors. It is the content that distinguishes a museum from a private collection. A museum is like a lung of a great city; each Sunday the crowd flows like blood into the museum and emerges purified and fresh. (see Bataille, 1986: 25)

Since Bataille's original writing in the 1930s, the museum has found new ways of injecting itself with the lifeblood of its visitors via the web and, more recently, social media. This has also necessitated new ways of thinking about audiences, and ways to count and evaluate their relationship to the museum. These new forms of engagement with the museum, such as social media and the web, fundamentally challenge ways of knowing audiences and the claims made about the value of museums.

How do museums identify their "public" and why do they equate public with audience? How does the museum use the term "public" in relation to people? How is the public conceptualized: as audience, as community, as individuals? The complexities of this conceptualization are highlighted in the example of "multiculturalism" in Australia from the 1980s to the mid-1990s. The need for multiculturalism was devised in Australia to address inequity and exclusion on the basis of ethnicity and culture in government policy. Similar to gender, community and class, identifying awareness of yet another category of inequity indicates inadequacies in the notion of "public." Multiculturalism is a term that was generally accepted by the museum community in Australia, in some cases perhaps only because it was government policy and it was not possible for some museums to reject or ignore multiculturalism. While the term has been consigned to a particular

Museums and the Public Sphere   by Jennifer Barrett
© 2010 Jennifer Barrett

period in Australia's recent political history, it is important to consider what multiculturalism implied for museums, democracy, and the notion of the public sphere. Despite the passing of the term "multiculturalism" from government policy, like gender, class and race, this does not mean that the original issues multiculturalism was devised to address have been resolved.

A discourse about the democratic basis of museums involves a process of identifying gaps in the ideology and the claim of museums to be open and accessible to all. Like other areas of social and cultural policy, this method of identification (multiculturalism, social exclusion, pluralism, and diversity) indicates a desire to not only render museums more democratic but also the need to reconsider how we understand the formative role of the term "public" in the museum context.

This chapter is a critical exploration of the use of visitor studies to understand "audiences" as the public. By investigating the role of subjectivity in visitor studies programs and material produced by museums, I reveal the limitations of methodologies used to identify and understand the public as audience. The chapter concludes that the relationship between the rhetoric of the museum and the real ways in which communities form and identify themselves is at odds. With a more nuanced approach to the site-specific publics and understanding of community, we may see the museum develop its competency to articulate the public in ways that are recognizable and commensurate with the "real world."

Michael Warner (2002: 15) offers useful insights on research about publics as being "essentially interpretative and form sensitive." He calls for "an understanding of the phenomenon of publics that is historical in orientation and always alert to the dynamics of textuality" (Warner, 2002: 15). This is argued in contrast to what he sees as a social science model where "the public is simply an existing entity to be studied empirically and for whom empirical analysis has to mean something more definite, less interpretative, than attention to the means by which fiction of the public is made real" (Warner, 2002: 15). Indeed, some authors argue that museums in the twenty-first century "are less concerned about their moral or political agency than they are about visitor numbers on their funding streams. Even so, museums continue to have significant agency both in reproducing contemporary cultural preoccupations and in modifying them with new or different ideas" (Bolton, 2006: 13.1). According to Warner (2002: 12), the "idea of a public is motivating, not simply instrumental. It is constitutive of the social imaginary." Engaging with the public necessitates engaging with the "conditions that bring them together" (Warner, 2002: 12). Intertextuality is necessarily required for this complex and significant task. With this in mind, the chapter begins by reviewing the work of Pierre

Bourdieu, a central influence in the development of research on visitors to museums. The chapter then considers the ways that museum professionals have come to know the visitor. This section summarizes a range of approaches, including visitor studies, segmentation studies, and barrier analysis. The following section of the chapter presents critiques of these practices. This leads to the essence of the chapter, which is about "doing museum research differently." How the museum research is to be different is then presented through a number of subsections, namely community, community and public spheres, and communities of practice.

The Influence of Pierre Bourdieu

One of the most influential thinkers and researchers in the field of museum studies was Pierre Bourdieu (1930–2002). Bourdieu's contribution included a major international study of museum attendance, including the activities and perspectives of different classes, in the mid-1960s. This extensive research was to influence museum theory and practice for many years, and is still very relevant. The theorizing around this empirical research is also crucial. Bourdieu and his co-authors provided insights into important debates about the "public" that museums are attempting to attract, and how these people engage with various museums. This section of the book introduces Bourdieu's empirical study, his main theoretical contributions and the critiques that have been made of Bourdieu's work. This last point is crucial, because Bourdieu's empirical work was mainly undertaken in the mid-1960s, and although his work is still relevant in museum studies today, many changes have occurred since this time, both within museums and in the wider social context (Prior, 2005).

In 1964 and 1965, Pierre Bourdieu, along with Dominique Schnapper, Alain Darbel, Francine Dreyfus and many other research assistants, conducted a "systematic survey of the European museum-going public, its social and educational characteristics, its attitudes to museums and its artistic preferences" (Bourdieu and Darbel, 1990: 5). The study was undertaken in five countries (France, Greece, Holland, Poland, and Spain), with the main survey alone in March and April of 1964 involving 9,226 questionnaire respondents in 21 French museums selected on the basis of their measured quality and the number of annual visitors. The study also included 250 in-depth interviews, a verificatory survey and studies of the duration of visits and its relationship to the knowledge of paintings (Bourdieu and Darbel, 1990).

The main findings from the full study included the revelation that there were important class differences in the attitudes towards, and the attendance of, museums. People in the upper socioeconomic category attended museums and galleries more often, from an earlier age and alone compared with people from working classes. Having agreed to participate in the study, they were also far more likely to answer all the questionnaire than working-class respondents, and when they did not answer particular questions, it was the "naïve" question that was blamed whereas working-class non-responses on particular questions were interpreted as being derived from ignorance (Bourdieu and Darbel, 1990).

Bourdieu and Darbel (originally 1969) concluded that the apparent naturalization of art appreciation and knowledge concealed important processes that enabled some people, and limited the ability of other people, to display their knowledge and appreciation of art. The upper classes felt comfortable being in art galleries and museums because they had learned how to be so. In this sense, Bourdieu and Darbel (1990: 111) highlighted the shift in boundaries from the "strictly economic differences created by the pure possession of material goods through the differences created by the possession of symbolic goods such as works of art or through the search for symbolic distinctions in the manner of using these goods. . . ." They linked this very closely with the "true functions" of museums:

> If this is the function of culture, and if the love of art is the clear mark of the chosen, separating, by invisible and insuperable barrier, those who are touched by it from those who have not received this grace, it is understandable that in the tiniest details of their morphology and their organization, museums betray their true function, which is to reinforce for some the feeling of belonging and for others the feeling of exclusion. (Bourdieu and Darbel, 1990: 112)

The idea that there is a "true function" of museums is about questioning the appearance of museums being open to all. Bourdieu and Darbel claimed that this is:

> false generosity, since free entry is also optional entry, reserved for those who, equipped with the ability to appropriate the works of art, have the privilege of making use of this freedom, and who thence find themselves legitimated in their privilege, that is, in their ownership of the means of appropriation of cultural goods . . . . (1990: 113)

Bourdieu continued this theme of social distinction, particularly in his 1979 book *Distinction: A Social Critique of the Judgement of Taste*, which was translated into English in 1984 and was very influential in the museum world. He claimed that: "art and cultural consumption are predisposed, consciously and deliberately or not, to fulfil a social function of legitimating social differences" (Bourdieu, 1984: 7). While there are very few direct references to museums in this book, Bourdieu reiterates an important point from his co-authored 1969 publication: ". . . the art museum admits anyone (who has the necessary cultural capital), at any moment, without any constraints as regards dress, thus providing none of the social gratifications associated with great 'society' occasions" (Bourdieu, 1984: 272).

According to Bourdieu, an inability to acquire cultural capital limits access to museums. The acquisition of cultural capital, Bourdieu (1984: 101) argued, was a process that was part of creating a lifestyle, and lifestyles originated in class habitus (i.e., the "internalized form of class condition and of the conditionings it entails"). The habitus enabled certain practices, such as attending museums (particularly art museums), to be rendered natural when, in fact, they were deeply class derived.

Bourdieu's work has been highly influential in the English-speaking world, both in museum studies and in its wider social application (Fyfe, 2004). Fyfe and Ross (1996) use some of Bourdieu's concepts in their study of museum visitation in the contiguous towns of Stoke-on-Trent and Newcastle-under-Lyme in the Potteries region of England. Their in-depth interviews highlighted the importance of place. They concluded that "class formation does not occur independently of place . . . it occurs partly through the medium of geographical migration" (Fyfe and Ross, 1996: 148). This has important implications for museums; they are both part of the place in which people live but they also interpret place, and this raises a question about "whose sense of place are they to acknowledge?" (Fyfe and Ross, 1996: 130). Fyfe (1998) extends this notion of the variance between and within museums. "Museums are not monoliths" is his first sentence in its entirety (Fyfe, 1998: 325). This point is echoed by Prior (2005: 130), who claims that "Bourdieu operates with a vague and monolithic version of the institution" which is "a static and unreflexive upholder of a tightly-bound high culture." In probably his most strident criticism of Bourdieu, Prior (2005: 130) wrote that this characterization of museums "lacks subtlety and accuracy." Prior's criticism is supported by the historical evidence, where the history of museums and museology highlights the variance in museum ideas and practices over time, within a single institution, and in the many articles and debates that later led to changes in museum practice.

Bourdieu's work is not without other critics. Among them is Vera Zolberg (1990, 2003) who critiqued the emphasis on class, the "fluidity of the categories" used and the failure to "incorporate the most striking feature of the arts; their changing nature, their construction and recon-struction, resulting in their crossover character" (Zolberg, 2003: 300). Nick Prior (2005) and Tony Bennett (2007) both question the existence of homologous tastes across different fields, such that it could be said, as Bourdieu did, that there are clear distinctions arising from a unified habitus. Bennett (2007: 201) highlights Bourdieu's own life as being derived from a divided habitus: "coming from lowly social origins to achieve high scholarly distinction." Prior (2005: 135) notes the rigidity of Bourdieu's categories, in particular that of class, but rather than rejecting Bourdieu's ideas, advocated that they be "warped and quickened without loosing (sic) their explanatory value." He calls for "a Bourdieu" who can devise categories that can "keep up with an accentuated modernity" and be flexible enough to deal with "the embodied inequalities of gender, class and ethnicity [that] are relatively durable but also frequently reconstructed" (Prior, 2005: 135).

While not harboring pretenses of being a new Bourdieu, I concur with Prior's call for an approach to museum studies, and social life generally, that can account for the changing nature of museums, is grounded in a rigorous understanding of history and contemporary museum practices, and is visionary so as to account for changing discourses and technologies. Such an approach cannot emerge from a monolithic understanding of museums, or from an emphasis on class or from the universalizing of culture that ignores distinctions based on class, ethnicity, gender, place, and so on. I contend that a nuanced reconsideration of the concepts of public, public space, and the public sphere are critical starting points from which a new and relevant museum studies approach can be based. Part of this reconsideration involves the questioning of work done to date on the concept of a "visitor" to the museum.

Ways of Knowing the Visitor

The idea of researching museum visitors, and indeed non-visitors to museums, is valid. Museums Australia Inc. (2002) distinguished between "research," which is about uncovering new facts or principles, and "evaluation," which provides feedback on the merit or worth of a specific program or exhibit.

Carol Scott (1994: v) wrote that "evaluation is one means by which museums can establish a channel of communication with their audiences and thus produce better exhibitions." She was focusing on the development and assessment of specific exhibitions, and advocated a four-stage model of evaluation, which is discussed below. The evaluation at various stages may comprise quantitative and qualitative research techniques. This can be seen in the following subsections where we summarize different forms of research and evaluation.

Audience research

Audience research looks at actual and potential visitors to museums, with a view to enabling museums to make decisions on policy, programming, and marketing. It uncovers both motivations and barriers to visitation, and is also used to demonstrate wide societal access to museums. It can also function as a form of performance monitoring and quality control.

There are various types of audience research. These include:

- *Visitor studies:* This involves profiling the audience. An example is the use of cross-sectional studies to provide a snapshot of visitation at a particular point in time. The specific snapshot should be balanced by longitudinal studies that reveal variability and build an idea of visitor base and visitation patterns over time.
- *Segmentation studies:* This approach acknowledges the differences between individuals and attempts to group "like audiences" to uncover each segment's motivations and expectations. The role of these studies is to gain competitive advantage by catering for specific segments.
- *Barrier analysis:* This research recognizes that not everybody visits museums. It seeks to identify who does not visit, and why this is the case. The aim is to reduce the existence of actual and/or perceived barriers to visitation.
- *Visitor counts:* This approach is used to determine the proportion of total visitors in various areas, at peak times. This then enables better planning of exhibitions and staffing arrangements, for instance.

There are also various methodologies used in audience research. The reasons for undertaking the research should determine the type of data collection and methodology employed. At its simplest, there is a division between quantitative and qualitative research methods, but it is important to note that these are not mutually exclusive and some of the better studies use a combination of quantitative and qualitative methods in an effective manner.

The quantitative methods include large samples for surveys, often based on random sampling, which produces generalized findings leading to general assumptions. Techniques used include questionnaires and exit surveys. The limitations of such approaches include the potential under-representation of certain groups, such as children, non-English-speaking people, and so on.

Image 4.1   Installation view, *The Arts of Islam: Treasures from the Nasser D Khalili Collection*, Art Gallery of New South Wales Sydney Australia. Photo Jenni Carter, 2007

Qualitative methods rely on smaller samples, are more time intensive, and often yield an understanding of attitudes, motivations and opinions. The disadvantage of these methods is that they produce quotes and other information that cannot be readily quantified and therefore presented graphically or in statistical form to decision-makers. These are termed "subjective" measures, and involve collecting "psychographic" data. They are essential to segmentation studies.

Exhibition evaluation for museums and galleries

Evaluation assesses the merit or value of museums and exhibitions, but seems to focus on exhibitions. In museums, the main criterion for assessing merit or value is accessibility.

According to Scott (1994), accessibility is assessed in four stages:

- *Front-end evaluation – concept stage*: Qualitative methods are employed, usually using focus groups, to obtain a cross-section of opinion.

- *Formative evaluation – design stage*: This is undertaken when deciding how best to communicate the exhibition message and story, and tests elements of the proposed design from the visitors' point of view. This involves the use of qualitative methods.
- *Remedial evaluation – concurrent with the running of the exhibition*: It assesses, using quantitative methods, the patterns of usage to detect if the exhibition is "working." Changes can then be made to the exhibition.
- *Summative evaluation – post exhibition*: Using a range of visitor feedback sources, this judges the outcomes of the exhibition and whether it achieved its aims.

While there is an emphasis on museum research and evaluation along the lines of what has been presented above, it is also pertinent to explore the critiques of the above types of studies.

Critiquing Visitor Studies

Much of the evaluation that currently takes place with regard to museums conforms to what Sue Allen et al. (2007) identified as reducing complexity, rather than embracing complexity. The "reducing complexity" approach (Allen et al., 2007) is empirically founded, utilizes primarily quantitative research methods and aims to reduce results to simplified ideas that can then be applied universally. The main techniques used include interviews, observations and questionnaires, usually applying random sampling of visitors and carried out by consistently following a set protocol. There are many limitations of this approach, which have been identified by Allen et al. (2007) and are applicable in contexts beyond museum-based research. For example, can empirical methods be used to measure, and generalized assumptions be made, about the motivations, levels of engagement and learning of a wide variety of visitors?

In essence, these techniques seek to create a controlled environment where research follows a scientific model to identify causal relations, and is then used to inform future policy and practice. It is, however, hard to conduct controlled experiments on museum visitors because such studies intrude on natural behavior. It is also difficult to arrange the environment so that direct comparisons can be made between different museum contexts (Allen et al., 2007: 231).

These factors mean that the conclusions reached through the "reduced complexity" approach are necessarily limited in their usefulness to museums, as they are in other contexts. I would argue, however, that many visitor studies practitioners are not acutely aware of these limitations. For example, in *Museum Methods*, it is stated that so-called "objective measures" – such as demographics, socioeconomic information, and participation data – are "... fairly easy to obtain so they often form the mainstay of audience research" (Ferguson, 2001: 4). This statement implies that these methods are often employed for reasons of convenience, rather than because of their theoretical soundness.

Another reason for the appeal of these quantitative evaluation techniques is their appearance of "objectivity." The experience of being seduced by metrics is not confined to museums. As Judith Mastai (2007) noted in her chapter titled "There is no such thing as a visitor," the gradual withdrawal of government funding to museums (specifically in Europe and North America) has forced these institutions to conceive of visitors as "customers," and to incorporate commercial marketing strategies at all operational levels to realign the museum to meet the wants of customers in order to survive financially. The focus on counting visitor numbers, and promoting exhibitions for their commercial appeal rather than for the quality of the material culture or the importance of the issues, is, according to Mastai (2007), about the need of museums to earn money. It is not an altruistic desire but "... the need to better understand the visitor has risen ... to attract the customer and gain their allegiance through membership, while ensuring they spend as much money as possible each time they visit the museum" (Mastai, 2007: 174).

Parallel to this, communities with a developing interest in museums have also developed greater capacity to relate to audiences and challenge the practices of museums. Indigenous communities in Australia, for instance, have played a major role in challenging the nineteenth- and early twentieth-century ideology of museums by insisting on new ways of understanding the relationship between museums and source communities. The notion of the museum as a "keeping place," which communities may choose to use or modify for their own purpose, is one such way that indigenous communities in Australia have challenged museums. Of particular note is how the community was self-defined and representative. These changes in museums were also linked to social movements formed by communities. They engaged with forms of representation and changed the museum practice in such a way that strong professional ethics now guide museum professionals to engage with communities, not only indigenous communities, on their terms. Consequently, museums in Australia have modified their practices. What is perhaps unrealized about this particular example is how self-identifying communities, as such, were engaged. In other words, would the shift have occurred in the same way if indigenous communities were interpreted as audience or visitor, as individuals aggregated?

By way of contrast, Allen et al. (2007) identify "embracing complexity" as an approach that recognizes the "multiple realities" of visitor experiences, the plethora of perspectives that visitors bring to museums and the many meanings generated when different people are exposed to a common stimulus.

One mode of research in this approach is "naturalistic inquiry," which favors extended and rich observations over a large sample size. Importantly, this approach is employed in the "natural" setting, rather than attempting to isolate the variables, as is likely to be done with approaches that seek causality (i.e., the reducing complexity approaches).

In contrast to the reducing complexity approaches, which are often designed to answer a specific question in a cost- and time-effective manner, naturalistic inquiry is often time intensive. Similar to anthropological studies over an extended time period, naturalistic inquiry tends to employ "persistent observation" and explores "details of the phenomena under study to a deep level [because this] may reveal important or surprising results" (Allen et al., 2007: 238).

This embracing complexity approach does not, in itself, lead to high-quality research in museums. In order to identify good research, and to deal with the volume and complexity of data gathered, four measures have been put forward to assess the trustworthiness of the results (Allen et al., 2007). These are:

- "credibility" (whether the results are believable to those who took part in the study);
- "transferability" (whether the findings can be applied to other settings);
- "dependability" (which involves reviewing the consistency of the inquiry process over time);
- "conformability" (how well the results are supported by events inde-pendent of the researcher: e.g., by referencing previous studies).

Given that the scope of such research can be beyond the resources of the researcher(s), one popular form of research that embraces complexity is to use case studies. This involves a small number of subjects and highly contextualized data collection and analysis (Allen et al., 2007). The challenges of conducting effective case studies, as with other academic disciplines that employ this methodology, include case selection, establishing parameters, appropriate and accurate data collection over time, and interpreting and analyzing context-specific data (Allen et al., 2007). Case studies are appropriate to use in some situations but, like other forms of research discussed here, may be done well or poorly depending on how the above issues are addressed.

It is important to address a related issue here, which the authors identify as having a major impact on how and why museum visitor research is conducted – cultural variability. Hence the chapter addresses culturally responsive research and evaluation. While it is possible to present a list of qualitative research methods and discuss their strengths and weaknesses, I argue that there is a need for museums to engage with fundamental concepts, which should be central to this area of research methods concerned with the museum's engagement with the public and being public.

If we accept that the term "public" – as it relates to the public sphere, public space, and museum – changes over time, then the methods for understanding this relationship need to change too. In a quest to seek out a closer relationship with "the people," to shift from using the term "public" to "community" does not simply result in museums being more democratic than their predecessors. While audience, community, and public are too easily used interchangeably (as I have argued elsewhere: Barrett, 1998), it appears that the introduction of community has been assumed to be more democratic: a way of getting closer or more intimate with "the people." A closer look at the idea of community reveals similar limitations to the term "public." This means embracing complexity, and using the research methods discussed earlier in this chapter. Part of embracing complexity involves exploring in greater detail the concept of community, and what it may mean for museums to construct publics other than as audiences or consumers.

The Concept of Community and its Application to Museums

Given the limitations present in the above evaluation of culture and practice, limitations amplified by the funding culture in which museums exist, the question arises as to how museum research may be improved. This question is addressed by looking at the concepts of community, communities and the public sphere and communities of practice in the museum sector. A more nuanced understanding of these concepts provides a foundation for better quality research work in and about museums, and avoids the tendency to resort to romanticized notions or to simply replace one term (public) with another (community) and attempt to continue as before.

Understanding community

When public space is the focus of museological discourses, more often than not it is used loosely to describe spaces that are deemed as democratic by a community and/or a government body. The conflation of the idea of the public with what is authorized as public government also becomes apparent. This conflation is a common way in which the term "public" has been conveniently used, creating confusion about its many meanings. This is very different from the idea of the public sphere discussed by Habermas – which is the sphere between government and individual citizens. The concept of a critical body of people between government and the individual citizen is a highly desirable and a fundamental characteristic in almost any form of social organization and is a concern for advocates of participatory or associative democracy (see Mouffe, 1993, 2000).

An important consequence of this assignment of the public sphere to government is the invention, or rather transference, of the critical role of the public sphere to another level of social life – the community. The concept of community often becomes the more important level for initiating democracy although, unlike place, it is often neglected as a complex concept. The space with which community is conflated within such processes is "place" – a more local "grassroots" invention, closer to the people, a place with which the individual citizen is more familiar; a place in which the "community" will presumably feel more comfortable and be able to engage in exchanges necessary for "real" democracy. But are these characteristics of community merely assumptions and are these expectations of community based on the idea of the public sphere (which is transferred from what was once a critical public sphere)? As Edward Casey (1997) points out, the very word "society" stems from socius, signifying "sharing," and sharing is achieved in a common place. Communing together in specific places is within "a bounded institutionally sanctioned place," the sphere of public appearance (Casey, 1997: xiv). What is it that brings people together and "binds" them to form community?

A discourse that is counterpart to place is community. Community becomes the embodied element of place, distinguishing it from space. Places are inhabited, lived in by people who, by the nature of their location, can become part of a community – knowingly or unknowingly. In the words of Peter Rowe:

> [o]ver time, apartments, houses, and other physical characteristics of an urban neighborhood are modified or constructed until the space of the community becomes a place with its own distinctive characteristics and aura. (Rowe, 1997: 129)

Rowe suggests that space is "humanized" through the process of place-making by a community. Community is imbued with the potential to transform spaces into places. The term "community" thereby becomes equated with "place," particularly in "socialist-feminist accounts of women in community action" (Rose, 1993: 45). As Gillian Rose indicates, the term "place" is "laden with warm and positive connotations and formulations which stress the importance of spatial location to community" (1993: 174). Community is used to consider the individual in the context of social life in space; in other words, "a sense of personal satisfaction as well as a sense of community are both inescapably grounded in place" (Rose, 1993: 174).

The terms "community" and "public" are often used interchangeably, despite their differences in meaning. The slippage can cause considerable ambiguity, but like the space/place debate, one term is more frequently used to denote a more humanized formation of the public sphere – community. By understanding the formation of community and place it is possible to gain a better understanding of the way in which social life functions to generate different formations of the public sphere.

Community is neither more nor less conceptual than public, as indeed place is also abstract and real. However, neither community nor place have been identified as significant discourses through which the public sphere is considered in relation to the workings of democracy, and yet both concepts are used to demonstrate democracy at its most "genuine" moment (Harvey, 1990; Oakes, 1997; Goheen, 1998).

The prevailing interpretation of community is as a phenomenon arising through choice. Common interpretations of community fall within the parameters of the term as defined by Raymond Williams's (1976) *Keywords*.[1] To use an example from my country, in discourses on Australian culture, community may connote amateur, alternative politics and culture. The addition of the term "Australian" changes the implied meaning, so that community can also be equated with "the Australian people" or "the Australian community." This difference in meaning, it seems, is one of the fundamental issues in debates on the way in which democracy works in Australia. "Community" is mobilized by, and in, all sectors of social life and at all levels of government (non-government organizations, community of nations, and non-constituted community organizations). As noted by Neil Smith (1993), differing interpretations of the same term, "community," are used in significantly different ways to mean distinctly different things.

Community is not always distinct from other forms of social organization, such as the nation. While community politics aims to critique the homogenizing effect of a national culture, its relationship to the state, and the rhetoric often employed by exponents of community as discussed below, undermine this claim (Anderson, 1991). It is also the case that community is used at another level again: community of nations, international community (see Iveson, 2008). A blurring of boundaries that is possible between the rhetoric of nationalism and of community-based politics also demonstrates the importance of explicating the notion, and its changing meaning in different contexts arising from its interaction with other social formations.

In his unraveling of "community," Williams defines it as:

> the warmly persuasive word [used] to describe an existing set of relationships or the warmly persuasive word [used] to describe an alternative set of relationships. What is most important perhaps, is that unlike all other terms of social organization (*state, nation, society,* etc.) it seems never to be used unfavorably, and never to be given any positive opposing or distinguishing term. (Williams, 1976: 66, emphasis in original)

Williams's community identifies the relationships between people as comprising community, whether the "community/ies" consent or not to such a relationship. His definition suggests a rather polemical view of the possible meanings for the term. Williams outlines the way in which the two meanings are in opposition to each other: an alternative set of relations set up in "opposition" to "existing" relations.

Interpretations of "community" as amateurish, and an alternative form of social politics, often go unchallenged, according to Williams's definition (Williams, 1976).[2] For Williams, an easy qualification of the term "community" is impossible. Community may be bound together through a common geographical location. It is also acknowledged, however, that "ethnic groups are often referred to as communities, irrespective of whether they occupy already identifiable territories" (Johnston, 2000: 81). However, having "emotional ties" or "communion" with others is also acknowledged as another aspect of the term "community," where the social, and potentially the cultural, is also significant (Johnston, 2000). The concept of a "sense of belonging" to a locatable geographical "community" or "place" can also be used to mean a sense of belonging to a community that is not necessarily locatable geographically. Such an understanding of community, however, continues to be considered within a material context, thus polarizing the different notions of community, as outlined above.

What becomes evident in the accounts of community, as with accounts of the term "public," is the complexity of these terms. The terms "community" and "place" are inextricably connected to the production of not only material spaces, or groups of people, but also conceptual discourses. As I have outlined, the central concern in much discussion on place and community has been a response to the problems arising from universalist conceptions of the public sphere, and in turn, public space. Moreover, many of these accounts do not consider the key discourses they are critiquing, namely the dominance of universality, and the use of reason and rationality in thinking about the public sphere and democracy. Similarly, when key discourses such as Habermas's theory of the public sphere are used to develop, or to assist in understanding, public space as it relates to democracy, little attention is paid to the role of space in his theoretical or empirical treatment of the public sphere. Using the concepts of community and place as strategies to critique Habermas's universalist account is only useful for thinking about different models of social organization if "community" can be sufficiently developed to avoid universalism. This is the basis of work by theorists such as Chantel Mouffe (2000), who attempts to develop a new model for democracy that does not rely on the universalizing model of consensus.

Philosopher Jean-Luc Nancy provides an account of the term "community." He explains how its two most significant meanings are based on the German history of the word: "community" as a self-defined group (by choice), and as a group defined by common external circumstances, or not by choice (Nancy, 1991a, 1991b). He interprets the notion of community as having multiple meanings. In the first instance he refers to the notion of community coming from "the left" (a term he argues that also needs significant reviewing). To "the left" the "political as such, is receptive to what is at stake in community," as opposed to "the right" where "the political is merely in charge of order and administration" (Nancy, 1991a: xxxvi). Nancy reinterprets, or expropriates, the term "community" by articulating the distinctive differences in definitions of the same term. He argues for the differentiations to be identified and rethought in a more specific way – by "being separated." What he could also be suggesting is a separation of the meaning of community from the more nostalgic definitions provided by Williams:

> [Thinking of the community] as essence – is in effect the closure of the political. Such a thinking constitutes closure because it assigns to community a *common being*, whereas community is a matter of something quite different, namely, of existence in as much as it is *in* common, but without letting itself be absorbed into a common substance. Being *in* common has nothing to do with communion, with fusion into a body, into a unique and ultimate identity that

> would no longer be exposed. Being *in* common means, to the contrary, *no longer having, in any form, in any empirical or ideal place, such a substantial identity, and sharing this* (narcissistic) "*lack of identity.*" (Nancy, 1991a: xxxviii, emphasis in original)

In this sense, Nancy's concept of community allows for an interaction between seemingly contradictory notions of community. According to Nancy, a contradictory notion of community may be a situation where the community exists because of its "lack of identity" with a place, for instance (Nancy, 1991a: xxxviii). This differs from the human geography definitions I have examined, which tend to argue that communities share a common identity, which constitutes their community status. In many of the human geography discourses on place and community, community commonly lacks power. The lack of identity, however, can be used to consider more strategically the ways in which identity politics can be re-presented and re-interpreted within community politics.

Nancy appears to be arguing for a more particular, or limiting, notion of community that will be more liberating. Nancy's community resembles an alternative public that is potentially a model for "situated democracy" using "situated reason." According to him, to assign community as a "common being" (commonly lacking in culture or place) confines and limits the political possibilities of community:

> How can the community without essence (the community that is neither "people" nor "nation," neither "destiny" nor "generic humanity," etc) be presented as such? That is, what might a politics be that does not stem from the will to realize an essence? (Nancy, 1991a: xxxix)

Community, as constructed by the state, detracts from or dissolves certain political possibilities of community that exist when community is formed by choice. For Nancy (1991a: xxxvii), for instance, "the political is the place where community as such is brought into play." Community is the site where "authentic" notions of democracy are acted out, or tolerated in their various formations. Community becomes a form of direct democracy: community as process.[3]

For Nancy, community becomes

> a kind of broadly pervasive democratic consensus [which] seems to make us forget that "democracy," more and more frequently, serves only to assure a play of economic and technical forces that no politics today subjects to any end other than its own expansion. (1991a: xxxvii)

In contrast, for J.F. Lyotard it is possible that community is not necessarily recognizable or knowable. Community in this context vacillates between being a concept and a process – a noun and a verb. Lyotard states:

> I am not speaking of something that we could attribute to politics itself, of an intention to make forgotten. Intention has nothing to do with it. It's rather a question of "short-term memory," of that temporal disposition included in the rules governing a civil or citizenly community of whatever kind, and which requires that something in it be forgotten. What we could say is forgotten, of course, is that this community remains intractable (intraitable) to the treatment of political unity; or again, that this treatment has in appearance to be renewed "from time to time," while in reality it has to be renewed all the time, perpetually. (Lyotard, 1991: 42–43)

Following these arguments, it is necessary to work towards re-inventing community so as not to forget that it is a process, not a fixed "thing" in itself. Concepts of community are fluid, as demonstrated by the relationship of community to the state, which varies within different historical contexts. Community is not a thing in itself, but it becomes a conduit for the individual to the public sphere. Such a concept of community might enable the "formation and maintenance of progressive political alliances ... [and maybe] the consolidation of old communities of resistance or perhaps the creation of alternative political possibilities" (Keith and Pile, 1993: 36). Community of this kind can be both a characteristic of representative democracy and the process through which the public sphere is regenerated.

Community and public spheres

The terms "community" and "public" are often used interchangeably, though their meanings differ in significant ways. "Public" is a term more evocative of power and institutions for Nancy. The slipperiness of the terms and the consequent conflation of meanings shift and obscure the power relations that underlie the realities of experience in and for community and public.

> For these reasons, this use value, this product, which is the "public sphere," is the most fundamental product that exists. In terms of community, of what I have in common with other people, it is the basis for processes of social change. This means I can forget about the concept of politics if I neglect the production of a public sphere. This is a claim to legitimacy that we must carefully insist upon and oppose against the many private needs – despite the fact that disappointment with the bourgeois public sphere, its failures,

betrayals, and distortions, has led many leftist groups to reject a public sphere altogether. (Kluge, 1991: 69)

The more obscure and less defined sphere is the community sphere. It is also apparent that an oppositional public sphere seems to rely on and is similar to concepts of community. Community appears to illuminate the practice of other spheres. In this context community is inevitably linked with the production of the public sphere. It functions between the private and public spheres. The inadequacies of the public sphere are adopted and re-formed within the community sphere, and an interdependence is formed. In effect, the term "community" may overlap significantly with the notion of competing publics outlined above. This overlap may be due to scale and/or conceptual underpinnings of the two terms. What I have attempted to demonstrate is the way in which the public sphere may be complicated by an understanding of its relationship to the notion of community.

Alexander Kluge's explanation is useful here. Kluge distinguishes between two types of public spheres. The "pseudo public sphere" involves exclusions and "only represents parts of reality, selectively and according to certain value systems" (Kluge, 1991: 68). The "oppositional public sphere," on the other hand, is described as "a type of public sphere that is changing and expanding, increasing the possibilities for a public artic-ulation of experience" (Kluge, 1991: 67). The private sphere is defined by Kluge (1991) as being characterized by the notion of private ownership and of individual experience. In a more elaborate account of the public sphere, Oskar Negt and Kluge (1993: xlviii) argue that community is an "aggregate of individual spheres that are only abstractly related." Inclusion of the distinct characteristics that form the private sphere is integral to a critique of the pseudo public sphere and therefore to a critical and practical approach to an oppositional public sphere. Kluge's "pseudo public sphere" resembles Habermas's "liberal public sphere."

An oppositional public sphere comprises what Nancy Fraser (1990: 61) calls "competing public spheres." Fraser critiques the limitations of Habermas's "account of the bourgeois conception of the public sphere [which] stresses its claim to be open to all," particularly in his early writings on the public sphere:

> Moreover the problem is not only that Habermas idealizes the liberal public sphere but also that he fails to examine other, non-liberal bourgeois, com-peting public spheres. Or rather, it is precisely because he fails to examine these other public spheres that he ends up idealizing the liberal public sphere .... (Fraser, 1990: 60–61)

The notion of the liberal model of the bourgeois public sphere is historically understood in terms of exclusions, constructed on the basis of universalizing notions of the bourgeois European male in the nineteenth century. The bourgeois notion of the public sphere has traditionally deemed some cultural forms, practices, and issues as private and therefore not qualifying for inclusion in the public sphere. This process of exclusion has enabled the bourgeoisie to construct a distinctive public culture, which distinguished it from other cultural forms, and practices that formed, according to Fraser, the "competing counter-publics." It is useful to consider the way in which community art, public art and the art museums critique the exclusive notion of the "pseudo" and "bourgeois" public sphere to varying degrees, with differing publics and practices in mind. The notion of public might be more clearly illuminated by considering a theorized analysis of community and its limitations.

A number of other important points are worth raising here for clarity. The public sphere tends to be constructed as made up of private citizens, who form communities, which, in aggregate, constitute the public sphere. An argument for the oppositional public sphere must also negotiate with the community sphere, otherwise the legitimacy of the oppositional public sphere seems unsustainable, and difficult to distinguish from any of the articulated forms of the public. It may be difficult to ascertain the differences between oppositional, or counter-public, spheres and community. Oppositional public spheres for Fraser (1990: 61) are "competing public spheres." This notion of the public sphere as comprising competing public spheres potentially incorporates the formative role of community in a differentiated model of the public sphere.

Community can question the very notion of reason and rationality. The impact of community can change public life and consequently democracy without having to practice any principle of relation to universal reason.[4] In this sense, alternative publics become regular contributors to renewing the public sphere. Alternative publics do not necessarily have to remain alternative. The public sphere may be capable of adjustment (either by co-option of the alternative publics or by the public sphere being reformed by such an inclusion of alternative publics). Habermas's bourgeois public sphere was, after all, once an oppositional public sphere.

An important possibility with community is that it does not always seek representation in the public sphere. Alternative publics do not necessarily serve the cause of democracy directly. Alternative publics cannot, and do not, necessarily enter the "democracy" of the dominant public sphere. It is also the case that self-representation of community remains unresolved for many theorists of democracy when representation in the public sphere is not automatically instigated by those whose interests the alternative public sphere chooses to represent – for example, homeless people, young people, single parents. A dominant public may refrain from assimilating these alternative publics into any one notion of the public sphere, may purposely leave loose ends, so they can define what it is not. It then seems possible that alternative publics in Western democracies can co-exist even when the "difference" is not comprehended by the mainstream. The flow-on effect of this may alter the way in which the public sphere is understood in traditional terms, with its universalizing tendencies. Such a strategy also enables us to see the limits of the dominant forms of the public sphere. Seeing the public sphere as a more disordered practice in Western societies, trying to understand its limits, is to render alternative publics not assimilable, but heterogeneous.

Understanding community as alternative publics makes visible many incongruities in the practice and ideology of the public sphere. Alternative publics are signs of the limits of the public sphere – elucidating the borders, making the invisible visible, showing difference and sameness – thereby challenging the argument of the idea of the "reason and rationality" as it has been understood. In terms of the practice of this dominant public sphere, I question whether the essential characteristics of such ideology – reason and rationality – actually produce a unified public sphere in the first instance when community can always be formed. This requirement for a rational principle marks the incisive connection between contemporary and liberal constellations of the public sphere and democracy, and its theory and practice. It is possible that there are minimal levels of consensus (or misunderstanding of reason) that enable the public sphere to be enacted. It is conceivable that beyond this, there are always contestations in the practice of the public sphere.

While the concept of community may have offered an alternative to more universalizing concepts such as public, this book reveals that community, like the public sphere, has both limitations and advantages. The limitations of community are that its essentialist connotations may preclude critique, whereas a more nuanced, or situated, understanding of the term "community" counters universalizing concepts such as the public sphere or nation. The next subsection of this chapter explores a particular community of practice, that of museum professionals. It is acknowledged that this so-called community is an aggregation and is itself composed of many communities. How can we use this nuanced under-standing of community to develop more appropriate museum practice for the twenty-first century?

Communities of practice

Writing in the early 1990s, influential author Stephen Weil (1990) doubted that museum work would be lauded as a profession due to its diversity: the diversity of disciplines among museums and the diversity of the knowledge and skills required within any particular museum. Weil also argued that while museums' associations in the US have been successful in fulfilling their political role, and less successful in enforcing standards of conduct, they have completely failed in relation to the academic training that is currently offered for entry into the field. In order to have professional status, those who work in museums must take on some responsibility for the preparation of students for museum work. This problem involved the "enormous and unsupervised proliferation in recent years of so-called 'museum studies' programs and the question of whether these programs were the best preparation for people who were to be working in a museum" (Weil, 1990).

In 1990 there was no formal system by which to accredit or evaluate the 325 museum training opportunities offered in the US. Weil praised those that were under able leadership, provided students with the opportunity to study with well-respected museum practitioners and offered the chance to obtain practical experience through internships in well-managed museums. According to Weil, the majority of people who held "responsible positions" in museums in 1990 had never had any specific training in museology. He suggested that the thousands of dollars spent on "museum studies" might better be spent on discipline-based programs. Ultimately, he believed, it would be a "terrible mistake" to control the entry of new practitioners to the field by "licensing or certification procedures." There is a "remarkable variety of backgrounds and remarkable variety of paths, and ... most importantly ... museums workers are called upon to perform an equally remarkable variety of tasks" (Weil, 1990: 83).

Weil's acknowledgement of the diversity of the sector and its contribution to the work of the museum is in keeping with developments that occurred in the late twentieth century. Traditionally in museums the scholar curator was supported by a large number of non-professional support staff: manual workers mainly undertaking security, cleaning and building maintenance (Boylan, 1989). The conservator was also identified as a core position in the museum profession and the director of a museum, a scholar of repute (Anderson, 1990). For a variety of reasons, the curator is no longer a single authoritative voice (see Chapter Five). There is a new generation of museums – the responsibility of non-profit organizations, which operate without the permanent support of government. There are also new types of museums (including immigration museums, community museums and social history museums) that highlight how the concept of a museum has changed as a result of dialogue between academics and museums, communities, changing societal expectations and contemporary electronic technology (particularly the Internet and possibilities of digitization).

The new museums, and the restructured museums, raise numerous issues about museum education and the relationships between museum professionals, educational institutions, and the state. Suzanne MacLeod writes about the problem of tension between governments or boards and the forces of curators and academics, between scholarship and visitor-centered public programming. She defines museum studies as "an area of enquiry made meaningful through the participation and active involvement of individuals and communities in training and education, research and practice" (MacLeod, 2001: 51). She discusses the problem of the "theory vs. practice dichotomy," and the difficulties of providing university-based training of relevance within the museum sector (MacLeod, 2001: 52). She proposes a three-dimensional conceptual model for thinking about museums studies – made up of the different dimensions of museum practice, museum studies training and education, and museum studies research – where universities, museums, practitioners and scholars form a "community of practice" (MacLeod, 2001: 54). This concept clearly coheres with one of the concepts of community discussed in this chapter, but the detailed discussion on community highlights the complexities of developing a "community of practice" among people who work, are preparing to work, or are educating other people to work, in museums.

Conclusion

The relationship between the rhetoric of the museum and the real ways in which communities form and identify themselves is at odds here. With a more nuanced approach to the site-specific publics and understanding of community, we may see the museum develop its competency to articulate the public in ways that are recognizable and commensurate with the "real world." This so-called "real world" includes the importance of cultural capital, as developed by Pierre Bourdieu, in which museums (particularly art museums) are in theory open to all, but accessible only to those who know how to decode the morphology and objects of the museum.

This chapter has identified the complexities of the term "community" and discussed how we should embrace complexity – rather than reducing it by using a "language of closure" and/or the adoption of research methods that systematically reduce complexity. Visitor studies, similar to the counting of visitors to the museums in London that was criticized by Jevons (originally 1883), often aggregate visitors as an audience and do not engage with the complexity of visitors and non-visitors to museums.

The discussion on community, particularly in relation to the diversity of interests within the museum sector and the engagement with various publics (variously constructed as audiences, customers, and so on), provides us with an entry point into the next chapter, where we explore the potential and obligation of the museum to be a public intellectual. The next chapter contains historical material about the public intellectual role of museums in the past; then, drawing upon our understanding of communities and the challenge to the traditional authoritative intellectualism personified by the museum curator, we explore ways for museums to engage appropriately as public intellectuals in the twenty-first century.

Notes

1 Williams's (1976: 65–66) "Community" provides a historical account of the word "community." Interestingly, the word "public" is not included in *Keywords*. However, it is referred to in Williams's outline of the history of the word "society." The significant difference between the words "community" and "public," according to Williams, is that the term "community" is more closely affiliated with political action and implies a self-defining group. He also notes that the word has "few negative connotations in contemporary society."

2 While Williams's definition of "community" in *Keywords* is useful, it is also limited and perhaps overly simplistic, considering more recent theorizing on notions of community and public, where an increasing range of possibilities for interpreting notions of community exist, particularly in relation to art practice and production.

3 Communitarians focus on the notions of the "civic minded citizen concerned with common good":

> The communitarians object that it is an impoverished conception that precludes the notion of the citizen as one for whom it is natural to join with others to pursue common action in view of the common good . . . It only allows for an "instrumental" community, a community in which individuals with their previously defined interests and identity enter in view of furthering those interests. (Mouffe, 1991: 71)

4 See Dipesh Chakrabarty (1997) for a discussion of subaltern histories and their function in relation to grand historical narratives. In particular, it is his account of

the politics of co-option of subaltern histories into grand narratives, or into narratives that contest and replace a single historical narrative that interests me. The implication of his argument in this instance is that any alternative history still functions in relation to the "Grand historical narrative," which points to the paradox of history per se. I think that it is possible to see the same paradox operating with the public sphere and democracy.

5

The Museum as Public Intellectual

The intellectual function of the museum, as a site of public culture, is crucial for the continued existence of the museum. This chapter examines the role of the museum professional and the role of the museum as public intellectual, as producer and facilitator of public culture. It identifies the discourse that positions curators as the barrier to museums being "public," but raises questions about the efficacy of such an approach. A range of possibilities is considered, from the demise of curators as we once knew them, through to new forms of collaboration that reposition curators and/or introduce the non-expert to the curatorial team. The chapter also considers how curatorial practices, individual or collaborative, contribute to the role of the museum as public intellectual and whether, from this point of view, museums today are any different to their nineteenth-century predecessors.

In the previous chapter, I outlined how significant outcomes of the new museology included the emergence of the role of education and the new ways in which the visitor was no longer seen as a *tabula rasa*, as occurred in the nineteenth century. Thanks to some of the better visitor studies, visitors and audiences have become active producers of knowledge in the museum context. To a great extent, these developments were at the expense of the role of the curator. In effect, the curator was pronounced as the barrier between the people and the museum. The curator was alleged to have assumed too much about his/her public, was too authoritarian, and unaccountable. The work of curators was not often publicly acknowledged in the representational spaces of the museum. Of course, this varied between museums and galleries.

While not acknowledged in the sector, some of the methodological issues raised about visitor studies, I argued, emerged as a result of the way in which the public was conceptualized – as often interchangeable with audience, community, viewer, and visitors. More recently, however, as we have seen, museums negotiate new forms of interaction with the people via social

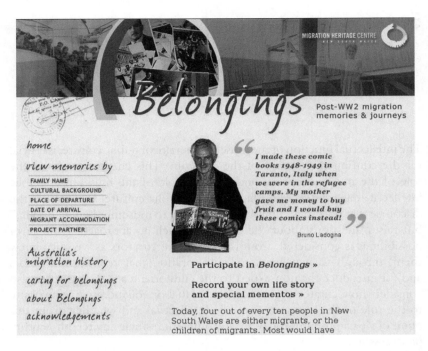

Image 5.1   *Belongings* homepage 2009. Migration Heritage Centre NSW. The NSW Migration Heritage Centre at the Powerhouse Museum is a New South Wales Government initiative supported by the Community Relations Commission for a Multicultural New South Wales. www.migrationheritage.nsw.gov.au

media and the Internet. This renders ways of "knowing the public" even more tenuous on the one hand and productive on the other. Two trajectories are of interest in this chapter: How do museums deal with their ever-expanding claim to interact and represent "everyone" and be accessible to "all"? To answer this question, we begin by considering various discourses about "the curator."

The Curator

Earlier discourses about the relationship between museums and the public were characterized by the belief that the curator was pivotal to the history of the authoritative museum; the all-seeing, all-knowing role in the museum that set the museum apart from its constituents. In recent times, some museums have responded to this authoritative museum discourse by abolishing the name or role of curator from their institutional position description. Arguably, the most high-profile example of such a response was the National Museum of Australia when it first opened in Canberra in 2001. The National Museum of Australia has since returned to using the job title of curator. The Australian Museum, in Sydney, has also had collection managers rather than curators, as well as exhibitions produced collaboratively by teams with a team leader.

Is it an accurate assessment to interpret the rise of other museum professionals being at the expense of the curator? As outlined in the previous chapter, perhaps this discourse explains the rise throughout the late twentieth century in the number of museum education professionals (particularly in the areas of visitor studies and public programs) and their managers.

By the late 1970s, it was apparent that changes in museum studies at a tertiary level in an international context were being reflected in other disciplines, including social history, feminist and social art history, and archaeology (Museum Education Association of Australia, 1977).[1] It is difficult to discern whether the disciplines, as they were practiced in the academy, influenced the professional related practice of these areas or if the changes were more closely related to general political and social changes. It is not my intention here to unravel the causes of these changes. I suggest, however, that change is a more complex series of relationships than single events. In the case of museum studies, as practiced in the academy, these changes reflected new concerns in academia that included democratizing culture and its institutions.

The international context has also informed museum studies around the world. In 1979, the International Council of Museums (ICOM) International Committee for the Training of Personnel met in Leicester (England) to continue discussions from the first ICOM Conference – held in Brussels, Liége, and Antwerp in 1978 – about the training of museum professionals. They identified three reasons why this topic was important. The first two were: "the very unequal development of training from one country to another [and] the opportunity to make a general proposal of such training programmes drawn up according to a universal, theoretical scheme which could then be adapted according to national requirements" (Cuypers, 1979: 6). The third reason was the ability to follow up with "a discussion on means, methods, and techniques used for this training" (Cuypers, 1979: 6).

The emphasis is on a general museum studies, rather than creating specialists in a specific field. A general syllabus with the capacity and integrity to encompass disciplines in the human and natural sciences was needed because while "university trained people leave the university as fully qualified zoologists or art historians, very often they have no museum training in museum studies – neither general training nor practical experience" (Cuypers, 1979: 6).

In this context, the general syllabus at a university level was expected to meet minimum requirements. Allowing for differences between nations, a general curriculum was accepted by the meeting as: the international museum context, collection management, museum management, and museum services.[2] While Leicester University appears to have led this direction of curriculum development, they did consult internationally with museum studies programs.

A review of seminars and conferences about museum studies from the 1970s, 1980s, and 1990s reveals an expectation that the industry should guide the museum studies programs. Reflecting trends in Britain, a 1989 symposium in Sydney insisted on this character of the relationship (Museum Studies Unit, University of Sydney, 1989). The publication from the Museum Training Symposium outlines the need to understand the impact of increasing numbers of non-museum professionals entering the museum sector (in areas such as finance and marketing), the importance of ensuring that graduates are able to work within communities and in various regions (urban and remote), with local government and other funding agencies (see Williams, 1989). In-service training for museum staff, voluntary staff and boards of management were considered, as was the development of management skills and training, and management and care of indigenous cultural material in the sector. There appears to be an emphasis on training the professional as distinct from training and education. The emphasis on the core aspects of "museology" prevails (i.e., museum context, collection management, museum management, and museum services). In this sense the "profession" is perhaps perceived to be the main beneficiary of museum studies training as distinct from "whether they are really creating better museums and improving the community's use of its cultural resources" (Winkworth, 1989: 30). In turn, museum studies reflected the intellectual values of a professional practice that saw museums as being storehouses of objects, a research focus and an understanding of the history of the museum that had been up until that time more or less unquestioned. A combination of academic and industry specialists delivered curricula. Students were encouraged, in some courses required, to do internships. It appears that museum studies programs were generally autonomous departments.

The invention of the "new museology" in the late 1980s reflected a profound shift in the museum studies literature. A profession engaged in academia around the idea of praxis developed the new museology (Vergo, 1989). With the term "new museology" used loosely these days, it is worth looking again at precisely why it came about, as a critique from within the sector, and its impact on scholarship and teaching in relation to museums. With the "new museology," Vergo attempted to develop new methods for:

> studying museums, their history and underlying philosophy, the various ways in which they have, in the course of time, been established and developed, their avowed or unspoken aims and policies, their educative or social role. (1989: 1)

Vergo and contributors to the volume from the sector and academia, signaled a new direction to demystify the role of the museum by revealing how the museum constructs knowledge and to significantly redress the museum's understanding of the importance of visitors as active agents in the production of knowledge. These developments saw the rise of education departments and visitor studies in museums. In the twenty-first century, museums exist within new political and cultural contexts. The museums are arguably more accessible, both intellectually and physically, to the public and to their communities of interest than in previous centuries. In particular, museum sectors in countries such as Canada, New Zealand, and Australia responded to critiques of their role in the process of colonization and appropriation of material culture. The responses are evident in a range of policy debates – for museums, their related professions, and governments – primarily relating to social inclusion and particularly repatriation.

Also of significance is how developments in social and cultural policy reflected similar concerns about access and provision of public services to communities. In academia, new art history (i.e., social and feminist), social and public history, gender and cultural studies became better known for their tendency to unsettle the canons. Museums did not exist outside of these developments in social and political life. Museums, in this context, also became prime sites for engaging with the critiques of power for these areas of the academy in particular. It is at this point, I argue, that these developments are also central to the reconfiguration of many museums and the intellectual frameworks used in the museum context. In other words, the academic disciplines central to museum scholarship and practice were also challenged in debates by these new approaches in the museum world. For example, in Australia, Canada, and New Zealand, critical developments in art history, anthropology, and history have been central to the reconception and presentation in museums of natural history and social history and vice versa (Message, 2006; Healy and Witcomb, 2006; Karp et al., 2006). International developments in museum and museum studies curricula and research reveal how the role of the curator was synonymous with the history of the authoritative museum. Therefore, in order to move away from the authoritative museum model, the resulting strategy was to bring into the museum new types of professionals to help facilitate more inclusive democratic institutions of culture. In other words, to be truly democratic the sector and a number of individual museums questioned the role of the curator. As outlined in the previous chapter, perhaps this discourse explains the rise in the number of museum education professionals, visitor studies and public programs, and associated managers.

According to Shelton:

> Formerly accepted universal truths have lost the legitimacy they once possessed, and with them, the intellectual legitimation behind narratives has been displaced to the institution's performance in relation to externally imposed objectives. (2006: 76)

How does the existence (or otherwise) and the practice of a curator relate to museology and the position of a museum in relation to other organizations and pressures? One connection between them is the pressures of externally imposed objectives, which often conflicted with what may be seen as traditional curatorial practice. These conflicts became embodied in the new museology. According to Macdonald (2006: 2), today there are three key components to the new museology that affect how museums perceive themselves, and are perceived externally:

- First, the idea that object meanings are contextual rather than inherent.
- Second, museums and their activities cannot be separated from "mundane" notions of entertainment or market concerns.
- Third, the experience and understanding of exhibitions, and other forms of museum communication, are variable rather than fixed or predetermined.

One result of the new museology was a move towards visitor studies and evaluation as a means of uncovering the motivations, needs, and interpretive frameworks of visitors. However, Macdonald (2006) notes that there now seems to be a shift away from this preoccupation and a restitution of respect for museum curators and directors who use their specialist expertise to challenge and inspire audiences in unexpected ways. The following subsections examine in greater detail the changing role of the curator within debates about the role of the museum as a public intellectual. The various roles of the curator discussed below are not mutually exclusive, and in some cases there will inevitably be overlap between these apparently distinct categories in the lived experience of curators.

The curator as the dispenser of knowledge

Eilean Hooper-Greenhill, argued that museums are "instrumental technologies with the functionality of enshrining the specialist, academic knowledge of the 'curator' as 'truth' (Hooper-Greenhill, 2000: 166). More recently, she has also come to see that:

> conceptually, some curators are inclined to see themselves as facilitators for learning rather than sole dispensers of knowledge. Shifts in the understanding of the learning process in schools, and the consequent recasting of the role of the teacher as facilitator, can be observed in museums. Exhibitions, and even collections, are now sometimes the product of joint efforts between audience and museum worker. (Hooper-Greenhill, 2000: 200)

The discourse surrounding the changing role of the curator is worth investigating here. For instance, in *Thinking About Exhibitions*, Section 4, entitled "Curators or caterers," the lead essay by Lawrence Alloway outlines:

> A curator is never the person in charge of the museum ... Curator's duties include 1. Acquiring work for the museum, 2. Supervising its preservation in store, and 3. Displaying it, putting it on exhibition ... they make a creative effort and do the research necessary in deciding what to show ... the curator selects what he/she wants to present and calculates the feasibility of the project ... when he/she puts on an exhibition his position changes: as the exhibition is visited it is assessed as part of the museum's output. Thus the curator is at the interface of the museum as an institution and the public as consumers. (Alloway, 1996: 221)

Alloway points to the pivotal role of the curator and believes curators are engaged with all aspects of the production of exhibiting collections and exhibitions. More recent accounts of changes to the role of the curator suggest they no longer are entrusted with such diverse roles, particularly their understanding of the relationship between object and public address. This has now been directed towards visitor and audience research.

In the same volume, Nathalie Heinich and Michael Pollok, writing about the crisis in the curatorial profession in France, have this to add:

among the four crucial tasks which define the job (safeguarding the heritage, enriching collections, research and display), the only one which would allow a certain personalization ... is the presentation to the public. (Heinich and Pollak, 1996: 235)

In earlier incarnations of the curator outlined above, the presentation to the public was seen as central to the role of the curator. The curator had a role not dissimilar, I argue, to that of a public intellectual. My interest here is not to defend whether all curators successfully carried out such engagements, but to indicate that this shift in how their role was described implies that, of all areas within the museum profession, the curators did not understand the public and therefore produced significant barriers for the museum to engage the public. In other words, too much power was in the hands of curators when there was an increasingly diversified sector, and others in the sector believed they had valuable contributions to make to the curatorial process. Significantly, the implication was that curators did not know how to communicate to the public but others in the museum sector did.

The demise of the curator as the dispenser of knowledge has occurred for a number of reasons, many of which are discussed below in relation to alternative curatorial practices. Within anthropological museums, and no doubt other museums as well, one factor eroding curatorial authority is the advent of an "audit culture" and the corresponding rise of museum administrators in the quest to make museum operations more transparent and accountable to the taxpayer. According to Shelton:

> Behind what might be seen as many museums' retreat from anthropology, and the fragmentation of any singular or dominant academic paradigm for ethnographic displays, lies a significant organizational shift that has displaced power and influence away from a curatorial coterie into the hands of professional managers and administrators. (2006: 76)

It is to this concept of the curator – as a person who is responsible for ensuring that the displays bring in the visitors – that we now turn.

The curator as cultural powerbroker

In the weekend arts pages of *The Sydney Morning Herald*, Joyce Morgan stated "they're the behind the scenes cultural powerbrokers charged with picking the public mood. Sydney's arbiters of the arts tell how they decide what we see" (2004). Readers learn about how "risk is expected of organisations if they are to do more than present museum pieces"

(Morgan, 2004). But, who takes these risks? And what is meant by "more than present museum pieces"?

The article went on to ask:

> ... how is success measured? Is it determined simply by producing bums on seats and a bottom line in the black or by less tangible measures such as an ability to make an imaginative response to our world? (Morgan, 2004)

Noel Kelly (2007) outlines an alternative, perhaps more narrow, view of the role of the art curator. He assumes that if the project management skills of the curator are up to scratch, the exhibition will automatically be a success on opening night. In this article, once again focusing on art curators, a methodology for exhibition development is set out, with the curator acting not only as a creative partner with the artist, but also as the manager and coordinator responsible for the smooth realization of the project.

Interestingly, audience expectations and needs are not addressed by Kelly (2007) as a concern for the curator – the assumption is that if the curator's project management runs smoothly, the project will have automatically been successful once opening night comes around. Is this indicative that, perhaps much more so than in other disciplines, art curators are still operating in an environment shielded from the overt visitor focus in non-art museums?

The curator as facilitator

In addition to their traditional tasks, Sheppard and Williams (2000) highlight the growing expectation that curators be across all facets of museum operation, including community awareness, technology, finance, public relations, and management. They provide the requirements of museum professionals for the twenty-first century:

> a broad understanding of learning and how people learn; a breadth of social and interpersonal skills, especially listening skills; an ability to conduct audience research and evaluation; a willingness to apply what you learn through evaluation; an interest in your communities and an openness to diverse opinions; a talent for negotiating discussion to permit, evoke, and validate many different viewpoints; and a knowledge of contemporary business practices. I haven't even touched on management, including marketing. Be well read; look for connections between objects and the bigger ideas they represent; have subject expertise, but be courageous enough to express a point of view, and generous enough to entertain divergence and controversy; and

finally, sustain a continuing passion for the idea of museums as forums for all people. (Sheppard and Williams, 2000)[3]

In the extract above, the authors outline the basic requirements for all aspiring museum professionals. One assumes that specialist skills will have to be acquired on top of these general attributes. In this example, museum professionals, including curators, are expected to be across all facets of museum operation and be in possession of an advanced social, cultural, and community awareness and understanding. Sheppard and Williams (2000) add to the list: technological know-how, managerial skill, and financial awareness.

The curator cannot perform all of these roles at the same time, nor have equal depth of knowledge and ability to undertake each of these tasks. In essence, the curator has to become a facilitator, both within the community of museum professionals and in his/her relationship to the public. The curator is no longer the undisputed dispenser of knowledge, but uses the above skills to negotiate competing agendas and beliefs. The curator facilitates.

The curator as an appropriate participant

A number of authors have identified ways in which curatorial practice can work with other participants and knowledges in respectful ways. Christine Kreps (2008) explores the concept of appropriate museology – that is, the use of curatorial know-how to foreground and give expression to indigenous ideas about collection and display. Appropriate museology is inspired by concepts and movements in the field of international development, notably "participatory" approaches to development and the use of "appropriate technology" (i.e., technology appropriate to the culture and resources of the people and to the environment in which it is being used).

Participatory approaches to development have existed for approximately 40 years. They emerged as a response to the limitations of top–down, macro-level approaches. The move towards a bottom–up, people-centered approach involved the intended beneficiaries in all phases of a project, especially in the decision-making process. This was partly to include local knowledge, and also to build on the idea that when local people have a greater stake in a project they are more interested in securing good outcomes. This concept has been used in many areas of development, including community forestry, in order to provide livelihoods and to move towards sustainability (Shrestha and McManus, 2007).

Kreps (2008)
nology into the
created for use
in heathcare pr
management, th
initiatives. Krep
local notions of
According to
"approaches to
made appropria

An importar
societies, such
practices for m
training appro:

This approac
professional ı
allow much
curatorial tra
in their own

Kreps sees po
together with
"many societie
models of muse
museum devele

Kreps advoca
into account th
museum process
practice accordiı
cultural environ:
bined with profe
appropriately cu
value and transm

For Kreps, app
practices and stra
contexts and cono
logical traditions s
tions where suitaı
indigenous model:
structures or spaces

of valued objects), curaᵗ
preservation.

Kreps also emphasize
the context of preservi
curatorial traditions for
facilitating local owners
engagement is a key str
community. Here Krep
engagement also gener
however, is whether co
whether the communit
museums. The questio
should see museums as
in their own communi

The above discussio
tion and perpetuation (
revisit the role of the c
looks in more detail at

Image 5.2 *Talkba*
and cartoonist Dav
Australia. Used wit
www.nma.gov.au

torial methods, and concepts of cultural heritage

s the positive role of "appropriate museology" in
ng intangible cultural heritage – as indigenous
rm part of that heritage. For Kreps (2008: 35),
hip of the museum using participatory models of
ategy to meeting the needs of the museum and its
os is advocating that community-based models of
rate interest in the museum. What seems unclear,
mmunities are seeking agency via the museum, or
es are giving social agency and public address to the
n that seems to be omitted is why the community
the preferred site rather than maintaining traditions
ty contexts.

n about community engagement and the conserva-
of intangible cultural heritage highlights the need to
urator in museums. The next section of this chapter
the curator and the public in the twenty-first century.

ck Classroom 'Political Satire' forum with John Safran
id Pope. Photo George Serras, National Museum of
h the permission of the National Museum of Australia

The Curator and the Public Revisited

What explains the twenty-first century tendency to return to using the description of curator as one of many specialists in the museum? Perhaps it is a new-found appreciation of the role of the curator as other roles in the museum also come under similar scrutiny. It may now be safe to acknowledge the importance of their intellectual contribution (Macdonald, 2006). Does the apparent return of the curator mean that museums are engaging appropriately with the many diverse publics, and what is the appropriate role of the newly restored curator in this process?

What many of the authors discussed above seem to suggest is that processes of working with communities and their cultural practices may benefit museums. I believe that they do benefit museums, but this benefit cannot be at the expense of communities. What does this mean for the position of curator? I am not arguing that we should do away with the specialist curator; indeed, the opposite. The curator becomes the conduit, facilitator, or respondent to a community's interest in a program, exhibition, or collection. This still requires curators with specific knowledge of collections, collecting, and exhibiting practices. Indeed, these roles are crucial to working with communities to develop their capacity to engage with the museum and vice versa. With this need for specialization in mind, we now turn to look at the debates about curators, curatorial practices, and public engagement in different disciplines. For the purposes of this book, the disciplinary approaches presented below are art, social history, and anthropology. While this range of disciplines highlights the variations in museums, it is important to point out that I am not attempting a comprehensive outline of the various disciplinary approaches and the curatorial debates going on within them. Rather, the examples chosen are indicative of the broad range of ideas relating to curatorial practices and the various extents to which not only theoretical developments, but also government policies, financial constraints, and other forces, are influencing curatorial output – that is, the presentation of collections to visitors.

A Selection of Disciplinary Approaches

Art museum curators

Art curators and, indeed, curators across museum disciplines, employ different modes of practice. How do the various disciplinary curatorial roles differ? Is the universal term "curator" artificially simplistic in view of the many kinds of museums and "curatorial" functions that pertain to them?

As discussed above, Noel Kelly outlines a view of the role of the art curator that emphasizes the need for project management skills. He assumes that if the project management skills of the curator are sufficient, the exhibition will succeed.

Kelly (2007) presents a methodology for exhibition development, with the curator acting not only as a creative partner with the artist, but also as the manager and coordinator responsible for the smooth realization of the project. Interestingly, audience expectations and needs are not addressed here as a concern for the curator. This is presumably a result of Kelly's assumption that if the curator's project management runs smoothly, the project will automatically be successful. While project management skills are undoubtedly vital, I argue that communication with different publics requires more than project management skills.

There are other approaches to curatorial practice in art museums. For example, in a newspaper article by Reyhan Harmanci (2006) an exhibition experiment is discussed "where [four] curators are themselves artists, with their material being the artists' work." They were asked to use an artist's work as the medium for "creating" their own "artwork": the exhibition itself. This is but one example of the increasingly active, creative, and perhaps intrusive role of contemporary art curators in the co-creation of artworks in the context of how they are publicly perceived. The exhibition "The Caretakers: 'Four on One'" by Michael Zheng comments on what he perceives as the increasingly direct role curators play in art production.

> "I invited four curators, all professionals, from different backgrounds," says Zheng, "to first agree upon one artist. Then they would each curate one week's show. The show will have four different views, from different perspectives."

In this case, Zheng's exhibition demonstrates the extent to which contemporary art curators are able to orchestrate displays in order to facilitate very particular perceptions of the material on exhibition. This seems to be a direct contradiction to trends in other curatorial disciplines. Is this indicative of a growing chasm between art and other forms of curatorship? This raises an interesting question that is beyond the scope of this book: has art curatorship become isolated from the debates surrounding other museum collections?

Social history

In Australia, McShane (2008) outlines the influence of not only museological theory but also government policy and funding on the development

Image 5.3   *Garden of Australian Dreams, opening day at the National Museum of Australia.* Photo George Serras, National Museum of Australia. Used with the permission of the National Museum of Australia, www.nma.gov.au

of the National Museum of Australia. This broadens the context for analyzing the changing role of the curator to include consideration of prevailing political attitudes, policies and funding allocations, in addition to developments in theoretical museological debates. As noted by McShane (2008: 1): "The rise of social history as a disciplinary genre has a close temporal fit with museum developments in the Western world, especially at a national level, since the 1960s."

McShane demonstrates this point with reference to the early history of the National Museum of Australia covering the first 20 years (1981–2000) prior to its opening in 2001. According to McShane, this was:

> a dynamic period of museum-making, cultural policy formation and structural economic change. The interplay between these three elements produced a complex institutional ecology that did much to shape the development of the collection and demands on the Museum's interpretive modes. (2008: 1)

The issue of agency is crucial here for the museum, and indeed the role of curator. Although the invention of social history (and oral histories) has been a useful method in the museum context because of its democratic appeal, McShane (2008:1) questions the coherence of "social history for which the museum had agency." However, methodologically it is this very character that has been questioned. The architecture of the museum was also influenced by the desire of the inaugural director and calls for the museum to be more democratic in form than its nineteenth-century predecessors. The implication is that for curators to use methodologies that are more accessible to museum audiences and related communities of interest is somehow compromising the coherency and intellectual authority of the museum. Despite the museum's charter to be a forum for discussion, the National Museum of Australia (which opened in 2001) has been criticized for changing its forms and practices.

Anthropology

Shelton (2006) includes a discussion about the way in which recent theoretical debates have been integrated into the presentation of anthropological and ethnographic collections, where ideas relating to cultural and identity politics, postcolonialism and inclusion of non-Western perspectives have particular relevance. The section on "post-narrative Museology, 1994–2005" particularly deals with the adoption of non-traditional,

Image 5.4   Jean-Marie Tjibaou Cultural Centre, New Caledonia. © ADCK-Centre Culturel Tjibaou/Renzo Piano Building Workshop, Architectes/John Gollings

cross-disciplinary approaches to representation of anthropological collections in museums such as the Musée du Quai Branly, Paris:

> While an aesthetic approach was agreed to be necessary to affirm the universality of artistic creation, geographical and comparative criteria were introduced to structure the organization of collections in the new galleries. (Dias, 2001: 90–93) (Shelton, 2006: 75)

However, Shelton argues that intellectual anthropological debates on the presentation of collections have been supplanted by predominantly visual displays, which do little to interrogate the political and cultural significance of collections. For example, the Museum of Mankind in the UK, which closed in 1994, had its collections incorporated into the British Museum:

> The new galleries are examples of the subordination of interpretation to aesthetic presentation ... The adoption of "white cube" designs for the commercially sponsored African galleries clearly confirms a distinct shift in exhibition strategies away from the use of the heterogeneous and more intellectually articulated genres which the museum had pioneered to more circumspect ocular experiences. (Shelton, 2006: 75)

This, and the accompanying material about the opening of the quai Branly, reflects a trend away from the traditional, academic and scientifically grounded interpretations of anthropological material towards more of a visual arts display – a sign that the interpretive strategies demanded of curators, in the light of contemporary theoretical debates, are perhaps just "too hard" to incorporate effectively in practice. This raises another question of relevance to any discussion about museums being public intellectuals: are the theoretical complexities and contingencies too difficult not only for curators to present, but also for visitors to assimilate?

According to Shelton, another factor eroding curatorial authority in anthropological museums, particularly in Europe, is the advent of an "audit culture" and the corresponding rise of museum administrators. This culture has arisen as part of the quest to make museum operations more transparent and accountable to the taxpayer. However, as noted earlier, this has also resulted in a shift of power and influence "away from a curatorial coterie into the hands of professional managers and administrators" (Shelton, 2006: 76).

A number of museums in Canada and the United States of America have responded well to these challenges. These include the Museum of Anthropology at the University of British Columbia and the National Museum of the American Indian (NMAI) in Washington. In relation to greater accountability and transparency, many of these museums have responded by collaborating with indigenous peoples in the care and curation of cultural objects in museums and their education and public programs. A central aim for museums such as the NMAI is to re-present and interpret First Nation cultures. "Having control over the tangible objects in museums plays a role in having control over the intangibles" (Clavir, 2002: 76).

In Australia, these new ethical approaches were employed in the Macleay Museum's 2008 exhibition about the history of the Anthropology Department at Sydney University, which highlights the theoretical approaches and limitations of traditional ethnographic research and the wider social and political implications of these studies (Image 5.5). It was followed in 2009 with an exhibition curated by indigenous people, which dealt with the social impact of anthropologists on the communities they studied (Image 5.6). Other museums in Australia, such as the National Museum of Australia, which opened in Canberra in 2001, have policies and practices that demonstrate how working with indigenous communities throughout all aspects of the museum has changed the conceptual form and practices. Rather than encouraging indigenous communities to come into the museum (giving museums agency), the community cultural practices of the community have changed the way the museum functions. Indeed, as I have indicated elsewhere in this book, due to the history of colonialism in Australia and the role of museums in the colonial project, museums across the disciplines are well aware of the museum's origins and capacity as a publicity tool, as a form of public address. To some extent these practices also reflect many aspects of appropriate museology outlined by Kreps above. This may also be the case for other museums in the Pacific cited in Chapter Three.

A wide array of curatorial approaches is now being employed in relation to anthropological collections. These respond to the new reflexivity, ethical concerns and notions of plurality that have entered into anthropological consciousness as a result of various theoretical developments. It is worth considering that these innovative approaches signal a new responsibility on the curator to be constantly mindful, politically astute, and conceptually creative, as well as retaining his/her expertise with the collection. If anything, this points to the need for a greater emphasis on the intellectual role of the curator, rather than diminishing it.

Image 5.5 Exhibition *People, Power, Politics: the first generation of anthropologists at the University of Sydney*, 2008. Photo courtesy Sydney University Museums/Rebecca Conway

Image 5.6 *Makarr-garma: Aboriginal collections from a Yolngu Perspective, Macleay Museum* 2009. Photograph: Michael Myers 2010

Image 5.7   Book cover *The Changing Presentation of the American Indian: Museums and Native Cultures* by the National Museum of the American Indian, Smithsonian Institution. Reproduced courtesy of the University of Washington Press

Conclusion

The capacity of the museum to be a public intellectual, a role once deemed to be the domain of curators alone, has been challenged in recent years. In some cases, this has resulted in the (temporary) demise of "the curator." More frequently, as I argue above, it has resulted in a reshaping of the position and duties of the curator. It is certainly possible for curators to be barriers to "the public," but they are not inherently so. Curatorial practices based on an ethos of participation, respect, a recognition of diversity and a belief in healthy intellectual debate are more likely than traditional authoritative practices to reposition the museum as a public intellectual in the contemporary context.

In many ways, recent iterations of the curator and curatorial practices demonstrate the effectiveness of museums as sites of the public sphere. The expansion of curatorial practices has demonstrated that the curator was not necessarily the barrier to effective public engagement, although some individuals may have been. Rather, these curatorial practices have enabled the museum to regain its position as an institution of public culture, of intellectual development, and as a facilitator of debate among diverse publics. In summary, museums are important spaces for the performance of the public sphere in the twenty-first century.

Notes

1 This conference publication includes appendices such as the International Council of Museums Working Party on *Training Museum Educators*, NY, 1972. "ICOM is the international organisation of museums and museum professionals which is committed to the conservation, continuation and communication to society of the world's natural and cultural heritage, present and future, tangible and intangible. . . . It carries out part of UNESCO's programme for museums" (http://icom.museum/mission.html).
2 See ICOM (1979: 62–63). These areas were also reflected in ICOM's *Basic Syllabus for Museum Training* (1972) and used for the development of a *Treatise on Museology*.
3 Transcript from Sheppard and Williams's talk at the Museum Careers Seminar for Smithsonian Center for Museum Studies (CMS), first published in the January 2000 issue of the *CMS Bulletin*.

Conclusion

If the public sphere is to be more than a term consigned to "the spectral half-life of a word that abides inside quotation marks" (Robbins, 1993: x) then we need to question its efficacy. At the beginning of this book I asked to what and to whom are museums relevant? The usual response is "the public." But what if there is no such thing as "the public"? "Public" is a term that has been used for many years, and was the foundational concept for the idea that museums and their collections should be open and accessible to all, rather than the private property of wealthy collectors who could store their treasures. Rather than abandoning the term "public," or attempting to preserve the term as it was understood in the modern era, *Museums and the Public Sphere* has salvaged it, but not in a universal way. This salvaging does not result from a fear of its loss, fear that we cannot do without it, but from the recognition that many of its replacements encounter the same basic issues. Merely substituting terms such as community, audience, and visitors conceals, but does not escape, the central concern of this book that it is necessary to continually monitor and adapt the idea in response to a changing world. *Museums and the Public Sphere* has examined the museum as a site of public address, as an institution whose structures, forms of management and professional roles, practices, and programs are all underpinned by the term.

Museums are important institutions and spaces of the public sphere. I argue that despite being overlooked in disciplines discussing the emergence of the public sphere, there is a lineage of museum practice that engages with "the public" on public matters. The museum is a cultural public sphere. As this book has shown, concepts of the public, the issues that engagement should focus on and the process of engagement have changed over time. Understanding such changes and how they affect what we *now* expect of the term "public" requires us to focus on ideas that are at the core of contemporary museums.

Contemporary museum images by artist Thomas Struth mirror the images of people in museums in previous eras by Louis-Léopold Boilly and Hubert Robert. All three artists have produced images that show people viewing paintings which depict symbolic moments in the history of France, particularly recalling the emergence of the bourgeois public sphere and the material context in which this occurred. Their subject matter is the act of viewing in a museum with others; such images demonstrate the functions of the museum as a site of publicity, as a site capable of representing its past and present simultaneously. In discourses on public space, this artistic practice and the view of the museum as a site of public address have been overlooked because neither have been understood as being capable of engagement with public discourse. Instead, the museum has been interpreted as a space of the state. Yet, I argue, the consequences of this looking, such as contributing to public discourse, may go well beyond the electronic and material space of the museum.

Before discussing future possibilities for rethinking concepts such as "public" and "community," I summarize the book and some of the key themes below.

Museums and the Public Sphere

Chapter One presented discourses of democracy in Habermas's concept of the public sphere as it relates to museums. In a modified framework that is not based exclusively on rationality and literary discourses, the public sphere can become a more diverse, site-specific concept: that is, a sphere comprising groups in continual motion. Habermas's public sphere is the most often cited reference to the notion of "public" as it is used and understood in relation to museums. With respect to the public sphere, museums that use the term "public" in a way to denote the nineteenth-century formation are certainly maintaining the notion of the museum in its early public form. This form closely resembles the public sphere identified by Habermas. However, what is more productive, I have argued, is a conception of the public emerging from this history that takes into account the way in which publics of different scale and interests operate in museums as a cultural public sphere.

This necessitates what may be termed a "post-Habermassian" conception of the public sphere. Such an approach requires us to develop a more nuanced understanding of the term "community." The switch from public to community does not necessarily resolve many of the issues about relevance, inclusion, diversity; nor is the term "public" irrevocably damaged such that it cannot be modified as I have discussed. The danger of using "community" to redeem the museum where communities are already practicing and producing culture elsewhere can potentially be a form of appropriation by the museum. The term "community" is equally as complex as the term "public" within a museum context.

Rethinking the term "public" is crucial for museum professionals and commentators on public space because it opens possibilities for democratic processes rather than focusing on the institutional provision of public space. It is important to understand concepts such as "public" and the "public sphere" so that the limitations of these concepts can be taken into consideration when expectations about *what* museums can do, and *how* they can do it, are established. The first chapter of this book extended the theoretical understanding of this concept and provided a foundation for subsequent chapters.

The pivotal role of the idea of *the public* in the historical development of the museum was explored in Chapter Two. This enabled us to understand how citizens were shaped and how ideas and practices related to the public were shaped. In looking at this history through the lens of the idea of the public, we can see how people may constitute themselves as a public through the performance of being *in public*. This requires vision, a concept that has until now been largely neglected in representations of the public sphere. This chapter demonstrated how the museum has been historically constituted as a public space. This construction of museums emphasizes a history of transition from princely collections to the publicly available institution – attempting democracy. It examined how the museum emerges from the nineteenth century as a cultural institution with an important role, working with competing notions of the term "public" as it develops a new relationship to the state. The production of new cultural material with which to represent and educate the population accompanied this transition. As a result of this history, the modern museum has been interpreted as a significant site for the enculturation of the bourgeois public sphere. It also presents the museum as a cultural public sphere.

In Europe, the modern museum, and its role in modern democracy, gained popularity as both a material space and as an idea. The role of the museum in research and public education was paramount. Despite the rhetoric of democracy, the modern museum maintained display practices of the monarchy and the clergy. The display practices did little to indicate dissent within the disciplines of art history, archaeology, anthropology, and history; nor were the museums subject to significant questioning by a public sphere about their social or political function.

Assumptions about the public nature of museum space are often made because of the democratic basis of the history of museums. Yet, as Chapter Three demonstrated, the relationship between the materiality of democratic public space and the discourses about democracy are little understood in museology. Conversely, in much of the literature on public space, little has been made of the museum as a public space. Presumably, this is because of assumptions about its limitations inherited from its late eighteenth-century form and an aversion to the political capacity of aesthetics to engage with the politics of the public sphere. Chapter Three outlined the relationship between space and democracy in the museum context and highlighted how museum professionals engage with audiences and attempt to make the space accessible and open to all, but are limited in their capacity to do so. I argued that efforts to understand the limitations of the museum as a space of public address and debate are not merely academic but go to the core of claims by the modern museums to be democratic, and the desire of new museums actually to be democratic. For almost two centuries, new ways of thinking about the idea of the museum have attempted to reconceptualize the museum as a more inclusive public cultural institution. In the late twentieth century, the need to significantly rethink the concept of the museum emerged through a discourse now known as "the new museology." At the core of the new museology was the discourse of "access" (intellectually and physically) to the museum for greater proportions of the population. A parallel discourse was developed to reposition the history of the museum – from an institution that had profited from inappropriate technologies to an institution capable of accommodating multiple histories and cross-cultural exhibitions. The acts of collecting and display have come under particular scrutiny.

In recent years, as a response to valid criticisms about imperialistic practices of appropriation from indigenous people and other communities, many museum theorists and practitioners have adopted the new museology. This approach emphasized the need for further modification of museum practices to accommodate and engage with community aspirations, again signaling another strategy to honor the public nature of the museum adequately. In many ways these developments in recent years with indigenous communities and otherwise marginalized communities reflect the changes that occurred in the eighteenth and nineteenth centuries, when "the people" became the new owners of princely collections and, as I have indicated earlier, new works of art were commissioned to better represent the emerging citizenry. Thomas Struth's work clearly reminds us how these issues of public address and knowing the public in the museum context resemble past formations (see Image 6.1).

Image 6.1   Thomas Struth, *Tokyo National Museum, 1999, Tokyo*. C-print, 179.5 × 277.0 cm. © 2010 Thomas Struth. (From Struth's *Museum Photographs*. Struth foregrounds the audience, this time in front of an iconic image from the French Revolution by Eugène DELACROIX (Charenton-Saint-Maurice, 1798 – Paris, 1863) July 28: Liberty Leading the People, Salon of 1831.)

I have also argued that museums are necessarily engaged in not only spatial discourses of the public sphere but also visual notions of the public sphere. Visual discourses of democracy and its limitations are sharply evident in the history of museums, by what appears in museums, and by what does not. Visuality is a form of publicity and public address with which the museum engages. In opposition to the stance of several authors discussed in this book, visuality is not so particular as to warrant exclusion from the realm of public address we find in museums.

Despite arguments excluding the role of aesthetics in discussions about public space, the role of aesthetics reveals a more complex public sphere than the universal one discussed earlier in this book. Indeed, the absence of aesthetics from discourses of public space merely polarizes and over-simplifies the situation. In a recent consideration of the history of "commonality" of art museums, Andrew McClellan argues that:

> Politics compromises the quality of disengaged aesthetic contemplation that the public has come to value and that museum's sponsors are content to pay for. For better or worse, a celebratory but de-politicized global humanism, is as much as we can expect from our art museums in the near future. (McClellan, 2008: 52)

I have argued that the political potential of the aesthetic, not only in art museums, as a discourse of the public sphere is underestimated by Habermas and in various discourses I discussed relating to the definition and use of public space. The oversight reduces the complexity of the museum as a site of public address. The interplay that occurs in museums between spatiality, visuality, and experience, I argue, does have the capacity to position museums as a space of public address. If they are genuinely in the public realm, like the terms "community" and "public", the meanings created in and by museums are not fixed. Museums cannot escape being a political sphere whenever they are deemed public.

The ways in which audience is conceptualized by museum professionals and museum studies was the focus of Chapter Four. The chapter began with an overview of the work of the influential theorist Pierre Bourdieu, and highlighted his analysis that accused museums of "false generosity." While they purported to be accessible to everybody, Bourdieu demonstrated that the upper classes visited museums more frequently than working-class people, who lacked the necessary cultural capital to decode the museum building and its objects. Despite claims of being democratic and accessible, art museums, in particular, were seen to be elitist. As a way to overcome allegations of elitism, museum professionals in many countries have sought feedback from users of museums through the introduction of visitor studies, audience research, and myriad methodologies to better understand museum attendance. These practices are founded upon, and raise, questions about how people come to museums with experiences and cultural practices that can contribute to the museum as a space for the production of knowledge and culture (material and intangible). As a plethora of literature has indicated, the technique of visitor studies has been used to assess the proposals and exhibiting practices within museums, to develop education and public programs, and to market the activities of museums. While museums have developed strategies to better "know" and understand "the audience," there is potential to embrace differences between conceptions of the audience and the public. As part of our understanding of terminology and its importance to museum practices, it is worth emphasizing that "audience" can be meaningless units if their limitations as a signifier of the museum's core constituents are not understood. As museums deal with the necessity of developing new methodologies to assess and understand how social media and the Internet have challenged conceptions of museums, forms of engagement and public address and audience, an understanding of these differences is vital. The limitations of the methodologies used to identify and understand the public as audience – where private individuals are surveyed to learn about their opinions, rather than these viewpoints emerging through public discourse – were examined in Chapter Four. An interdisciplinary approach to conceptions of public and community can reveal more about the public sphere than a notion of audience within visitor studies and audience research alone.

The desire "to know" and understand the audiences was, for Vergo (1989), a response to criticisms within the museum sector (at least in the United Kingdom) about museum practices. These practices were often based on assumptions about the pre-eminent role of curators. Chapter Five presents evidence of critical changes in curatorial practices, and how in some cases the position, role, and title were considered undesirable. Questioning of the curator's role in museums, from being an authoritative producer and dispenser of knowledge to be reconfigured (and sometimes retitled) to render the role more accountable and facilitative, has been a hallmark of reflexive museum practices. The chapter addressed questions about how museums function as public intellectuals and contribute to public debate in the twenty-first century. This is particularly pertinent as communities, in effect, are also expected to become curators and to teach museums. The modernist approach of the authoritative curator is not feasible for reasons presented in this book, but how will the new form of museum be more democratic? I argued that the role of the museum curator, and the role of the public intellectual, as a producer and facilitator of public culture, offers potential to create new knowledge without appropriating the knowledge, material culture and identities of communities. In order to avoid allegations of appropriation, a more reflexive use of the term "public," and an awareness of how it permeates all aspects of museum culture and museum studies, is required. *Museums and the Public Sphere* highlights how the term "public" was mobilized in the eighteenth and nineteenth centuries, and how conceptions of "public" have changed over time to incorporate a more diverse configuration, such as counter-publics.

The expectations museums create by using the term in a non-specific way are not tenable; nor are they met by exchanging the word with community. In *Museums and the Public Sphere* I have argued that the interchanging of "public" with "community" may be fraught, especially if it extends the potential for appropriation. I have proposed a more viable strategy for understanding what is at stake in the practice of attempting to be more democratic, more inclusive. This has involved a close examination of the productive literature on the public sphere and public space, relishing the richness of its complexity and what it offers. Drawing initially on the influential work of Jürgen Habermas, the concept of the public sphere was reworked by exploring the writings of Habermassians and critics, and then considering it within the museum context.

Museums and the Public Sphere promotes vigilance with a concept central to the history of the museum idea. Some museums have identified specific communities as collaborators, not just as audience or producer of cultural material, but communities that have a stake in the functions of museums and programs and as a place of public address. This museology is particularly suited to the concept of embracing complexity (Allen et al., 2007). The museum should, and can, be a productive cultural public sphere in social life.

Museum Futures

The recent proliferation of museums is likely to continue into the future, despite funding constraints in many countries. The development of new museums whose intended audiences are currently marginalized, the trend towards more commemoration of events, and the desire to attract tourists and inward investment will all contribute to an increase in the number of new museums in the developed countries. Simultaneously, many existing museums will be redeveloped, expanded, and "rebranded" to achieve relevance (again). This is partly in response to the same forces creating new museums.

There will be more museums in countries that do not share much of the heritage of the existing museums in developed countries. Some of the newly rich Arabian oil states have consciously planned a development strategy that extends beyond exploiting their finite reserves of oil; they are using the revenue generated from the sale of this fossil fuel to develop a range of cultural industries. Museums are central to their cultural industries planning, which includes both the establishment of new museums and the importation of branches of existing universal survey museums, such as the Louvre. Newly powerful countries such as China, and perhaps in the future India, will display their power through museums, similar to European countries and the United States of America in the nineteenth and twentieth centuries. This is already occurring, with the creation of a massive museum complex known as M+ (Museum Plus) on reclaimed land in West Kowloon, in the Hong Kong Special Administrative Region. Earlier conceptions of this development included branches of the universal survey museums and the likely engagement of an internationally recognized museum architect, before public pressure led to the plans being abandoned in favor of a locally driven process of consultation, discussion, and development.

Issues of repatriation are also likely to be foregrounded, and highly controversial. Claims for heritage and possession will broaden from a relationship between universal (and sometimes university and city-oriented museums) with indigenous people to include relationships between universal survey museums in the United Kingdom, France, Germany, and the United States of America with powerful museums, strongly supported by government, in the People's Republic of China.

These museums are emerging not just in a different era, but also in different cultural contexts from the museums of so-called developed countries. The notions of "public," "being public," and "public space" will inevitably be different in relation to these museums.

There will always be a role for what is becoming known as "the traditional museum" – a building displaying artifacts for the education and entertainment of visitors. Over time some of these museums will choose to adapt to new technologies and embrace the complexities that this development entails. In fact, there are few examples of museum display techniques and curatorial practices that a curator from the nineteenth century would immediately recognize. Those examples that do exist, such as the Pitt Rivers Museum in Oxford and Sir John Soane's Museum in London, are museums of museums. They are valuable in this discourse too. In the future, museums are likely to be as diverse, if not more so, than the museums that currently exist, and this should be celebrated. A plethora of museums, engaged with their diverse publics and with each other through traditional communications and the innovative use of digital technologies, is a desirable vision of the future.

The engagement with social media is both a challenge and opportunity for the future of many museums. The digitization of collections, use of the Internet and social media, as I have argued, while appearing to be a gateway for new forms of "audience engagement," have revealed the limitations of the methods used in museums to understand audiences and publics. In many ways, developments in the use of the Internet and social media in museums have moved faster than policy and planning (for instance, how do we interpret engagement and avoid listening only to the most frequent bloggers?). The potential of social media to usher in a new era in museum practice brings new pressures, not only in the securing and allocation of resources but also in how museums argue that these practices enable the museum to be *more* public than its predecessors. Social media have caused, and will continue to require, changes from the pre-digital era practices of museums, but they will not be a panacea for the challenges facing museums today and into the future. Social media are not immune to fundamental questions asked of museums. Embracing the complexities inherent in concepts such as public, public space, public sphere, and community will still be required.

Rather than seeing the passing of the modernist idea of a museum – that is, the museum as a traditional institution and idea in the way it was understood in the nineteenth and early twentieth century – museum practice shows this power relationship changing, albeit unevenly, around the world. Museums will continue to reflect the attitudes of dominant systems of knowledge and power in broader society and so as these change so do museums. There are times, it should be pointed out, as in the case of the work on repatriation in the 1970s and 1980s, when museums were ahead of institutions of the state. As these developments were influenced by and in many ways tied to social movements such as civil rights, they worked with these discourses to make change in the museum sector. Collaboration and reciprocity were central and remain so in this field. As disciplines of knowledge have evolved and developed, museums change.

In conclusion, many ongoing public debates around the world are re-examining the role of the museum in contemporary societies, and effecting changes in museums. As an institution, contemporary museums are always in a "period of transition" and attempts are continually made to renew them. As with previous times in museum history, it is a period complicated and made complex and contradictory by the range of demands made on the museum – to be representative, to consider the political thinking, collecting and display practices, issues of representation, and the new technological world in which we live and which links us in new ways.

Museums and the Public Sphere provides a conceptual base on which to interpret the museum as a cultural public sphere in its many guises, including when it is only appearing to be accessible and democratic. Democracy is a process, not a thing in itself. To consider the museum as fixed is to consider democracy as fixed, as universal. In this sense, museums, like democracy, are subject to competing interests. Without rethinking the basis of democracy and museums, it is apparent that museums will never become public or *truly* democratic. *Museums and the Public Sphere* is, I trust, a contribution to help us rethink the use of the core concept underpinning the history of the modern museum and its contemporary role as an institution of democracy.

References

Alexander, E.P. (1979) *Museums in Motion: An introduction to the history and functions of museums*, American Association for State and Local History, Nashville.

Allen, S., Gutwill, J., Perry, D.L., Garibay, C., Ellenbogen, K.M., Heimlich, J.E. Reich, C.A., and Klein, C. (2007) Research in museums: Coping with complexity. In Falk, J.H., Dierking, L.D. and Foutz, S. (eds) *In Principle, In Practice: Museums as Learning Institutions*, Altamira Press, Lanham, UK, pp. 44–56.

Alloway, L. (1996) The great curatorial dim-out. In Greenberg, R., Ferguson, B.W., and Nairne, S. (eds) *Thinking About Exhibitions*, Routledge, New York and London, pp. 221–230.

American Association of Museums (1999) Museums FAQ. Available at www.aam-us.org/aboutmuseums/abc.cfm#how_many (accessed October 29, 2009).

Anderson, B. (1991) *Imagined Communities*, Verso, London and New York.

Anderson, D. (1990) What shall we do with the curators? *Museum Management and Curatorship*, 9, pp. 197–210.

Anderson, G. (2004) *Reinventing the Museum: Historical and Contemporary Perspectives on the Paradigm Shift*, Alta Mira Press, Oxford and Lanham, MD.

Arendt, H. (1958) *The Human Condition*, Chicago University Press, Chicago and London.

Ashley, S. (2005) State authority and the public sphere: Ideas on the changing role of the museum as a Canadian social institution, *Museum and Society*, 3 (1), pp. 5–17.

Ashton, P., Connors, J., Goodall, H., Hamilton, P., and McCarthy, L., (2000) Australians and the past, *The Public History Review*, 8, University of Technology, Sydney, pp. 157–167.

Barker, E. (1999a) Exhibiting the canon: The blockbuster show. In Barker, E. (ed.) *Contemporary Cultures of Display*, Yale University Press in conjunction with The Open University, New Haven and London, pp. 127–146.

Barker, E. (1999b) Museum in the community: The New Tate. In Barker, E. (ed.), *Contemporary Cultures of Display*, Yale University Press in conjunction with Open University, New Haven and London, pp. 178–199.

Barrett, J. (1998) Community, public, audience: Complex and critical transactions. In Alison Beale and Annette Van den Bosch (eds) *Ghosts in the Machine: Women and Cultural Policy in Canada and Australia*, Garamond Press, Toronto, pp. 147–162.

Barrett, J. (2001) Gardens: Making space for the public. In Barrett, J. and Butler-Bowdon, C. (eds) *Debating the City: An anthology*, Historic Houses Trust, Sydney, pp. 84–98.

Barrett, J. and McManus, P. (2007) Civilising nature: Museums and the environment. In Birch, G. (ed.) *Water Wind Art and Debate*. University of Sydney Press, Sydney, pp. 319–344.

Barringer, T. (2006) Victorian culture and the museum: Before and after the white cube, *Journal of Victorian Culture*, 11 (1), pp. 133–145.

Bataille, G. (1986) *Museum*, Annette Michelson (trans.), *October*, 36, pp. 24–25. Original published in French in 1930.

Baudelaire, C. ([1863]1986) *The Painter of Modern Life and Other Essays*, J. Mayne (trans. and ed.), Da Capo Press, New York.

Bazin, G. (1967) *The Museum Age*, Desoer Publishers, Brussels.

Benhabib, S. (1992a) Models of public space: Hannah Arendt, the Liberal Tradition, and Jürgen Habermas. In Calhoun, C. (ed.) *Habermas and the Public Sphere*. MIT Press, Cambridge, MA, pp. 73–98.

Benhabib, S. (1992b) *Situating the Self: Gender, Community and Postmodernism in Contemporary Ethics*, Polity Press, Cambridge.

Benhamou, F. and Moureau, N. (2006) From ivory towers to museums open to the community: Changes and developments in France's cultural policy. *Museum International*, 232, pp. 21–27.

Benjamin, W. (1973) *Illuminations*, H. Zohn (trans.), Fontana, London Original published in 1955.

Benjamin, W. (1978) *Reflections: Essays, Aphorisms, Autobiographical Writings*, Demetz, P. (ed.) and Jephcott, E. (trans.), Schocken Books, New York.

Bennett, T. (1988) Museums and 'the people'. In Lumley, R. (ed.) *The Museum Time Machine: Putting Cultures on Display.* Comedia/Routledge, London, pp. 63–85.

Bennett, T. (1993) Shaping the Public. In Barrett, J. and Crayford, M. (eds.) *Hypothetically Public*, Lewers Bequest and Penrith City Council Art Gallery, Sydney, pp. 7–12.

Bennett, T. (1995) *The Birth of the Museum: History, Theory, Politics*, Routledge, New York and London.

Bennett, T. (1998) *Culture: A Reformer's Science*, Sage, London.

Bennett, T. (2004) *Pasts Beyond Memory: Evolution, Museums, Colonialism*, Routledge, London and New York.

Bennett, T. (2006) Civic seeing: Museums and the organization of vision. In Macdonald, S. (ed.), *A Companion to Museum Studies*, Blackwell, Oxford, pp. 263–281.

Bennett, T. (2007) Habitus Clivé: Aesthetics and politics in the work of Pierre Bourdieu, *New Literary History*, 38, pp. 201–228.

Berman, M. (1983) *All That is Solid Melts into Air: The Experience of Modernity*, Verso, London.

Berman, M. (1986) Take it to the street: Conflict and community in public space, *Dissent*, Fall, pp. 476–485.

Bhabha, H. (1994) DISSEMINATION: Time, narrative and the margins of the modern nation. In *The Location of Culture*. Routledge, London and New York, pp. 139–170.

Blackmar, E. (2006) Appropriating "the Commons": The tragedy of the property rights discourse. In Low, S. and Smith, N. (eds), *The Politics of Public Space*, Routledge, New York, pp. 49–80.

Bolton, L. (2006) The Museum as Cultural Agent. In Healy, C. and Witcomb, A. (eds), *South Pacific Museums: Experiments in Culture*, Monash University ePress, pp. 13.1–13.13. DOI: 10.2104/spm06013.

Bonython, E. and Burton, A. (2003) *The Great Exhibitor: The Life and Work of Henry Cole*, Victoria and Albert Museum Publications, London.

Boullée, É.-L. (n.d.) Architecture, essay on art. In Janson, H.W. and Janson, A.F. (eds) (1997) *The History of Art*, 5th edn, Thames and Hudson, London, pp. 934–935.

Bourdieu, P.([1979]1984) *Distinction: A Social Critique of the Judgement of Taste*, R. Nice (trans.), Harvard University Press, Cambridge, MA.

Bourdieu, P. and Darbel, A., with Schnapper, D. ([1969]1990) *The Love of Art. European Art Museums and their Public*, Beattie, C. and Merriman, N. (trans.), Stanford University Press, Stanford, CA.

Boylan, P.J. (1989) Museum training in an international perspective. In Van Mensch, P. (ed.) *Professionalising the Muses: The Museum Profession in Motion*, AHA Books, Amsterdam.

Buck-Morss, S. (1989) *The Dialectics of Seeing: Walter Benjamin and the Arcades Project*, MIT Press, Cambridge, MA.

Burt, N. (1977) *Palaces for the People: A Social History of the American Art Museum*, Little, Brown, Boston, MA.

Calhoun, C. (ed.) (1992) *Habermas and the Public Sphere*, MIT Press, Cambridge, MA.

Calhoun, C. (1997) Plurality, promises, and public spaces. In Calhoun, C. and McGowan, J. (eds) *Hannah Arendt and the Meaning of Politics: Contradictions of Modernity*, University of Minnesota Press, Minneapolis and London, pp. 232–259.

Cartledge, P. (1998) Defining a *kosmos*. In Cartledge, P., Millett, P. and von Redden, S. (eds) *Kosmos: Essays in Order, Conflict and Community in Classical Athens*, Cambridge University Press, London, pp. 1–13.

Casey, E.S. (1993) *Getting Back into Place: Toward a New Understanding of the Place-World*, Indiana University Press, Indianapolis.

Casey, E.S. (1997) *The Fate of Place: A Philosophical History*, University of California Press, Berkeley, Los Angeles, and London.

Çelik, Z., Favro, D., and Ingersoll, R. (eds) (1994) *Streets: Critical Perspectives on Public Space*, University of California Press, Berkeley, Los Angeles, and New York.

Chakrabarty, D. (1997) Minority histories, subaltern pasts, *Humanities Research*, VI (winter), pp. 17–32.

Chakrabarty, D. (2002) Museums in late democracies, *Humanities Research*, IX (1), pp. 5–11.

Chang, Y. (2006) Cultural policies and museum development in Taiwan, *Museum International*, 58 (4), pp. 64–68.

Clarke, T.J. (1985) *The Painting of Modern Life*. Thames and Hudson, London.

Clavir, M. (2002) *Preserving What Is Valued: Museums Conservation and First Nations*, University of British Columbia Press, Vancouver.

Clifford, J. (1999) Museums as contact zones. In Boswell, D. and Evans, J. (eds) *Representing the Nation: A Reader. Histories, Heritage and Museums*, Routledge, London.

Cole, H. (1857) Extracts from an introductory address on the functions of the Science and Art Department. Reprinted in Siegel, J. (ed.) (2008) *The Emergence of the Modern Museum: An Anthology of Nineteenth Century Sources*, Oxford University Press, Oxford pp. 245–246.

Crooke, E. (2007) *Museums and Community: Ideas, Issues and Challenges*, Routledge, London.

Crow, T. (1985) *Painters and Public Life in Eighteenth-Century Paris*, Yale University Press, New Haven and London.

Crow, T. (1994) Figures of revolutionary virtue. In Eisenman, S.F. (ed.) *Nineteenth Century Art: A Critical History*. Thames and Hudson, London, pp. 188–205.

Crow, T. (1995) *Emulation: Making of Revolutionary Artists for Revolutionary France*, Yale University Press, New Haven and London.

Cuno, J. (2004) The object of art museums. In Cuno, J. (ed.) *Whose Muse? Art Museums and the Public Trust*, Princeton University Press and Harvard University Art Museums, Princeton, NJ, and Cambridge, MA, pp. 49–75.

Cuypers, J.-B. (1979) Introduction of the President. In International Council of Museums International Committee for the Training of Personnel, *Methods and Techniques of Museum Training at University Level*, Report of a Symposium held in Leicester, England, 16–22 September, p. 6.

Dana, J. (1917) *The Gloom of the Museum*. The New Museum Series, The Newark Museum Association/The American Association of Museums, Newark, New Jersey. Reprinted in Anderson, G. (ed.) (2004) *Reinventing the Museum: Historical and Contemporary Perspectives on the Paradigm Shift*, AltaMira Press, Lanham, MD, pp. 13–29.

de Certeau, M. (1984) *The Practice of Everyday Life*, University of California Press, Berkeley.

Deustche, R. (1988) Uneven development: Public art in New York City, *October*, 47, pp. 3–52.

Deustche, R. (1996) *Evictions: Art and Spatial Politics*, MIT Press, Cambridge, MA, and London.

Dibley, B. (2005) Museum and redemption. Contact zones, government and the limits of reform, *International Journal of Cultural Studies*, 8, pp. 5–27.

Dixson, T. S. (1919) *Australian Museum, Sydney; Lecture on its Origin, Growth and Work*. Printed copy of a lecture delivered on 10 June 1919, Australian Museum, Sydney.

Duitz, M. (1992) The soul of a museum: Commitment to community at the Brooklyn Children's Museum. In Karp, I., Mullen Kreamer, C., and Lavine, S.D. (eds) *Museums and Communities: The Politics of Public Culture*, Smithsonian Institution, Washington and London, pp. 242–261.

Duncan, C. (1995) *Civilizing Rituals: Inside Public Art Museums*, Routledge, London.

Duncan, C. and Wallach, A. (1980) The universal survey museum, *Art History*, 3(4), pp. 448–469.

Eagleton, T. (1990) *From the Polis to Postmodernism, The Ideology of the Aesthetic*, Blackwell Publishers, Oxford.

Eisenman, S.F. (1994) The generation of 1830 and the crisis in the public sphere. In Eisenman, S.F., with T. Crow, B. Lukacher, L. F. Nochlin and Pohl, K. (eds) *Nineteenth Century Art: A Critical History*, Thames and Hudson, London, pp. 188–205.

Eley, G. (1992) Nations, publics, and political cultures: Placing Habermas in the nineteenth century. In Calhoun, C. (ed.) *Habermas and the Public Sphere*, MIT Press, Cambridge, MA, pp. 289–339.

Euban, J.P., Wallach J.R. and Ober J. (eds) (1994) *Athenian Political Thought and the Reconstruction of American Democracy*. Cornell University Press, Ithaca.

Falk, J.H. and Dierking, L.D. (2000) *Learning from Museums: Visitor Experiences and the Making of Meaning*, Altamira Press, Walnut Creek.

Ferguson, L. (2001) An introduction to audience research, *Museum Methods*, Sheet 7.1, Museums Australia Inc., Canberra.

Flower, W. (1898, reprinted 1972) *Essays on Museums (and other subjects connected with natural history)*, Books for Libraries Press, Freeport, New York.

Foster, H. (ed.) (1988) *Vision and Visuality: Discussions in Contemporary Culture No. 2*, Bay Press, Seattle.

Foucault, M. (1965) *Madness and Civilization: A History of Insanity in the Age of Reason*, R. Howard (trans.), Pantheon, New York.

Foucault, M. (1970) *The Order of Things: An Archaeology of the Human Sciences*, Routledge, London.

Foucault, M. (1973) *The Birth of the Clinic: An Archaeology of Medical Perception*, Alan Sheridan (trans.), Vintage, New York.

Foucault, M. (1977) *Discipline and Punish: Birth of the Prison*, Alan Sheridan (trans.), Pantheon, New York.

Foucault, M. (1980) Questions on Geography. In Gordon, C. (ed.) *Power/Knowledge: Selected Interviews and Other Writings 1972–1977*, Pantheon Books, New York, pp. 63–77.

Foucault, M. (1984a) What is enlightenment? In Rabinow P. (ed.) *The Foucault Reader*, Pantheon Books, New York, pp. 32–50.

Foucault, M. (1984b) Space, knowledge, power. In Rabinow, P. (ed.) *The Foucault Reader*, Pantheon, New York, pp. 146–165.

Foucault, M. (1986) Of other spaces, *Diacritics*, 16 (spring), pp. 22–27.

Foucault, M. (1991) *The Order of Things: An Archaeology of the Human Sciences*, Routledge, London.

Francis, M. and Hester, R.T. Jr. (eds) (1990) *The Meaning of Gardens: Idea, Place and Action*, MIT Press, Cambridge, MA and London.

Fraser, N. (1989) *Unruly Practices: Power, Discourse, and Gender in Contemporary Social Theory*, University of Minnesota Press, Minneapolis.

Fraser, N. (1990) Rethinking the public sphere: Contribution to the critique of actually existing democracy, *Social Text*, 25–26, pp. 56–80.

Fraser, N. (1992) Rethinking the public sphere. In Calhoun C. (ed.) *Habermas and the Public Sphere*, MIT Press, Cambridge, MA, pp. 109–142.

Frisbee, D. (1985) *Fragments of Modernity: Theories of Modernity in the Work of Simmel, Kracauer and Benjamin*, Polity Press, Cambridge.

Fyfe, G. (1996) A Trojan Horse at the Tate: Theorizing museum as agency and structure. In Macdonald, S. and Fyfe, G. (eds) *Theorizing Museums*, Blackwell Publishers, Oxford and Cambridge, MA, pp. 203–228.

Fyfe, G. (1998) On the relevance of Basil Bernstein's Theory of Codes to the sociology of art museums, *Journal of Material Culture*, 3 (3), pp. 325–354.

Fyfe, G. (2004) Reproductions, cultural capital and museums: Aspects of the culture of copies, *Museum and Society*, 2 (1), pp. 47–67.

Fyfe, G. and Ross, M. (1996) Decoding the visitor's gaze: Rethinking museum visiting. In Macdonald, S. and Fyfe, G. (eds) *Theorizing Museums*, Blackwell Publishers, Oxford and Cambridge, MA, pp. 127–150.

Fyfe, N.R. (1988) *Images of the Street: Planning, Identity and Control in Public Space*, Routledge, London and New York.

Gallup, A.B. (1908) The children's museum as an educator, *Popular Science Monthly*, 72, pp. 371–379. Reprinted in Genoways, H. and Andrei, M.-A. (eds) (2008) *Museum Origins: Readings in Early Museum History and Philosophy*, Left Coast Press, Walnut Creek, CA, pp. 155–159.

Genoways, H. and Andrei, M.-A. (eds) (2008) *Museum Origins: Readings in Early Museum History and Philosophy*, Left Coast Press, Walnut Creek, CA.

Goheen, P.G. (1998) Public space and the geography of the modern city, *Progress in Human Geography*, 22 (4), pp. 479–496.

Gregory, D. (1989) The crisis of modernity? Human geography and critical social theory. In Peet, R. and Thrift, N. (eds) *New Models in Geography*, Unwin Hyman, London, pp. 348–390.

Griffin, D., Anderson, M., and Parisseon, L. (eds) (forthcoming), *Museums in Australia: 1975–2007*, National Museum of Australia, Canberra.

Habermas, J. (1964) The public sphere: An encyclopedia article, P.U. Hohendahl (trans.) (1974) *New German Critique*, 3, pp. 45–48.

Habermas, J. (1976) *Legitimation Crisis*, Thomas McCarthy (trans.), Heinemann Educational, London. Originally published in German.

Habermas, J. (1981) Modernity vs. postmodernity, *New German Critique*, 22, pp. 3–14.

Habermas, J. (1983) Modernity — An incomplete project. In Foster, H. (ed.), *The Anti-Aesthetic: Essays on Postmodern Culture*, Bay Press, Seattle, pp. 3–15.

Habermas, J. (1984) *The Theory of Communicative Action, Volume One: Reason and Rationalization of Society*, Thomas McCarthy (trans.), Polity Press, Cambridge.

Habermas, J. (1987) *The Theory of Communicative Action, Volume Two: The Critique of Functionalist Reason*, Thomas McCarthy (trans.), Polity Press, Cambridge.

Habermas, J. (1989) *The Structural Transformation of the Public Sphere: An Inquiry into a Category of Bourgeois Society*, Thomas Burger (trans.), MIT Press, Cambridge, MA. This work was originally published in German as Habermas, J. (1962) *Strukturwandel der Öffentlichkeit*, Hermann Luchterhand Verlag, Darmstadt and Neuwied, Federal Republic of Germany.

Habermas, J. (1992a) Further reflections on the public sphere. In Calhoun, C. (ed.) *Habermas and the Public Sphere*, MIT Press, Cambridge, MA, pp. 421–461.

Habermas, J. (1992b) Questions and counterquestions. In Bernstein, R.J. (ed.) *Habermas and Modernity*, MIT Press, Cambridge, MA, pp. 192–216.

Habermas, J. (1996) Modernity: An unfinished project. In Passerin d'Entreves, M. and Benhabib, S. (eds) *Habermas and the Unfinished Project of Modernity: Critical Essays on The Philosophical Discourse of Modernity*, Polity Press, Cambridge, pp. 38–55.

Habermas, J. and Levin, T.Y. (1982) The entwinement of myth and enlightenment: Re-reading dialectic of enlightenment, *New German Critique*, 26, Critical Theory and Modernity (spring-summer), pp. 13–30.

Hansen, M. (1993) Foreword. In Negt, O. and Kluge, A. (eds) *Public Sphere and Experience: Toward an analysis of the bourgeois and proletarian Public Sphere, Theory and History of Literature*, Labanyi, P., Owen Daniel, J. and Oksilloff, A. (trans.), University of Minnesota Press, Minneapolis, pp. ix–xli. Original published in German in 1972.

Hansen M.H. and Raaflaub K. (eds) (1995) *Studies in the Ancient Greek Polis*, Franz Steiner Verlag, Stuttgart.

Harmanci, R. (2006) The Caretakers: 'Four on One': The curator's role has become influential. This show puts the spotlight on them. *The San Francisco Chronicle*, (online), Datebook Section, Visual Art Picks, 10 August. Available at: www.stephaniesyjuco.com/reviews/review.sfgate_reyhan_8_06.html (accessed April 3, 2008).

Harrison, C. and Wood, P. (1993) The idea of the modern world. In Harrison, C. and Wood, P. (eds) *Art in Theory 1900–1990: An Anthology of Changing Ideas*, Blackwell Publishers, Oxford, pp. 123–129.

Hartley, J. (1992) *The Politics of Pictures: The Creation of the Public in the Age of Popular Media*, London and New York.

Harvey, D. (1990) *The Condition of Postmodernity. An Enquiry into the Origins of Cultural Change*, Blackwell, Oxford.

Harvey, D. (1993) From space to place and back again. In Bird J., Putman, T., Robertson, G. and Tickner, L. (eds) *Mapping Futures: Local Cultures, Global Change*, Routledge, London, pp. 4–29.

Harvey, D. (2003) *Paris, Capital of Modernity*, Routledge, New York.

Harvey, D. (2006) The political economy of public space. In Low, S. and Smith, N. (eds) *The Politics of Public Space*, Routledge, New York, pp. 17–34.

Healy, C. and Witcomb, A. (2006) (eds) *South Pacific Museums: Experiments in Culture*, Monash University ePress, pp. 13.1–13.13. DOI: 10.2104/spm06013.

Heinich, N. and Pollak, M. (1996) From museum curator to exhibition *auteur*: Inventing a singular position. In Greenberg, R., Ferguson, B. W. and Nairne, S. (eds) *Thinking About Exhibitions*, Routledge, New York and London, pp. 231–250.

Held, D. (1996) *Models of Democracy*, 2nd edn, Polity Press, Cambridge, and Blackwell Publishers, Oxford.

Henare, A.J.M. (2005) *Museums, Anthropology and Imperial Exchange*, Cambridge University Press, Cambridge.

Heumann Gurian, E. (2005) *Civilizing the Museum: The Collected Writings of Elaine Heumann Gurian*, Routledge, Oxford and New York.

Hohendahl, P.U. (1974) Translation and notes of Habermas, J. (1964) The Public Sphere: An Encyclopedia Article, *New German Critique*, 3, pp. 45–48.

Hohendahl, P.U. (1992) The public sphere: Models and boundaries. In Calhoun, C. (ed.) *Habermas and the Public Sphere*, MIT Press, Cambridge, MA, pp. 99–108.

Hooper-Greenhill, E. (1992) *Museums and the Shaping of Knowledge*, Routledge, London.

Hooper-Greenhill, E. (1994) *Museums and Their Visitors*. Routledge, London.

Hooper-Greenhill, E. (2000) *Museums and the Interpretation of Visual Culture*, Routledge, London.

Horkheimer, M. and Adorno, T. (1972) *Dialectic of Enlightenment*, John Cumming (trans.), London, Verso. Original published in German in 1944.

Howell, P. (1993) Public space and the public sphere: Political theory and the historical geography of modernity, *Environment and Planning D: Society and Space*, 11, pp. 303–322.

Hunt, J.D. (1992) *Gardens and the Picturesque: Studies in the Histories of Landscape Architecture*, MIT Press, Cambridge, MA.

Ingram, D. (1994) Foucault and Habermas and the subject of reason. In Gutting, G. (ed.) *The Cambridge Companion to Foucault*, Cambridge University Press, Cambridge, pp. 215–261.

International Council of Museums (ICOM) International Committee for the Training of Personnel (1979) *Methods and Techniques of Museum Training at University Level*, Report of a Symposium held in Leicester, England, 16–22 September.

Iveson, K. (2008) *Publics and the City*, Wiley-Blackwell, Oxford.

Jay, M. (1985) Habermas and modernism. In R. Bernstein (ed.) *Habermas and Modernity*, MIT Press, Cambridge, MA, pp. 125–139.

Jay, M. (1988) *Scopic Regimes of Modernity*. In Foster, H. (ed.) *Vision and Visuality, Discussions in Contemporary Culture*, No. 2, Bay Press, Seattle, pp. 3–23.

Jay, M. (1994) *Downcast Eyes: The Denigration of Vision in Twentieth-century French Thought*, University of California Press, Berkeley.

Jevons, W.S. (1883) The use and abuse of museums, *Methods of Social Reform and Other Papers*, Macmillan, London, pp. 53–81. Reprinted in Genoways, H. and Andrei, M.-A. (eds) (2008) *Museum Origins: Readings in Early Museum History and Philosophy*, Left Coast Press, Walnut Creek, CA, pp. 99–109.

Johnson, P. (2006) *Habermas: Rescuing the Public Sphere*, Routledge, Oxon and New York.

Johnston, R.J. (2000) Community. In Johnston, R.J., Gregory, D., Pratt, G., and Watts, M. (eds) *The Dictionary of Human Geography*, 4th edn, consultant editor D.M. Smith, Blackwell Publishers, Oxford and Malden, MA, pp. 101–102.

Kant, I. (1952) *The Critique of Judgement*, J.C. Meredith (trans.), Clarendon Press, Oxford. Original published in German.

Karp, I. and Levine, S.D. (eds) (1991). *Exhibiting Cultures: The Poetics and Politics of Museum Display*, Smithsonian Institution, Washington and London.

Karp, I., Kratz, C.A., Szwaja, L., and Ybarra-Frausto, T. (eds) (2006) *Museum Frictions: Public Cultures/Global Transformations*, Duke University Press, Durham and London.

Karp, I., Mullen Kreamer, C., and Levine, S.D. (eds) (1992). *Museums and Communities: The Politics of Public Culture*, Smithsonian Institution, Washington and London.

Keane, J. (1988) *Democracy and Civil Society*. Verso, New York and London.

Keith, M. and Pile, S. (eds) (1993) *Place and the Politics of Identity*, Routledge, London.

Kelly, L. and Gordon, P. (2002) Developing a community of practice: Museums and reconciliation in Australia. In R. Sandell (ed.) *Museums, Society, Inequality*, Routledge, London, pp. 153–174.

Kelly, N. (2007) Curators: Best practice in project management, *The Contemporary Arts Review*. Available at: http://www.contemporaryartsreview.com/?p=(1 (17 (accessed February 3, 2008).

Kemp, W. (1994) The Theater of Revolution: A new interpretation of Jacques-Louis David's *Tennis Court Oath*. In Bryson, N., Holly, M. A. and Moxey, K. (eds.) *Visual Culture: Images and Interpretations*, Wesleyan University Press, Hanover and London, pp. 202–227.

Kluge, A. (1991) The public sphere. In Wallis, B. (ed.) *If You Lived Here: The City in Art, Theory, and Social Activism, A Project By Martha Rosler*, Dia Foundation, Bay Press, Seattle, pp. 67–70.

Koivisto J. and Valiverronen, E. (1996) The resurgence of the Critical Theories of Public Sphere, *Journal of Communication Inquiry*, 20 (2), pp. 18–36.

Koster, E. (2006) The relevant museum: A reflection on sustainability, *Museum News*, May/June, American Association of Museums. Available at: http://www.aam-us.org/pubs/mn/mn_mj06_relevantmuseum.cfm (accessed October 10, 2009).

Krens, T. (1999) quoted in Judith H Dobrzynski, Hip Vs. Stately: The Tao of Two Museums, *New York Times*, February 20, 2000, p. 20.

Kreps, C.F. (2008) Appropriate museology in theory and practice, *Museum Management and Curatorship* (online), 23 (1), pp. 23–41. Available at: http://dx.doi.org/(10.(1080/0964777070(1865345 (accessed July 4, 2008).

Landes, J.B. (1988) *Women and the Public Sphere in the Age of the French Revolution*, Cornell University Press, Ithaca and London.

Landes, J.B. (1992) Jürgen Habermas, The structural transformation of the public sphere: A feminist inquiry, *Praxis International*, 12 (1), pp. 106–127.

Landes, J.B. (1995) The public and the private sphere: A feminist reconsideration. In Meehan, J. (ed.) *Feminists Read Habermas: Gendering the subject of discourse*. Routledge, New York and London, pp. 91–116.

Latour, B. (2005) From Realpolitik to dingpolitik: How to make things public. In Latour, B. and Weibel, P. (eds) *Making Things Public – Atmospheres of Democracy*, MIT Press, Cambridge, MA, and ZKM, Karlsruhe, pp. 4–31.

Lefort, C. (1988) *Democracy and Political Theory*, University of Minnesota Press, Minneapolis.

Losche, D. (2009) Memory, violence and representation in the Tjibaou Cultural Centre, New Caledonia. In Stanley, N. (ed.) *The Future of Indigenous Museums, Perspectives from the Southwest Pacific*, Berghahn Books, New York and Oxford, pp. 70–77.

Low, T. (1942) What is a museum? *The Museum as a Social Instrument, American Association of Museums*, Metropolitan Museum of Art, New York. Reprinted in Anderson, G. (ed.) (2004) *Reinventing the Museum: Historical and Contemporary Perspectives on the Paradigm Shift*, AltaMira Press, Lanham, MD, pp. 30–43.

Lucas, F. (1908) Purposes and aims of modern museums, *Proceedings of the Staten Island Association of Arts and Sciences*, 2, pp. 119–124. Reprinted in Genoways, H. and Andrei, M.-A. (eds) (2008) *Museum Origins: Readings in Early Museum History and Philosophy*, Left Coast Press, Walnut Creek, CA, pp. 57–60.

Luke, T. (1992) *Shows of Force: Power, Politics, and Ideology in Art Exhibitions*, Duke, Durham, NC, and London.

Luke, T. (2002) *Museum Politics: Power Plays at the Exhibition*, University of Minnesota Press, Minneapolis.

Lyotard, J.F. (1991) A l'insu (Unbeknownst). In Miami Theory Collective (eds) *Community at Loose Ends*, University of Minnesota Press, Minneapolis, pp. 42–48.

Macdonald, S. (2002) *Behind the Scenes at the Science Museum*. Berg, Oxford.

Macdonald, S. (2006) Expanding museum studies: An introduction. In Macdonald, S. (ed.) *Companion to Museum Studies*, Blackwell Publishing, Oxford and Malden, MA, pp. 1–12.

Macdonald, S. (ed.) (2006) *A Companion to Museum Studies*. Blackwell Publishing, Oxford and Malden, MA.

MacLeod, M. (2001) Making museum studies: Training, education, research and practice, *Museum Management and Curatorship*, 19 (1), pp. 51–61.

Malraux, A. (1967) *Museum Without Walls*, S. Gilbert and F. Price (trans.), Secker and Warburg, London. Original published in French.

Marstine, J. (ed.) (2006) *New Museum Theory and Practice: An Introduction*, Blackwell Publishing, Oxford and Malden, MA.

Massey, D. (1994) *Space, Place and Gender*, Polity Press, Cambridge.

Mastai, J. (2007) There is no such thing as a visitor. In Pollock, G. and Zemans, J. (eds.) *Museums After Modernism: Strategies of Engagement*, Blackwell Publishing, Oxford, pp. 173–177.

McCarthy, T. (1989) Introduction. In J. Habermas, *The Structural Transformation of the Public Sphere. An Inquiry into a Category of Bourgeois Society*, MIT Press, Cambridge, MA, pp. xi–xiv.

McCarthy, T. (1992) Practical discourse: On the relation of morality to politics. In Calhoun, C. (ed.) *Habermas and the Public Sphere*, MIT Press, Cambridge, MA, pp. 51–72.

McClellan, A. (1994) *Inventing the Louvre: Art, Politics, and the Origins of the Modern Museum in Eighteenth-century Paris*, Cambridge University Press, Cambridge and New York.

McClellan, A. (2003) A brief history of the art museum public. In McClellan, A. (ed.) *Art and its Publics: Museum Studies at the Millennium*, Blackwell Publishing, Oxford, pp. 1–49.

McClellan, A. (2008) *The Art Museum: From Boullée to Bilbao*, University of California, Berkeley.

McGuigan, J. (1996) *Culture and the Public Sphere*, Routledge, London and New York.

McIntyre, D. (2006) The National Museum of Australia and public discourse: The role of public policies in the nation's cultural debates, *Museum International*, 232, pp. 13–20.

McKee, A. (2005) *The Public Sphere: An Introduction*, Cambridge University Press, Melbourne.

McShane, I. (2008) Museology and public policy: Rereading the development of the National Museum of Australia's collection, *reCollections*, 2 (2), pp. 1–12.

Meehan J. (ed.) (1995) *Feminists Read Habermas: Gendering the Subject of Discourse*, Routledge, New York and London.

Merriman, N. (1989) Museum Visiting as Cultural Phenomenon. In Vergo, P. (ed.) *The New Museology*, Reaktion Press, London, pp. 149–171.

Message, K. (2006) *New Museums and the Making of Culture*, Berg, Oxford.

Miami Theory Collective (eds) (1991) *Community at Loose Ends*, University of Minnesota, Minneapolis.

Mitchell, D. (1995) The end of public space? People's park, definitions of public, and democracy, *Annals of the Association of American Geographers*, 85 (1), pp. 108–133.

Mitchell, D. (2003) *The Right to the City: Social Justice and the Fight for Public Space*, Guilford Press, New York.

Mitchell, D. and Staeheli, L. (2006) Clean and safe? Property redevelopment, public space, and homelessness in downtown San Diego. In Low, S. and Smith, N. (eds) *The Politics of Public Space*, Routledge, New York, pp. 143–175.

Moore, C.W., Mitchell W.J., and Turnbally W., Jr. (1988) *The Poetics of Gardens*, MIT Press, Cambridge, MA, and London.

Morgan, J. (2004) *Sydney Morning Herald*, SPECTRUM, 25–26 September, Fairfax Publications, Sydney, p. 4.

Mosser, M. and Teyssot, G. (eds) (1990) *The History of Garden Design: The Western Tradition from the Renaissance to the Present Day*, Thames and Hudson, London.

Mouffe, C. (1991) Democratic citizenship and the political community. In Miami Theory Collective (eds) *Community at Loose Ends*, University of Minnesota Press, Minneapolis, pp. 70–82.

Mouffe, C. (1993) *The Return of the Political*, Verso, London.

Mouffe, C. (2000) *The Democratic Paradox*, Verso, New York and London.

Museum Education Association of Australia (1977) *A Conference of the Museum Education Association of Australia, Sydney, AGNSW*, April, Museum Education Association of Australia, Sydney.

Museum Studies Unit, University of Sydney (1989) *Papers of the Museum Training Symposium*, University of Sydney, 16–17 February.

Museums Australia Inc. (2002) *Evaluation and Audience Research*, Museums Australia, Canberra.

Nancy, J.-L. (1991a) *The Inoperative Community*, University of Minnesota Press, Minneapolis.

Nancy, J.-L. (1991b) Of being-in-common. In Miami Theory Collective (eds) *Community at Loose Ends*, University of Minnesota Press, Minneapolis, pp. 1–13.

Nathans, B. (1990) Habermas's "Public Sphere" in the era of the French Revolution, *French Historical Studies*, 16 (8), pp. 620–644.

Negt, O. and Kluge, A. (1993) *Public Sphere and Experience: Toward an Analysis of the Bourgeois and Proletarian Public Sphere, Theory and History of*

Literature, P. Labanyi, J.O. Daniel, and A. Oksilloff (trans.), Vol. 85, University of Minnesota Press, Minneapolis. Originally published in German in 1972.

Oakes, T. (1997) Place and the paradox of modernity, *Annals of the Association of American Geographers*, 7 (3), pp. 509–531.

Parry, R. (2007) *Recoding the Museum: Digital Heritage and the Technologies of Change*, Routledge, Oxon and New York.

Perry, G. and Cunningham, C. (eds) (1999) *Academies, Museums and Canons of Art*, Yale University Press in conjunction with Open University; New Haven and London.

Pollock, G. (1988) *Vision and Difference: Femininity, Feminism and the Histories of Art*, Routledge, London and New York.

Preziosi, D. (2003) *Brain of the Earth's Body: Art, Museums, and the Phantasms of Modernity*, University of Minnesota Press, Minneapolis.

Prior, N. (2002) *Museums and Modernity: Art Galleries and the Making of Modern Culture*, Berg Publishers.

Prior, N. (2005) A question of perception: Bourdieu, art and the postmodern, *The British Journal of Sociology*, 6 (1), pp 123–139.

Rabinow, P. (1989) *French Modern: Norms and Forms of the Social Environment*, MIT Press, Cambridge, MA.

Robbins, B. (ed.) (1993) *The Phantom Public Sphere*, University of Minnesota Press, Minneapolis.

Robinson, F.W. (2006) Learning by looking: The future of museums. In Genoways, H. (ed.) *Museum Philosophy for the Twenty First Century*, AltaMira Press, Lanham, MD, pp. 161–164.

Rose, G. (1993) *Feminism and Geography: The Limits of Geographical Knowledge*, Polity Press, Cambridge.

Rowe, P. (1997) *Civic Realism*, MIT Press, Cambridge, MA.

Ryan, M.P. (1990) *Women in Public: Between Banners and Ballots, 1825–1880*, Johns Hopkins University Press, Baltimore.

Ryan, M.P. (1992) Gender and public access: Women's politics in nineteenth century America. In Calhoun, C. (ed.) *Habermas and the Public Sphere*, MIT Press, Cambridge, MA, pp. 259–288.

Ryan, M.P. (1997) *Civic Wars: Democracy and Public Life in the American City During the Nineteenth Century*, University of California Press, Berkeley.

Sandell, R. (1998) Museums and agents of social inclusion. *Museum Management and Curatorship*, 17 (4), pp. 401–418.

Scott, C. (1994) *Formative Evaluation of an Exhibition about Innovation in Australian Industry*, Powerhouse Publishing, Sydney.

Sennett, R. (1990) *The Conscience of the Eye*, Knopf, New York.

Sennett, R. (1992) *The Fall of Public Man*, Norton, New York.

Sennett, R. (1994) *Flesh and Stone: The Body and the City in Western Civilization*, Faber & Faber, London.

Sheets-Pyenson, S. (1988) *Cathedrals of Science: The Development of Colonial Natural History Museums During the Late Nineteenth Century*, McGill-Queens University Press, Kingston and Montreal.

Shelton, A.A. (2006) Museums and anthropologies: Practices and narratives. In Macdonald, S. (ed.) *Companion to Museum Studies*, Blackwell, Oxford, pp. 64–80.

Sheppard, B. and Williams, P. (2000) Museum careers in the next millennium, CMS Bulletin, 7 (1) (online). Available at: http://museumstudies.si.edu/bull/jan00/careers.htm (accessed April 7, 2008).

Sherman, D. (1987) The Bourgeoisie, cultural appropriation, and the art museum in nineteenth-century France, *Radical History Review*, 38, pp. 38–58.

Sherman, D. (1989) *Worthy Monuments: Art Museums and the Politics of Culture in Nineteenth Century France*, Harvard University Press, Cambridge, MA.

Shrestha, K. and McManus, P. (2007) The embeddedness of collective action in Nepalese community forestry, *Small-scale Forestry*, 6 (3), pp. 273–290.

Siegel, J. (ed.) (2008) *The Emergence of the Modern Museum: An Anthology of Nineteenth Century Sources*, Oxford University Press, Oxford.

Simmel, G.([1903]1950) The Metropolis and mental life. In *On Individuality and Social Form*, University of Chicago Press, Chicago, pp. 324–39.

Simpson, M.G. (2001) *Making Representations: Museums in the Post-Colonial Era*, Routledge, London.

Smith, N. (1993) Homeless/global: Scaling places. In Bird J., Putman, T., Robertson, G. and Tickner, L. (eds) *Mapping Futures: Local Cultures, Global Change*, Routledge, London, pp. 87–119.

Smith, N. and Low, L. (2007) Introduction: The imperative of public space. In Low, S. and Smith N. (eds) *The Politics of Public Space*, Routledge, New York, pp. 1–16.

Sorkin, M. (ed.) (1992) *Variations on a Theme Park. The New American City and the End of Public Space*, Noonday Press, New York.

Spate, V. (ed.) (1980) *French Painting: The Revolutionary Decades 1760–1830*, Australian Directors Council, Sydney.

Staeheli, L.A. and Mitchell, D. (2007) Locating the public in research and practice. *Progress in Human Geography*, 31 (6), pp. 792–811.

Taylor, B. (1999) *Art For the Nation: Exhibitions and the London Public 1747–2001*, Rutgers University Press, New Brunswick.

van Aalst, I. and Boogaarts, I. (2002) From museums to mass entertainment: The evolution of the role of museums in cities. *European Urban and Regional Studies*, 9 (3), pp. 195–209.

Vergo, P. (ed.) (1989) *The New Museology*. Reaktion Press, London.

Vilain J. (1980) Louis-Léopold Boilly. In Spate, V. (ed.), *French Painting: The Revolutionary Decades 1760–1830*, Australian Directors Council, Sydney, pp. 26–29.

Von Falkenhausen, S. (1997) The Sphere: Reading a gender metaphor in the architecture of modern cults of identity, *Art History*, 20 (2), pp. 238–267.

Ward, F. (1995) The haunted museum: Institutional critique and publicity, *October*, 73 (summer), pp. 71–89.

Warner, M. (1992) The Mass Public and the Mass Subject. In Calhoun, C. (ed.) *Habermas and the Public Sphere*, MIT Press, Cambridge, MA, pp. 377–401.

Warner, M. (2002) *Public and Counterpublics*, Zone Books, New York.

Watson, S. (ed.) (2007) *Museums and their Communities*, Routledge, London and New York.

Weil, S. (1990) *Rethinking the Museum and Other Meditations*, Smithsonian Institution, Washington, DC.

Weil, S.E. (2002) *Making Museums Matter*, Smithsonian Institution Press, Washington and London.

Wenger, E. (1988) *Communities of Practices: Learning Meaning and Identity*, Cambridge University Press, Cambridge.

White, S.K. (1995) Reason, modernity and democracy. In White, S.K. (ed.) *The Cambridge Companion to Habermas*, Cambridge University Press, Cambridge, New York, and Melbourne, pp. 3–16.

Williams, M.-L. (1989) Non credit training. *Papers of the Museum Training Symposium held at the University of Sydney*, 16–17 February, Museum Studies Unit, University of Sydney, pp. 22–25.

Williams, P. (2007) *Memorial Museums: The Global Rush to Commemorate Atrocities*, Berg, Oxford.

Williams, R. (1976) *Keywords: A Vocabulary of Culture and Society*. Fontana, Glasgow.

Wilson, D. (ed.) (2003). *The Collections of the British Museum*, 3rd edn, The British Museum Press, London.

Wilson, E. (1991) *The Sphinx in the City: Urban Life and the Control of Disorder, and Women*, Virago Press, London.

Winkworth, K. (1989) Other concepts of training: Meeting the need of museums and their communities, *Papers of the Museum Training Symposium held at the University of Sydney*, 16–17 February, Museum Studies Unit, University of Sydney.

Witcomb, A. (2003) *Re-imagining the Museum: Beyond the Mausoleum*, Routledge, London.

Wolff, J. (1985) The invisible *flâneuse:* Women and the literature of modernity, *Theory Cultural and Society*, 2 (3), pp. 37–46.

Wood, J.G. (1887) *The dullness of museums, Nineteenth Century*, 21, 384–396.

Wright, P. (1989) The quality of visitors' experiences in art museums. In Vergo, P. (ed.) *The New Museology*, Reaktion Press, London, pp. 119–148.

Yanni, C. (1999) *Nature's Museums: Victorian Science and the Architecture of Display*, Johns Hopkins University Press, Baltimore.

Young, I.M. (1990) *Justice and the Politics of Difference*, Princeton University Press, Princeton, NJ.

Young, I.M. (1992) Social groups in associative democracy, *Politics and Society*, 20 (4), pp. 529–537.

Zolberg, V.L. (1990) *Constructing a Sociology of the Arts*, Cambridge University Press, New York.

Zolberg, V. (1995) What price success? *Museum International*, 47 (2), pp. 60–63.

Zolberg, V.L. (2003) Current challenges for cultural policy: New meanings of community, *The Journal of Arts Management, Law and Society*, 32 (4) (winter), pp. 295–307.

Zukin, S. (1995) *The Cultures of Cities*, Blackwell Publishers, Oxford and Cambridge, MA.

Acknowledgements

The need to think about what the term "public" means in relation to culture has been at the core of my work as an academic – participating in governance of my workplace, community organizations, and cultural institutions – for over a decade.

My interest in the public sphere began many years ago when I worked on public culture and democracy as they relate to community cultures, and art and public space. Central to this has always been a concern for what the terms "public" or "community" invoke.

The core subject matter of this book will be of no surprise to students of museum studies at the University of Sydney and in Hong Kong. Teaching subjects about the museum context and the ethics of cultural property has always been stimulating and rewarding. This has enriched my work and hopefully inspired those students.

I have always been encouraged by the debate that this topic stimulates and the genuine interest of my colleagues in academia, the museums and galleries sector, and students. Often these concepts are central to why people want to work in museums, engage in public debate, or to communicate this importance to others.

As the thinking associated with the life of a book and its production spans a few years there are many people to whom I owe particular thanks. I have been very fortunate to have research assistance from Helena Robinson and Bridget Berry, who both work across the academic and museum contexts. Elin Howe assisted with the research in the early stages of the project. Colleagues in museum studies, Chiara O'Reilly and Jane Johnston, I thank for their collegiality and ongoing interest in the book.

I owe sincere thanks to Helen Irving, for her long-term interest and critical engagement with the topic. Jane Jacobs, likewise, has provided generous feedback and support at critical times. There are many friends

Museums and the Public Sphere by Jennifer Barrett
© 2010 Jennifer Barrett

and colleagues to whom I owe thanks for continued support: Caroline Butler-Bowdon, Janet Carding, Annie Clarke, Lee-Anne Hall, Elin Howe, Jacqueline Millner, and John Petersen. The kind support of Margaret Harris, Geraldine Barnes, and Judith Keene at the University of Sydney is also greatly appreciated.

A University of Sydney SESQUI Grant assisted with the initial stage of the research in 2005. The School of Letters Art and Media later supported me with a Writing Fellowship in 2007 and a Research Grant in 2009 to assist with image permissions and copyright. In early 2009 Edinburgh University's Institute of Geography provided a pleasant and supportive environment in which to work. Thank you.

One of the challenges of museum studies is its interdisciplinarity: I am grateful to the anonymous referees for their different perspectives and interest in the core ideas in this book. *Museums and the Public Sphere* is richer for their contributions.

It has been a consistent pleasure to work with the editorial staff at Wiley-Blackwell: Jayne Fargnoli, whose interest in and commitment to this project I have greatly enjoyed and appreciated, and Margot Morse, for whose judgment and sense of timing I am grateful. To the patient and efficient copy-editor, Paul Stringer, and to the project manager, Louise Spencely, for bringing the project to a conclusion, go my thanks.

My family and friends, Winifred and Fergus Barrett, Garry Barrett, Robyn Dowling, Fiona Alvarez, the Guppy-Halls, Robert Biddle, Antony Dietrich, Chrissy Ryan, and Jan Cronin all deserve acknowledgment for their support of this book.

And last, but not least, my sincere appreciation to Caitlin – may your love of museums continue – and to Phil McManus, for reading and commenting on drafts, engaging in endless discussions (which will continue), and for his confidence that this book would some day be out of my system.

Jennifer Barrett
Sydney, July 2010

Index

academic disciplines and
museums 6
Acropolis Museum, Athens (Parthenon
Sculptures/British
Museum) 89
aesthetics 169
audience 169
and modernity 62
political potential of 166
and the public sphere 60–3
agency
of museums 157–8
agora 82–3, 88–9
alternative public spheres 37, 134,
137–8
American War of Independence 84
anthropology and museums 147,
150, 158–60
appropriate museology (Christina
Kreps) 152–5, 160
Arendt, Hannah
public sphere and freedom 87–8
art
and modernity 60, 63–5, 72
and the public sphere 61
art criticism
and the public sphere 24, 29, 30,
31–2, 37, 41
Art Gallery of New South Wales,
Sydney 108
*Arts of Islam: Treasures of the Nasser
Khalili Collection* 125

art history 166
and the public sphere 63–8, 72–8
art museum
history of 46, 51
artists
Boilly, Louis-Léopold 64–8, 71,
74, 79
Boullée, Éttienne-Louis 68
Daumier, Honoré 58
David, Jacques-Louis 68, 73–8
public space and the public
sphere 93–4
and the public sphere 60–5, 75
Ashmolean Museum 46
audience 119, 128–9, 141
audience research 124, 127
"embracing complexity" 126,
128–9, 140
Australian Museum 48, 55, 109
Australian War Memorial 88

Belongings 144, 109, 111; *see also*
New South Wales Migration
Heritage Centre
Benhabib, Seyla 18, 34, 38–9, 41
Benjamin, Walter 70–1; *see also*
Haussmann, Baron Eugene von
Bennett, Tony 6, 11, 47, 51–3, 58,
59, 85, 91, 101, 113
critique of Bourdieu 123
Foucault, public institutions,
governmentality 100

blockbusters　56
Boilly, Louis-Léopold　12, 97, 165
　The Public in the Salon of the Louvre,
　　Viewing the Painting of the
　　"Sacre" begun 1808　*17*
　Interior of a Parisian Café,
　　c.1815　66
Boullée, Éttienne-Louis, *Cénotaphe de*
　　Newton, 1784　18, *19*
Bourdieu, Pierre　3, 13, 120–3
　Alain Darbel and Dominique
　　Schnapper　51
British Museum　46, 59, 89, 91,
　　112–13, 159
　Elgin Marbles　89
　see also Acropolis Museum
Brooklyn Children's Museum　54–5

Chakrabarty, Dipesh　52, 57
citizens　52, 85, 87, 98, 105, 166
　and public space　82–3, 100–1
citizenship　52, 57, 83
civic laboratory (Tony Bennett)　113
civic seeing (Tony Bennett)　92
civil society　8, 23, 88, 101
Clifford, James　110–14
Cole, Henry　49–53
collectors　47–9, 51–7, 66
colonialism　160
common good　22, 23
community　2, 7, 10, 20, 42, 109–11,
　　114–15, 127, 129, 137–8, 170
　defining community　130–6
　Kluge, Alexander　136
　Lyotard, Jean Francois　135
　MacLeod, Suzanne　140
　Mouffe, Chantal　130
　Nancy, Jean-Luc　133–5
　and place　122, 130–4
　and the public sphere　119, 129,
　　130, 133, 135–8, 140, 165
　Rose, Gillian　131
　Smith, Neil　131
　Williams, Raymond　131–2

communities of practice　120, 139–40
competing publics　23, 27, 32, 33,
　　37, 43
contact zones　110–14
contested boundaries and cultural
　　spheres (critics of)　38–40
counterpublics/competing public
　　sphere　33–4, 136–7
critical limits and situated reason　34
criticism of the public sphere　22
　Fraser, Nancy　19–20
Crow, Thomas　63–6, 71–2, 74,
　　75, 77
cultural and spatial aspects of the public
　　sphere　21
cultural capital　121–2; *see also*
　　Bourdieu, Pierre
cultural public sphere　164
Cuno, James　56
curator　53–4
　as appropriate participant　152
　as facilitator　151–2
　and public intellectual　150
　　see also Chapter 5
　role of　145–6, 148, 150–2, 154–7,
　　159, 160, 162–3, 170
curatorial methods　144, 149, 150,
　　152–5, 159–60, 162–3

Daumier, Honoré　58
　Free Admission Day – Twenty-Five
　　Degrees of Heat, 1852　*35*
David, Jacques-Louis　12
　Le Serment des Horaces, 1784　*73,*
　　73–5
　The Tennis Court Oath　74–8
Degas, Edgar *Mary Cassatt at the*
　　Louvre: The Etruscan
　　Gallery, 1879–80 65, 69; *see*
　　also art and modernity
democracy　83–4, 95, 97, 105–6,
　　114–15
　and community　130–1, 133–5,
　　137–8

and culture 91
museums and 3, 16–17, 166–9
and public space 82, 86, 91, 93, 94,
98, 106, 115
and the public sphere 99
and representational public
space 86
democratic public space 81–2, 94
democratic sites, performative aspect
of 16
Deutsche, Rosalyn 94–6
digital/online – "museum without
walls," concept of 108
*Distinction: A Social Critique of the
Judgment of Taste* (Pierre
Bourdieu) 121–2
diversity 3

education
history of museums 48–51, 53, 58,
61, 69
embracing complexity, approach to
audience research 119,
128–9, 141
entertainment 50–1
entrance fees 53, 65, 69
evaluation
methods of audience
research 123–7
exhibitions 124, 127

First Nations 160
Flower, Sir William
museums and natural
history 51–2
Foucault, Michel 100–6
heterotopias 105–6
Frankfurt School 15, 18, 23
Fraser, Nancy 7, 19–20, 22, 35–40
and oppositional public
sphere 136, 137
French Revolution 84, 95
and Jacques-Louis David 72–8
Fyfe, Gordon 82, 122

Guggenheim, Bilbao 92, 104
Guggenheim, New York 104

Habermas, Jürgen 130, 134,
136, 137
communicative action 99, 102
and Foucault 102–6
limitations of Habermas's public
sphere 114
modernity 87–8
"Modernity: An unfinished project"
29–31
public space 82, 85, 97
public sphere 81, 96–9, 107, 165
publicity 95
STPS 7, 11–18, 26, 93
Haussman, Baron Eugene von
26–7
heterotopias 100; *see also* Foucault,
Michel
history and museums 166
history of museum 46
Hong Kong museum development:
West Kowloon Cultural
District 171
Hooper-Greenhill, Eilean 6, 100,
108–9, 113, 149
post-museum 109–13
Hohendahl, Peter 33–4, 36, 42–3
Hoving, Thomas 56

Imperial War Museums, Britain 88
inclusivity 3, 167
indigenous communities
(Australia) 127
intangible cultural heritage 154, 160
Internet (as public sphere) 9, 108–9,
111, 118, 140, 143–4, 169
and social media 169,
171–2

Jean-Marie Tjibaou Cultural Centre,
New Caledonia 158
Jevons, Stanley 50, 55

Kant, Immanuel   30–1, 40
Keane, John
  civil society   8
keeping place
  Australian Museum   127
Kluge, Alexander   15, 33, 42, 136
Kreps, Christine   152–4, 160; *see also*
  appropriate museology

Landes, Joan
  women and the public sphere   62,
  72–4
leisure
  and museums   54, 55, 58–9,
  68–9
Love of Art, The (Pierre Bourdieu, Alain
  Darbel, and Dominique
  Schnapper)   120–1

Macdonald, Sharon   148–9
Macleay Museum, University of
  Sydney   160
  *People, Power, Politics: The first
  generation at the University of
  Sydney*, 2008   161
  *Makarr-garma: Aboriginal
  collections from a Yolngu
  Perspective*, 2009   161
Malraux, Andre   56, 107–8; *see also*
  museum-without-walls
McCarthy, Thomas (public
  sphere)   24, 25, 34, 36, 39, 40
McClellan, Andrew   6, 11
Medici Palace, Florence   46
Metropolitan Museum of Art, New
  York   54, 65
Migration Heritage Centre of New
  South Wales, Sydney   109, 111
Mitchell, Don   85–90
modernity   26, 29–33, 37–8, 40
  and aesthetics   62
  and art   62–3, 70–2
  experience of modern life   98–9
  and public space   97–9, 103–4

spaces of   64–5, 68, 70–1
  and vision   65
"Modernity: An unfinished project"
  (Habermas)   29–31
Mouffe, Chantal   130, 133, 141 n3
Musée du Louvre   46, 47, 54, 57–8,
  63, 69, 75, 162
Musée du Quai Branly, Paris   104, 159
Museum of Anthropology, University
  of British Columbia   160
Museum of Mankind, Britain   159
Museum of Natural History, South
  Kensington (and British
  Museum collections)   113
Museum of World Culture,
  Sweden   104
museum-without-walls (*musée
  imaginaire*)   107–8; *see also*
  Malraux, Andre
museum
  directors   53–4
  the idea of   166
  as public intellectual   143–63
  as space for the public   99
museums
  art and public space   96
  and communities   119, 127, 129,
  138–40
  history of   45–59
  imperialism and colonialism   47–8,
  51, 53
  international growth of   51–6
  modern   52, 60
  modernist assumptions of   109–11
  and the public   13, 52–3
  as spaces of public discourse   101
  and the working classes   48–51, 57
museum studies   172–3

National Gallery, Washington DC   54
National Museum of American
  History   104
National Museum of the American
  Indian, Washington   160

Book Cover: *The Changing
Presentation of the American
Indian: Museums and Native
Cultures*, NMAI   162
National Museum of Australia,
Canberra   88, 104, 157–8, 160
*Talkback classroom, "Political Satire"
forum with John Safran and
cartoonist David Pope*, National
Museum of Australia   154
*Garden of Australian Dreams,
opening day at the National
Museum of Australia,
2001*   157
natural history museums, growth
of   42–8
Natural History Museum,
London   51–2
Negt, Oskar   15, 33, 42
"new museum," the (Kylie
Message)   113
new museology   3–4, 47, 56, 148,
153, 167, 170

Paris Exhibition   1867 52
pedagogic democracy (Homi
Bhabha)   52
performative museum   52
People's Republic of China   172
Pitt Rivers Museum, Oxford   48, 172
place
and community   122, 130–4
Pompidou Centre, Paris   104
post-Habermassian   22
post-museum   107, 109–13
Hooper-Greenhill, Eilean   99,
111–12
"post-narrative museology"
(Shelton)   158
postcolonial   111–12, 158
postmodern   111–12
Prior, Nick   120
and critique of Bourdieu   122–3
private   7–8, 21, 24–5, 27–9, 38–41

private collectors   45–6, 48–9, 51, 53
public   5–7, 10, 119, 143, 155, 150,
144, 170
idea of   166
and community   170
use of the museum   49, 57–9
public address   160, 154, 169
public culture   2
public debate   1
public discourse   18–19
public good (common good)   22
public museum   99
public opinion   21, 26
research methods   119, 125
public programs   145, 148
public space   6, 7, 9, 10, 12, 167
art and artists   60, 91
and cities   90–1
and community   10–11, 123,
129–30, 133
defining of   82
and modernity   98–9
public sphere(s)   6, 8, 10, 11–12,
16, 165
bourgeois   16
characteristics of   98
and community   131, 136–8
feminist critique of   37–8
and freedom   87–8
see also Arendt, Hannah
historical model of   18–19, 21,
24–7, 32, 38
liberal   19
norms   21–2
oppositional   22
Kluge, Alexander   137
and Nancy Fraser   136
promotion and publicity   21
public use of reason   21
"strong and weak" publics   19–20
use of reason   21–3
women and the   65, 72, 74
see also Landes, Joan; Fraser,
Nancy

rationality
    and public space   103
    and reason   20–6
reason
    and aesthetic (judgment)   99
    and rationality   20–6
repatriation   109, 127
representation   12, 16, 21, 25, 23, 30,
        34, 38, 40, 41
revolution, French and American
        84, 95
Robert, Hupert   97, 165
    *Projet d'aménagement de la Grande
        Galerie du Louvre en 1796*   31
Royal Society, London   52

Sennett, Richard   7, 22–3
Sir John Soane Museum, London   49,
        172
Smithsonian Institution of American
        History   89
social media   169, 172
South Kensington Art Museum   51
space
    and the public sphere   40–3
Spate, Virginia
    art and revolution   63, 66–8, 72–5
spatial   81, 96, 98, 100, 102, 114
spatial metaphors   106
spatial organization, relations   90, 104
spatial practices   107–14
spatiality and the public
        sphere   18–19, 169
*Structural Transformation of the Public
        Sphere (STPS)*   7, 15–18, 21–7,
        33–4, 40–1, 82
Struth, Thomas   165
    Hermitage 1, St Petersburg, 2005   2
    *Tokyo National Museum, 1999,
        Tokyo*   168

Taiwan
    museum development in   101

Tate Liverpool   90
Tate Modern, London   91
Te Papa Tongaweare, Museum of
        New Zealand   89, 104
Tenniel, John, *The Sunday Question.
        The Public-House: or The House
        For the Public?* 1869   59
traditional public space   88; *see also*
        Mitchell, Don

United States Holocaust Memorial
        Museum   96
universal survey museums   54
universal truths   148

vision   100–2
    and modernity   60
    and the public sphere   18, 36–8,
        40–3, 60
    and civic seeing (Tony
        Bennett)   168
visions of the public sphere   60, 62,
        64–5, 68, 71, 78–9, 151
visitor studies   5, 11, 13, 123–4, 126,
        128, 141, 143, 145, 147–8
visitors as customers/consumers   5,
        127, 149
    Museums Australia   124
    and Scott, Carol   125–6

Warner, Michael   7, 21, 41
Weil, Stephen   11, 139
Wood, John   50
World Trade Center New York
        (Kylie Message)   95
worldwide web and museums
        116, 172
Wright, Peter (*The New Museology*)   3

Zolberg, Vera   56, 122–3
Zukin, Sharon (public space,
        communities, and
        culture)   90–4